MW00694700

# VDI
# Design Guide

A comprehensive guide which will help you design
VMware Horizon Virtual Desktop Infrastructure solutions
based on the VMware Certified Design Expert methodology.

# VDI Design Guide

International Standard Book Number: ISBN 9781977535528

Version 1.0

# DISCLAIMER

This book represents an overview of how I think a Virtual Desktop Infrastructure (VDI) should be designed. Everything that I have written in this book is based on my own experience as an End-User Computing Architect. It is based on the successful outcomes of VDI projects I worked on. It will guide you through the process of running a VDI design project.

No customer is the same and no existing or new infrastructure is the same! This book and the examples in it should only be used as a guideline to approach and strategy for a project. Never copy the metric data for your own projects.

Always understand that when we refer to *design decisions* in this document, they are specific to the *use case* at hand and should be seen as such. The objective of this book is to take the reader through the design process. Use the framework!

Understand that we all need to come up with our own design decisions related to each project and each use case. Use this book as a guide of the lifecycle of a project. Use each chapter as a way to illustrate why this phase in your project is necessary, instead of learning this the hard way.

# ABOUT THE AUTHOR

My name is Johan van Amersfoort, and I am a Dutch, passionate, (bearded) VDI junkie. Since early 2014, I am part of the team at ITQ Consultancy in Wijk aan Zee, the Netherlands. In 2016, after a year of working really hard, I achieved the VCDX certification (238) on Desktop and Mobility.

Next to my passion for technology, I like to travel and see the world. My wife and I are especially attracted to places that offer great diving. Tiny critters such as sea horses, ghost pipe fish and all sorts of shrimps and crabs have been in front of my lens (since I never jump into the water without a fully charged camera). The passion for diving became even bigger when I saw my first shark. It was a great hammerhead in Thailand (which is extremely rare) and since then I am scratching sharks of my so called "shark bucket list". Tiger sharks, whale sharks, great whites, and threshers are examples of sharks I've seen in the past couple of years. A lot of people think I'm completely mad, but after seeing hundreds of sharks in their natural habitat, I'm sure they see me as a weird and friendly looking object.

When at home, I'm the head chef. In all four seasons my BBQs are used on a weekly basis. Big chucks of meat are the obvious masterpieces that leave the grill, but I must admit that I'm starting to enjoy the somewhat more delicate things, like clams, as well.

This book couldn't be finished without some great music to help me gain focus. Foo Fighters, Nothing But Thieves, Frank Denneman's "Chill the fuck out" playlist (with relaxing EDM tracks), and my own 90's Hip Hop playlist on Spotify are awesome to get into "The Zone" (a form of concentration that is required for me to write).

If you would like to read some more about my IT journey, check the Bio section at the end of the book or visit my blog on https://vhojan.nl.

Enjoy reading!

# FOREWORD

(by Shawn Bass, Chief Technology Officer, End-User Computing at VMware)

Some number of months ago, Johan reached out to me to ask if I was willing to write a foreword for a new VDI design book he was planning on writing. I was honored that Johan would ask me to write the foreword as we've only known each other for a few years having met at some community events. My second thought was "If I had a nickel for every time someone told me they were writing a book, I'd be rich!". In all seriousness, writing a book takes a huge amount of effort. I've thought about doing it myself several times over the years, but it's such a massive commitment. The closest I ever came was collaborating on a book jointly with Ruben Spruijt and Dr. Bernhard "Benny" Tritsch on Remoting Protocols and 3D Graphics. My contributions to that book were much smaller than Ruben or Benny's, but it was still a ton of work. I think people take for granted the amount of time and dedication that it takes to write a book and I do hope that if you find Johan's book valuable that you drop him a note to thank him for his efforts. I'll extend my personal thanks to Johan for all of the extended delays I put him through on scanning the book's contents and writing this foreword. I'm sure there were times when this foreword seemed less likely to finish than the rest of the book's contents ;). Thanks Johan!

With that out of the way, I want to say a few things about what I really like about the approach of Johan's book. While I didn't have time to proofread the entire book, I did spend time going through the structure, focus, and topics. I'll sum up my thoughts in three areas:

1) A focus on the why! A really great portion of this book focuses on "Starting with Why". For those who have not read the wonderful book by Simon Sinek named "Start with Why: How Great Leaders Inspire Everyone to Take Action," you should definitely add it to your list. I've seen far too many IT projects that were started for the wrong reasons and spending some time to

consider why you're embarking upon a particular project is always a great vantage point.

2) Learning from others. When I got started in community activities around 2004, I had already been doing Server Based Computing or RDSH for about 11-12 years. I cannot tell you the number of times that I would find assistance for technical problems in online communities like the Citrix Forums, BrianMadden.com's Forums, The Thin List, VMware's communities, etc. When I attended my very first BriForum in 2005, I recall being so star struck at people like Brian Madden, Rick Dehlinger, Benny Tritsch, Doug Brown, Thomas Koetzing, Jeff Pitsch and many others. To my surprise, my prior 12-15 months of heavy posting on the Citrix.com and BrianMadden.com forums had made me a new entrant to this community and many of the people that I idolized were all seeking to meet me at BriForum. What an amazing rush of feelings that brought to me and really helped to shape who I am today.

I owe great parts of career, my community and my friends to these early experiences. A huge thank you to all of those who influenced me to give back to the community. Johan is continuing this tradition by spending time in this book interviewing people that provide unique points of view and information sharing with his audience. It may seem like a small thing to do in a book, but honestly, this is something that makes this book truly wonderful.

3) Consultative Approach to Design – There are many books that give you instructional information on how to install or configure a product. This isn't that type of book. What this book aims to do is draw on Johan's years of experience at architecting and designing VDI environments and provide real-world guidance on the best ways to do so. I spent roughly 20+ years in consulting prior to joining VMware.

I believe that consultants have a unique experience having the opportunity to deploy technology in all different types of customer environments and often with different management/monitoring/security tools, different objectives on disaster recovery and business continuity, etc. These diverse environments provide a treasure trove of knowledge that is best when shared. I think Johan does a great job of sharing his experiences and to me sharing one's experience with others is part of what makes us great as a community. Thanks for sharing your experiences Johan!

# CONTRIBUTORS

There's no "I" in team" (except for the one in #TeamITQ). This book couldn't be finished without the help of some of the greatest (community) friends, ITQ colleagues and family. Without their help, it might have been unreadable (thanks Ray Heffer and Tobias Kreidl), lack important information or wouldn't be detailed enough. Chances are that it wouldn't even be finished in time or finished at all. I am forever grateful to these awesome people!

I would like to express a special thank you to Marco van Baggum, the guy who started working at ITQ a month prior to my first day at the most awesome company in the world. Marco and I went through the same journey from day one and after four years we are still going strong! Marco to me is one of the most knowledgeable architects, especially in the field of Software-Defined Datacenters and Software-Defined Networking.

Another special thank you goes out to the 15th VCDX-DTM, Sean Massey. I first met Sean at VMworld, during the VMware EUC Champion meeting back in 2016. It's pretty cool to meet people with shared passion for VDI. Sean is a great community friend and someone with the same drive I have, which is why I asked him to contribute to this project.

# MARCO VAN BAGGUM (VCDX 223)

My name is Marco van Baggum and Software-Defined Datacenter aficionado. I've started my IT career, fresh from school in 2002, at a rather small company as a service engineer repairing Fujitsu Siemens laptops. From there I worked my way up from repairing desktop to repairing servers, but then I saw the world of virtualization coming up and knew that it was time to make a move and hop on the virtualization train. I moved to a new company in a Technical Consultant role and started to work with customers and helping them to solve their IT challenges on various platform and various vendors. From Windows NT to Windows Server 2012, VMware ESX to Citrix XenServer, VMware View to Citrix XenApp (yes, I've done that too...), HPE to Dell, 3Com to Cisco and everything in between.

After continuing to grow in my role, I still wanted more and started looking how I could specialize more. I've always seen VMware as the leader in the virtualization field, so the choice where to specialize in was not difficult, but where... Which company could enable me in achieving my goal? Working at a customer I saw a name of a company come by which didn't ring a bell, so google to the rescue. The slogan of the company read "Passion for Technology", well that definitely triggered my interest. I applied for a job at ITQ and started a month later, almost at the same time as the author of this book Johan van Amersfoort!

It is a little bit hard to explain what happened next, but you could compare it with the best rollercoaster in the world. Learning and passing VCAP exams, working on achieving the vExpert status, working with peers on trying to achieve the VCDX status. And as the icing on the cake, earning my VCDX number #223 in 2016. I'm still far from ready to slow down, the world of SDDC is speeding up and getting more and more interesting. To conclude, I love the vCommunity, all the time and effort people put into creating all different kind of content for us all to consume. To everyone from the vCommunity, keep up the good work and help us to share knowledge! I hope to see you at one of VMworlds or any other events, just come over and say hi!

# SEAN MASSEY (VCDX 247)

My name is Sean Massey. I've been in Information Technology for 13 years, and I've spent the last eight years focusing on datacenter and end-user computing technologies. I am currently a Senior Technical Architect focusing on VMware end-user computing technologies for a consulting firm based out of Chicago, IL.

End-user computing is a technology set that I am passionate about. I enjoy the challenge of delivering business changing technology to organizations and end-users. I feel that end-user computing technology changes organizations and enables them to embrace the advances that we've seen in computing, mobility, and network technology.

I have been a VMware vExpert since 2014, and I've been involved with the VMware EUC Champions program since 2015. I'm also involved with the NVIDIA GRID community and the VMware User Group. I blog about end-user computing related topics at https://www.thevirtualhorizon.com.

I earned my VMware Certified Design Expert in the Desktop and Mobility Track in February of 2017.

I live just outside of Appleton, Wisconsin in the United States with my wife, Laura, my two children, and two cats.

I'd like to thank Johan for putting together this book and asking me to help contribute.

# ACKNOWLEDGEMENTS

The VMware end-user computing community is a great one of which I am very proud to be a part of. I would like to thank the following persons, as well, as they have contributed to a project that will hopefully act as an accelerator for more consultants and architects to become a VMware Certified Design Expert in the field of Desktop & Mobility:

- Ray Heffer
- Brian Gammage
- Simon Long
- Shawn Bass
- Fabian Lenz
- Erik Bohnhorst
- Jared Cowart
- Kim Harrington
- Ruben Spruijt
- Tobias Kreidl
- Brian Madden

The ITQ family is a tight one. The guidance of some of the brightest minds and mentors brings the best out of every person. I never thought that after four years of rollercoaster rides, something like this would be possible. Because of that, Francisco Perez van der Oord and Paul Geerlings have earned a special place on my wall of fame.

Writing a book could have a low *Wife Acceptance Factor* (*WAF*). This is because you will need to focus on writing and thus will miss out on certain things (like parties, birthdays and going to the beach on a sunny day). Because of her constant support and understanding that this project is a dream come true, she is awesome!

Last but not least, creativity is essential to make something look great. My brother Rick van Amersfoort is one of the most creative people I know and was responsible for the cover design.

# INTRODUCTION TO VDI

Since you are reading this book, I'm guessing that you are in some way interested in a virtual desktop infrastructure (VDI), based on VMware Horizon technology. That's great news, because now we share a common interest!

## WHAT IS VDI? (AND WHAT IS IT NOT?)

A virtual desktop infrastructure is a centrally hosted desktop infrastructure that provisions and presents desktops to an end-user. Those desktops are distinct virtual machines with their own operating system and resources like virtual CPU, virtual RAM and virtual NIC. A single virtual desktop isn't shared between multiple users at the same time. Each user has their own desktop on which he or she can work.

A virtual desktop is something utterly different from *Remote Desktop Services (RDS)*. An RDS session may have the same user experience as a VDI session, but in case of the RDS session, the resources are shared on a single RDS server. The RDS server has multiple concurrent sessions and every session allocates a few resources that the RDS server can offer. In the case a user runs an application that takes a lot of resources, the other user might have a negative user experience. So multiple users, share a single virtual (or physical) Windows machine. Remote Desktop Services basically is an evolved version of mainframes and terminals, dating all the way back to the early 1970's.

A VDI can either be hosted from your own on-premises datacenter as well as from an external datacenter (that you manage). Technically speaking, if you run your virtual desktops from a shared VDI service (like Horizon DaaS or Horizon Cloud on Azure) it is still VDI. But in that case, we call it Desktop as a Service (DaaS).

# WHAT IS VMWARE HORIZON?

The obvious answer to this question, is that it's VMware's VDI solution. But it's actually much more. Let's start off with some history.

In 2007, VMware invented the Virtual Desktop Infrastructure with its product called VMware Desktop Manager 1.0 (VDM). It was basically a way of running a desktop operating system on top of a hypervisor.

The one thing it missed was a broker service that connected users to virtual machines. For that specific reason, Propero was acquired in the same year, as they had a great solution that could fill that gap. That product was renamed to the service we know now as the Horizon Connection server. A funny side note is that some people that were part of Propero still work at VMware. Matt Coppinger (who you might have seen in many VMworld sessions on stage) is Director of Technical Marketing for EUC and Mark Benson is well known for his significant involvement in creating the Unified Access Gateway (UAG). VDM 2.0 was released in January 2008 which included the Connection server.

Since then, a lot has happened.

In version 3.0, VDM was renamed to VMware View, and using RDP as a desktop protocol.

In 2009, VMware View version 4.0 was released which contained the PC over IP (PCoIP) desktop protocol built by Teradici and gave the end-user a better user experience than RDP.

VMware View 5.0 was released in 2011 with 5.3.1 being the last version before VMware Horizon 6.0 was born in 2014. Horizon 6.0 was the first version that fully supported a multi-datacenter approach (using Cloud Pod Architecture) and had the ability to use a web browser as a client on an endpoint using the Blast protocol.

In March 2017, VMware Horizon 7 was released and again had tons of new functionality and scalability improvements. It was also the first version that had further developments with the Blast protocol as the primary connection protocol. Blast Extreme (as this was the new name of the protocol) had some significant improvements on latency tolerance, bandwidth usage and (secure) remote connectivity with the Access Point (which we know now as the Unified Access Gateway), a tunnel appliance for remote access instead of the View Security server.

Every version that came after Horizon 7 included more features to improve the Blast protocol (such as Blast Extreme Adaptive Transport), extensibility with endpoints and the user experience. It's a complete solution that is basically ready for most use cases.

The funny thing is that you can still find parts from the VDM era in the current Horizon solution. Some log files and directories still contain the name VDM.

The current Horizon portfolio, which this version of the book is based on (version 7.5), contains a series of products of which most of them were acquired in the past couple of years.

The following products are included in the VMware Horizon Enterprise edition:

- vSphere including vCenter – this is the trusted hypervisor and management framework that delivers and manages virtual machines (including virtual desktops).
- Horizon – this is the virtual desktop and remote application provisioning solution (and the main character in the book).
- User Environment Manager – VMware's answer in solving roaming profile problems and create a persistent user experience in non-persistent environments.
- App Volumes – the layering technology that could save you lots of time in deploying applications to virtual desktops.
- ThinApp – this is VMware's clientless application virtualization technology.
- vRealize Operations – the monitoring solution that is used to monitor health, performance and efficiency of the complete VDI platform.
- Identity Manager – a web-based portal that provides Single Sign-On (SSO) functionality and conditional access to the Horizon desktops and remote applications.
- vSAN – VMware's solution to enable Hyper-Converged Infrastructures (HCI) to use local storage in a host to act as a shared storage device.
- Horizon Help Desk Tool – A solution included in VMware Horizon which allows you to troubleshoot user sessions in near real-time.

Additionally, the following solution will be discussed in this book:

- NSX – VMware's network virtualization solution, which lets you manage your network from a software-defined perspective.
- VMware Cloud Foundation – the Hyper-Converged solution based on vSAN ReadyNodes and a full Software-Defined Datacenter (SDDC) stack.
- Liquidware Stratusphere – a desktop and application assessment solution by Liquidware.

- Goliath Technologies – performance and application monitoring solutions to troubleshoot user experience issues.
- NVIDIA Virtual GPU – enterprise-grade graphical acceleration solutions for datacenters and virtualization.

# PREPARATIONS

This might be the most boring chapter if you are eager to start designing and building your virtual desktop infrastructure. But it's *the most crucial* one if you want your project to be successful. The most depressing thing that could happen, is your CFO pulling the plug on your VDI project because it was far more expensive than everyone thought.

## START WITH WHY?

A question we always ask our customers is "Why?". Because VDI is quite often deployed for the wrong reasons. The most prominent misconception is that it is a lot cheaper (in terms of Capital Expenses or CapEx) than having to manage physical endpoints including Microsoft operating systems. It is true that if you implement VDI, the chances are that your endpoints might be much less powerful and much cheaper, like the Google Chromebook for example. But it all depends on the use cases that exist at your company. A developer might not be able to work on a Chromebook, and as the Chromebook is just browser-based, peripherals like a smartcard reader or integration features like Skype for Business might not work.

The downside in terms of investments is that the datacenter hardware that is required for a certain number of users might be a lot higher. Did we talk licenses yet?

Why should you build a solution like VDI? The answer isn't that simple. It can be due to a lot of reasons. The most common ones:

- Your operational expenses might be a lot lower due to central management, application layering and features like Just-In-Time (JIT) provisioning.
- VDI can improve your desktop security by using micro-segmentation, disabling interaction with the endpoint and using conditional access policies for access.
- The uptime or availability of your current (physical) desktop service needs to be improved.
- Security by containing user desktops and applications within the datacenter.
- Operational efficiencies (quicker support resolution time).
- Enable mobile work-force and Bring Your Own Device (BYOD).
- Disaster Recovery (DR).

First start to define the *why* before you continue with the rest. The *why* or main reason behind the project will help you in creating a business case, because it is the primary goal of the business case. If your *why* is to improve the availability of the desktop service, this comes with a price.

Let's Illustrate. Imagine your daughter asks you to bake a cake. You should ask her: *"Why?"* "Is it going to be a birthday cake, a Christmas cake or a wedding cake?"

As you might know, they are all cakes, but the *why* drives the ingredients we put into the cake and drives the end result.

Another way to see this is the user experience. During a project you will have to make many design decisions. Understanding the user experience requirements will either drive success or failure in VDI projects.

You should never forget *why* you are doing this. The *why* will be unique to every project.

# BUSINESS CASE

For whatever reason you (or your boss) might have to start a VDI project, it's a great idea to create a business case before you start designing. In some of the projects I worked on, customers didn't create a proper business case (with a failed VDI project as a result). The business case will validate if your *why* behind the project will be successful. One of my customers is a stockbroker in the Netherlands. They run a VMware Horizon-based VDI solution. Years back when they created a business case for VDI, it was quite simple. Their *why* behind the project stated that their stockbrokers must be able to work without any downtime and can't experience any negative performance. Application latency between the desktops and backend services couldn't be higher than five milliseconds (5 ms) – at all costs.

In this case, it was quite simple because any downtime or degradation in performance would cost them more in terms of lost income than the investment in VDI.

Compare this to any insurance policies you might have. An insurance policy will make sure that you are able to pay for any damage that you might have caused in case of an incident. Chances are higher that you won't have to use your insurance at all, but in case it is necessary, you can. The monthly fee might be high, but it is much lower than the amount of money you must pay in case of damage if you weren't insured.

I've seen some great business cases being created on the back of a coaster or on a napkin in a bar, but in most situations, this isn't always the best approach. Make sure that the business case is solid before you start your design to avoid disappointment and set the right expectations!

This is an overview of some of the topics that you need to think about when creating a business case. It might take more, but that is depending on your situation.

| Item | Explanation |
|---|---|
| Number of users | The number of users will determine a lot. The number of physical hosts, the number of licenses, the amount of work (and thus the number of admins), etc. Take concurrency, shifts and office hours into account, as well. |
| Use cases | The types of users that will be working on VDI. On an average, a higher density of task workers can be achieved on a single host, comparing to power users. |
| Growth | What growth is predicted in terms of users, sites, concurrency, for instance? This helps size the infrastructure. |
| Infrastructure hardware | What hardware is needed to run the infrastructure. This includes networking, storage, server hardware, etc. |
| Connectivity | Connectivity is required for every aspect of your infrastructure. Between datacenters, between offices, between networking components, between the VDI platform and remote users, etc. Also, don't forget your DR connectivity (such as separated fabrics in case of an ISP failure). |
| Datacenter costs | A datacenter filled with hosts consumes a lot of power, as will server racks at an external datacenter. Cooling, offsite backups, data center maintenance (water detection, fire suppression), monitoring and operational costs are essential for a complete business case. |
| Labor | VDI might save you on OpEx. On an average, one VDI admin can manage up-to 500 desktops, but this is |

| Item | Explanation |
|---|---|
|  | depending on the number of different use cases. |
| Licenses | Try to find out what the most efficient way of licensing is to your infrastructure: Enterprise vs Standard licensing or CPU vs User count. |
| Client hardware | Centralizing desktops may have a positive impact on your choice of endpoints. Less compute resources might be required on an endpoint, which could save money. The same for licenses. Linux-based thin clients don't require a Microsoft Windows license for the physical endpoint. |

A great way to calculate the Total Cost of Ownership (TCO) and Return on Investment (ROI), which drive a big part of the business case, is to use the online tool that VMware has developed.

https://euc-roi.vmware.com

# MISCONCEPTIONS

What marketing PowerPoint slides will show you, is that basically every use case can be implemented on VDI (including their own application set). While that is true in most cases, it might come with a price. In the ideal situation, all your users can run on a single *non-persistent* virtual desktop pool (based on *Instant Cloning*), all applications are distributed through *App Volumes* and user profiles are configured with *User Environment Manager*. If you only run straightforward applications and your entire workforce consists of a use case called *Task Users*, this might be the case. Unfortunately, in most cases it's not. That's where the complexity and OpEx (Operational Expenditure) misconceptions come from.

If you ask a random end-user computing architect, what the most complicated part of VDI is, with 99% certainty the answer will be

"Applications" (probably followed by "Printers"). From my experience, that's where your admins will spend 90% of their time on. The bigger the application landscape, the bigger your admin team will be. There isn't a real calculation of how many apps can be managed by one admin, but in my experience, I have seen an average of 100 apps handled by a single admin.

Most of this complexity comes from the fact it's not the question *if* an application will create conflicts but *when*. Conflicts with another application, conflicts with the operating system, conflicts with drivers are all examples of application-related challenges.

Depending on the number applications, the number of admins might be different. If your application landscape has a lot of complicated applications such as development suites that you need to manage, you will obviously need a bigger work force.

Another misconception is that VDI will lower the CapEx (Capital Expenditures) involved with your desktop strategy. While cheaper endpoints might be used by end-users in case of VDI, investments in datacenters, connectivity, host hardware will have a high impact on the TCO if you compare it to a decentralized desktop management and delivery model.

I'm not trying to scare you off, but you need to have the right expectations before you start designing.

# INTERVIEW WITH BRIAN GAMMAGE

In this book, I would like to give you the best advice possible. From a technical perspective that's reasonably easy, but from a financial perspective, it is somewhat harder since the only financial job I am really good at, is spending. And don't forget the business, of course. The business is essential in a business case since it is your most important stakeholder.

Nevertheless, I would like to share the best knowledge that is available and therefore I've asked Brian Gammage (Chief Marketing Technologist at VMware) for an interview about business cases. Brian has a vast track record as he has been working as a subject matter expert on this specific topic at both VMware as well as Gartner.

Me: Why should organizations invest in VDI?

Brian: Virtual desktop infrastructure is a mechanism to make an application accessible to a user in a way that breaks the dependency on the access device. Because of that, there is a range of reasons. It may be that you want to protect the application the way is accesses associated data to make it more broadly available. This is the case in many healthcare scenarios, particularly in North America, where obviously there are very clear restrictions and guidelines on how data can be accessed. The key is that you need to demonstrate compliance with these restrictions. So, it is an architecture which allows you to demonstrate that compliance automatically, so it makes it much easier to access systems as you move around a hospital environment. Another reason can be that it's just about extending access and making applications more freely available. And that can be useful, but it depends on the application. How many times did I have someone showing me proudly that they run a CAD application on their smartphone. Just because you can, doesn't mean you should. That reason is a little bit broader.

The real reason is the long term. Historically, it was done because of flexibility. Hardware being stuck to software and operating systems being stuck to applications, the complete desktop stack was very inflexible in terms of deployment. To become more agile, organizations were looking for ways to make their delivery of applications and access to applications more flexible. So, all of the historical reasons come from that side.

The very first time we saw desktop virtualization done, was at a customer in the UK who wanted to send the process of transcribing data from insurance forms in their database, offshore, to access lower-cost labor without having to send the database. They were looking for remote access mechanisms. Moving forward, I think it will become something different. Increasingly, as we see customers looking for the *digital workspace* (an environment where you can control the posture of access to individual applications, services and data on any device) your unit of investment is the individual, not the device. So, you will manage users (or identities) and not devices. Then, VDI will become the mechanism to package up and expose the applications you have to keep on using from previous generations of deployment and are not yet ready to expose directly. This is particularly relevant for in-house built applications, because commercially available applications are typically being modernized by their providers, so they can be more easily updated, used and purchased by their customers. Every organization has applications developed in-house, maybe 15 or 20 years ago, with no documentation. They were never designed with the context of mobility and those applications nowadays make, for instance, the tax office talks to the pension department or finance talk to accounts payable. These are usually business critical and stuck in the previous generation of technology. So being able to go on a journey towards a digital workspace and take those applications with you, you need that decoupling technology. And historically, VDI was a very use case-specific deployment model, while we are now seeing that it's becoming more of a general requirement.

Me: With that in mind, what would be the best way of convincing C-level management of investing in VDI?

Brian: Any investment case is made out of value versus cost. So, there are two elements there. First of all, what is the value going to get? Being able to access your application anywhere in a hospital while simultaneously demonstrating compliance with the regulation that allows you to access funding for treating patients from their insurers (which is the scenario with HIPAA in North America), is a real strong value-based business case. Because access to that funds in very critical.

Value, however, is in the eye of the beholder. The question is going to be: What are you trying to achieve? And then demonstrate the value of what you are trying to achieve. Enabling users to access a business process (which all applications are), in places and times they were otherwise not able to access that business process will probably mean that they are doing work that they were otherwise not able to do. And that, therefore, is a top line of revenue generating a contribution to any business, which can be valued.

But there is also a strong cost-based motivation. It's important to look at the cost-based progression of VDI. Most organizations have been investing in desktop infrastructures since the early 1980's. Progressively, as they have gone through, and refreshed, and replaced and upgraded that desktop infrastructure, they moved through a process where they are typically replacing existing functionality instead of extending it since the old thing is worn out, not because the new thing is giving something new. And that very much leads to a cost-based buying position. Particularly when you look at the recent operating system migrations which are the main reason for reinvesting in the desktop portfolio. I don't think any organization has migrated from Windows XP to Windows 7 because they explicitly wanted Windows 7 because it was fantastic. They migrated, because Windows XP was out of support. So, when you think you are just replacing instead of gaining a (marginal) value, then you look for cost savings. Historically, the cost-saving equation for VDI was all about OpEx. You take the desktop instances of distributed devices where you have to manage and intervene on them in many places and you bring them centrally where you simplify the process of management in the way that IT has always lived with value. Through automation and standardization. And so, you save on OpEx. At VMware, we have been building business cases for customers for six years and created between 1100 and 1200 business cases, so we have an awful lot of data. I can tell you from that data we know exactly how long our customers normally budget to manage a desktop image in a physical and a virtual environment. At the end of the day, that translates into a very important metric which is "How many IT staff you need per user", and that is OpEx. In a physical environment, it's going to be somewhere between 200 and 300 users which can be managed by a single member of the IT staff. 200 to 300 is depending on the ratio of desktops and laptops per user. Typically, you would need fewer people for desktops and more for laptops. When you move to virtual desktops, it's typically 1 to 500.

You are gaining efficiencies in operations. But historically, you were paying more money for the infrastructure. Because you were buying servers and storage and you were still paying for access rights for Windows and access devices. We tracked this data very carefully in the last number of years and there was a crossing point in 2014 with the release of Horizon 6 where we slashed the costs of the biggest single item, which was storage. Up until that point, the average storage costs per year, were $150 per user, just because enterprise storage is expensive. We introduced two technologies that slashed that. First of all, *Virtual SAN (vSAN)*, which allowed you to move out dedicated *Storage Area Networks (SANs)*, which were expensive because they were designed for performance and resiliency, into using low-cost storage components in the servers themselves. We saw that the average storage costs per user, dropped down by about 2/3. When we combined that with the layering technology of App Volumes, we were able to standardize the elements in the desktop image even further and that reduced the amount of storage required for the individual user (depending on whether he was using a persistent or non-persistent desktop) by somewhere between 30% for a non-persistent desktop and 70% for a persistent desktop. On average (based on the non-persistent vs persistent ratio) we call that a 40%. Suddenly, we saw that storage cost come down from $150 to $30 per user per year. And basically, in those two steps we saw that the capital costs of a physical desktop became more than the equivalent cost of a virtual desktop. That's including access to the software, operating systems and access devices. Those two things became critical, so the cost-argument really pivoted in 2014. Before 2014, it really was a case of a virtual desktop costs less over life, but costs more to buy. And pay more to save later is not everyone's business case. Suddenly, costing less to buy and less to manage became a much stronger business case.

So, how do you justify the business case? By figuring out what you are trying to achieve and what do your cost savings look like.

Me: What is the most underestimated side of a business case?

Brian: Security and risk management, and that is quite simple. How do you measure risk management? There is no established metric. The closest you would come, would be the OWASP framework used to establish the security profile of web-based applications. And that tends to work on the basis of likelihood, costs and impact, but it doesn't give you an objective measure. So, how do you measure the risk of something? I think it is a little bit like insurance. There are many times when as individuals, we renew our insurance premiums, and think: well, nothing happened on this in the past five years, is this really worth paying. But the minute something happens, you see the value. So, I think the most understated and underappreciated business value of VDI is information security and the additional protection that it gives you by the reduction of the risk profile.

Me: Do you think that this is also the reason why business cases fail or have a negative outcome, or would that be related to other reasons?

Brian: I think business cases fail, because people don't know how to make them. And that surprises me. Because as individuals, we all make business cases. When you buy a car, you start off with an idea of what you want. I start by doing my research by what they look like. The same with dishwashers. I don't know what dishwashers these days do, I am going to look at what the latest dishwasher-capabilities are. Then I am going to look at the prices of the dishwashers and I am going to work out what I want to pay. And in doing that, I am forming a rough equation of cost and value that's going to put me in a position. I think that most organizations don't go through that process in any kind of rigorous way and don't bring on board stakeholders. So, all they see is the cost and not the value. And I say that because I mentioned earlier that we produce lots and lots of business cases. Sometimes we produce a business case with a negative ROI and the customers still buy because they see the value. So, going through the process and exposing and having things on the table, I think, is really the principle. If you can't see what those items are, and you can't somehow form an idea of its value or cost, I don't think you can go through that equation. I don't think that business cases fail, I think lack of business cases fail.

Me: What do you think what the impact of cloud-based VDI versus on-premises VDI is, in the business case?

Brian: Yes, but again, the theme here is the lack of objectivity in creating the business case. We went through this principle about three years ago when we first made Horizon Air available broadly. I had a senior executive customer come through to me which said: "Brian, we are going to go with Horizon, I just can't decide on whether we build it ourselves or whether we buy it as a service. And here is the question, how should I think about that?". That actually, was the right question to ask because we sat back, and we thought "How should we think about it?". It isn't just about costs, it's about value. So, let me tell you. If you are deploying a cloud-based desktop, then you are fundamentally doing it for one of 3 reasons: Firstly, because of the predictability of your requirement is highly variable. If that's the case, then the business case of investing in the peak requirement makes no sense. Let's imagine that you run a ski-school in the mountains. In the winter, you employ 1000 people. But in the summer, you employ only 30. Each of those people is using a set of applications to record the progress of all of their students. There would be no business case of you investing in 1000 seats on-premises. You would probably invest in no more than 30 and the rest coming in as when you need them. So, predictability of requirement, therefore, becomes the first thing. On the other hand, if you run a manufacturing organization with very steady demand and supply relationship and a fixed set of people all the way through, then outsourcing a very stable requirement for you would have a very different cost/value/benefit relationship.

The second motivation is about speed to deploy. If internally it takes you longer because you need architects and all of that extended team to go through the deployment and the planning process, it may be that the extended team of the provider gets you up and running, faster than you could do it yourselves. So, if your principle is "There is a market opportunity over there, now, we need to be there. Every day is lost revenue", then your business case is made.

The third thing is that you maybe have a balance sheet strategy. This tends to happen less in commercial organizations than it does in government organizations. The balance sheet strategy is about not wanting to own anything. So, if you are actively trying to remove things from the balance sheet, then there is a value of taking this thing off the balance sheet. It is a financial strategy, and you might think that it sounds academic, but we see government organizations doing this across the world. It is important to remember that commercial organizations, typically don't have discontinuities in higher-level management. There tends to be a continuity. They might make a strategic change in direction at some point, but they're not likely to flip and change. Whereas in the world of politics and governments, we potentially bring in a new set of higher-level managers every four years or so. And one of the things we often see is that new people coming in, often want to show some differences than the people who came before. So, you do see it in that sector.
Three simple motivations: predictability, speed to deploy/bring it up and running and a balance sheet strategy impact the choice of cloud-based VDI versus on-premises VDI.

Me: What three takeaways would you have for organizations regarding business cases?

Brian: Make sure you build one first. Make sure that when you build one, you have a buy-in from all the stakeholders because there is no point in building a business case that one person understands. So, put in the work to understand what matters to you, how technology impacts your business and that the business case is connected with your overall business strategy. If your business strategy is to extend and open up new offices, any business case you build, should be connected to that strategy. So, first of all, build a business case with some diligence. As I said before, I don't see failed business cases, I see a lack of proper business cases.

Number two: be cautious. It's easy to assess things at the top-lead range of savings every time. If you know that the savings you can get from a particular technology is in the range of 30% to 70%, which is the example we used for App Volumes before, pick a number towards the bottom end of that range to set expectations. Because you want to exceed delivery in terms of savings, not underachieve, so your business case will be a success.

Finally, only include the right items and only include the items you can measure. If you can't measure it, don't include it. Because you won't be able to demonstrate any success in the business case that you built. If, for instance, you know you are rolling out a digital workspace and today you are seeing on average six password or credential support tickets with your support organizations per user, per year, use those things to justify the business case. Because you can demonstrate with external data where you can, that each support ticket typically cost $15. So that's $90 per user, per year that you are eliminating when rolling out a digital workspace. Use that and not something that is fluffy and can't be demonstrated.
So, to sum up: make the business case, get buy-in and only measure the things you can measure.

So now you took all hordes that were needed. If you are still convinced that VDI is the right solution for your workplace, you may continue to the cool stuff in the next chapters.

# DESIGN APPROACH

This is one of these parts of the process where a Jedi mind trick from Star Wars would be awesome. *"You will take this VDI architecture as I designed it"* while waiving your two fingers at the CIO of the customer.

A VDI design like it should be. No constraints to deal with, no risks to mitigate and just some simple and easy-to-implement requirements. An unlimited budget and as much bandwidth as possible. Yep, I'm still dreaming.

Even in a greenfield situation with a VDI environment following the basis of a VMware Validated Design (VVD), you will always have constraints, risks and certain requirements. Mostly because VDI nine out of ten times is purposely built to handle legacy applications.

To help you handle these design challenges, this chapter is all about designing VDI. To me, that's the most exciting part of a project. It's also the most challenging part because in most projects, requirements tend to change during the design phase, which could ultimately impact your design.

Therefore, why design VDI instead of not just building it? The answer is quite simple. Let's compare building VDI to building a house. I live in the coastal part of the Netherlands, in a small city called IJmuiden. I know for a fact that it's windy all year long, the air and rain are salty, and soil is mostly made up out of dune sand. My house is built on top of a concrete foundation including pilings that only go 2/3 meters (6 – 9 ft for people who don't use the metric system) deep. My house sits stable without any shifting. This is due to the stable, sandy soil.

Just ten Kilometers away, there is another small city called Velserbroek. The soil in Velserbroek is mainly mud. If the same construction as my house was chosen to build a house in Velserbroek, the house would most certainly shift and probably crack.

In this case, the type of soil that is used is a constraint that impacts your design. It automatically adds a risk to your design which needs to be mitigated.

With VDI designs it's entirely the same. First you need to create a plan. The plan will include your design goals and scope. You need to gather all requirements and constraints and identify risks. Next you will assess the existing infrastructure, hold interviews with different stakeholders (such as end-users, admins and managers) and finally should start creating a conceptual architecture. The following diagram describes the whole design process.

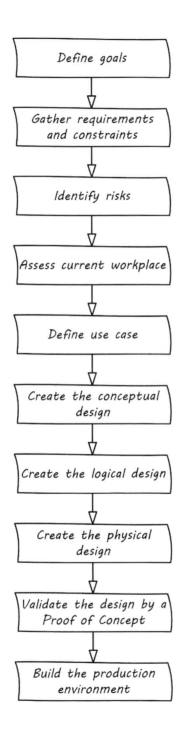

In the next sections, I will highlight some of the steps mentioned in the previous figure.

# GOALS

Defining the goals in your design should be one of the easiest parts of the design. What would you like to achieve with the solution? A higher uptime? Lower operational expenses due to the fast and easy provisioning of desktops and applications? The ability for users to work from home? All of these reasons are valid reasons to invest in VDI.

The goals will be a significant driver behind requirements. If one of the goals is that you want to give end-users the ability to work from home, this will automatically lead into suitable requirements such as "The VDI must be available from external locations".

Be sure that the goals in your design are **smart**. Smart is an acronym which you can use to guide your goal setting.

To make sure your goals are clear and reachable, each one should be:

- **S**pecific
- **M**easurable
- **A**chievable
- **R**ealistic
- **T**ime-sensitive

In case of the example of users being able to work from home, the goal itself is quite smart.

It's specific, because we know what we should design. It's measurable, because we know how to test if it works. If it's achievable depends on the constraints we have (which I will cover in a later section). If there isn't any internet connectivity available because our datacenter is in the middle of the desert, the goal isn't achievable (and not realistic).

The time-sensitivity is less important for our design goals as time-related aspects are quite often discussed in an earlier phase of the project.

# REQUIREMENTS

Goals, on average, will automatically create some of your first requirements.

Requirements-gathering is an essential part of the design process. Requirements will steer your design in a specific direction. For instance, if a company would like to have an availability of the VDI service of 99% (per year), it would mean that the service could have a downtime of no more than 3 days and 15 hours. In that case, it isn't necessary for the solution to be deployed in a multi-datacenter platform with active/active load balancing (because recovering the environment from a backup is quite feasible in that time).

If, on the other hand, the customer asks for the availability of four nines (99.99%), it is unlikely one datacenter will be sufficient. This means that the environment can only tolerate 52 minutes of downtime per year to still be compliant with the SLA.

The most important aspect for every requirement, is that it can be validated. So, if your customer has a requirement for 99.99% availability and you decide to build a single datacenter VDI, make sure you can validate that in case of a disaster you are able to recover within 52 minutes.

Another example is performance. If your customer has a requirement that the process from clicking on a remote desktop icon on an endpoint until the moment the user is presented with a desktop is one minute, make sure you can validate it.

For both requirements, it is also vital that they are monitored. You want to make sure that as soon as the load on a platform grows, you are still able to be compliant with the requirements in the design.

Requirements must always be accompanied by a design scope (or context). The number of users, working locations and infrastructure sizing (aggressive or conservative) are all examples of scope items. So, if you agree with a customer that they have a maximum of 2,000 users and during the deployment you are able to validate that the performance requirement for the logon process is compliant, you did a good job. But as soon as the customer decides to add an additional 1,000 users to the current platform without adding additional host/storage capacity, the infrastructure might violate the performance SLA. Therefore, make sure that the design scope and requirements are signed off by the customer.

Requirements can either be functional or non-functional.

A functional requirement describes *what* the system should do. For example:

- The user should be able to install software in his virtual desktop.
- The user should be able to use a USB headset for VOIP integration.

A non-functional requirement describes *how* the system should do it. For example:

- The VDI platform should have an uptime of 99.9%.
- Login on to the desktop should not take longer than 20 seconds.

Requirements can be categorized into qualities. The most common design qualities are:

| Design Quality | Explanation |
| --- | --- |
| Manageability | The effect of a design choice on the flexibility of an environment and the ease |

| Design Quality | Explanation |
| --- | --- |
| | of operations in its management. Sub-qualities might include scalability and flexibility. |
| Availability | The effect of a design choice on the ability of a technology and the related infrastructure to achieve highly available operation. |
| Recoverability | The effect of a design choice on the ability to recover from an unexpected incident that affects the availability of an environment. |
| Security | The effect of a design choice on overall infrastructure security. As a design quality, security may also indicate whether a design has an impact on the ability of a business to demonstrate or achieve compliance with specific regulatory policies. |
| Performance | The effect of a design choice on the performance of the environment. This does not necessarily reflect the impact of other technologies within the infrastructure. |
| Scalability | Depicts the effect the option has on the ability of the solution to be augmented to achieve higher sustained performance within the infrastructure. |

More design qualities can be found on the following Wikipedia page:

https://en.wikipedia.org/wiki/Non-functional_requirement

I will explain use cases in a later section, but let's take a use case called *road warriors* as an example and see what requirements drive this specific use case.

Road warriors are employees who spend at least 90% of their time outside the company offices. They need secure encrypted, access to business-critical applications such as the CRM and project management tools. Depending on the location of the customer and their business hours, road warriors might work outside of the standard business hours of the company.

We can extrapolate a couple of requirements from this use case scenario:

- The environment must be accessible from outside the company premises.
- The environment must be available outside of the company business hours.
- Connectivity between the user and the solution must be encrypted.

These requirements will be the basis for design decisions we are going to make in our logical design such as "Unified Access Gateways will be used to provide a desktop to external users". In this case, this decision is justified with the requirement that the VDI must be available from outside the company premises.

Some great advice I got from one of my VCDX panelists, is to sort the requirements based on importance and impact to the design. Look at the following requirements.

- The solution should have an availability of at least 99.95% (based on a year).
- The solution should be able to manage roaming user profiles.

The first requirement has a massive impact on the architecture. This is because in (nearly) all situations, this requires a secondary datacenter.

The second requirement has an impact on how profiles should be managed. A profile management solution such as VMware User Environment Manager (UEM) is required but because of the first requirement will most likely drive your design into a multi-site architecture, this also has a significant impact on the second requirement. This is because VMware UEM itself has some limitations when implementing it in multiple datacenters.

# CONSTRAINTS

A constraint is a restriction that limits you in your design scope and choices. The restriction acts as a requirement in the design. The most common constraints in a VDI design are already purchased hardware, bandwidth limitations or budget limitations.

In an ideal situation (which are mostly greenfield projects), the customer will purchase hardware after the design is signed off. Unfortunately, this isn't always the case. In most cases, the customer already has hardware (compute, storage or endpoints) that need to be incorporated into the design. In these cases, we have to deal with an unchangeable restriction that will drive our design in a particular area.

In Northern Europe, bandwidth limitations are a less common constraint these days as fiber optics are becoming cheaper by the day and ISP infrastructure is getting better and better. But still, in some projects such as the ones in the UAE, I had to deal with it.

Constraints make a project more challenging (and more fun) as it might become a puzzle to create a design that satisfies all of the requirements. Too many constraints might make it impossible to satisfy the customer's requirements, but it will be your job as an architect to help the customer in making certain choices.

If, for instance, they already have a storage device that you must use in the design which isn't able to handle all of your desktop storage resources during peak hours, this adds a risk to the design

That's what most constraints will cause. Most constraints will incorporate risks.

If your storage device isn't able to handle all of your desktop storage resources during peak hours, this adds a risk to the design.

# RISKS

In every project I have worked on, I encountered risks. In some projects, they were bigger than in others and in most cases, they aren't a deal breaker. A design risk to me is more of a challenge I'm facing that I can't solve with technology and I have no control over. It might be a danger to the design. The risk needs to be identified in the design and if possible, mitigated but at least acknowledged.

The most important reason to add a risk to the design, is to cover your butt if stuff goes wrong. Like I mentioned in the *requirements* section, risks also are bound to the scope of the design. If you design your environment for 2,000 users and the existing storage device doesn't allow you to scale beyond those 2,000 users, it might be a risk. In case the customer needs to be scalable as can be, this will most certainly pose a risk. If no scalability is required and the VDI will be sized for maximum use (at 2,000 named users with 1,500 concurrent) this won't be a risk.

Something that helps me create risk awareness amongst the stakeholders, is to create a risk heat map. The risk heat map contains all the project risks including the impact when things go wrong and the chance of it going wrong.

|  | Low impact | Medium impact | High impact |
|---|---|---|---|
| **High Chance** | | | |
| **Medium Chance** | | | |
| **Low Chance** | | | |

The next table describes the chance values and description.

| Chance value | Description |
|---|---|
| Low | Once every five years or less |
| Medium | Once every two years |
| High | Once every year or more |

The next table describes the impact values and description.

| Impact value | Description |
|---|---|
| Low | Impact on primary processes is limited |
| Medium | Possible damage to the image of the company<br>Possible high financial impact due to the recovery from disasters<br>Primary processes are directly affected, but workarounds are possible |
| High | Direct damage to the image of the company<br>Direct high financial impact due to the recovery from disasters<br>Primary processes are directly affected |

Let me give you an example of how to use the risk heat map:

One of the risks I encountered in a recent project was due to a bandwidth constraint. The customer had an on-premises datacenter that had a 1 Gigabit internet connection. That internet connection was used for both VDI-related traffic as well as other traffic such as hosted web applications, mail traffic and things like Spotify. The customer had 3,000 end-users that all had the ability to work from home. If all those users were office workers, we didn't face any challenges. But unfortunately, there were also quite a few designers and those designers don't have the same bandwidth requirements as the office workers. If all the end-users would be working from home because of a problem at the office, we would definitely have a challenge in terms of user experience.

In this case, the chance of something like this happening is very low. The impact could be medium as we could create a workaround to scale down the bandwidth settings and block sites like YouTube and Facebook. Users would still be able to work, but with a slightly different user experience.

Mitigating those risks as much as possible is essential. The most important way to do that is through design choices. When looking at the bandwidth constraints, the risk of users creating congestion on the WAN links, can be reduced if bandwidth policies can be created that will scale down the user experience in case of a failure. More about risk mitigation and design decisions in the *Design Decisions* section.

# ASSUMPTIONS

Let's start with the number one rule on assumptions. *An assumption is the mother of all **** ups.* Use assumptions as your very last resort in architecture designs. Unfortunately, sometimes you can't avoid them.

For instance, when working with session concurrency. Session concurrency information is an excellent example of something that can be collected during the assessment phase. It might be that the assessment took place during a less busy period (five weeks) of the year. Let's say that your assessment report contained information of 2,000 concurrent sessions in those five weeks. It might be the case that this is the maximum concurrent number of sessions during other moments as well, but you aren't sure. In this case, we assume that the maximum number of concurrent sessions is limited to 2,000. When you add this to your design, you are covered in case the 2,000 limit is exceeded and performance collapses (sure, you would size for future growth, but you get the point).

Hence, the first reason is to cover your butt in case of changing behavior within the organization you are designing the VDI for. The second reason you might use assumptions is to allow for supporting infrastructure that is required to build the VDI. For instance, VDI relies heavily on Active Directory, DHCP, DNS, KMS, etc. You want to ensure that these services are running and are healthy. In this case, you might use an assumption to let the customer know that these services need to be in place and running correctly. The same holds true for supporting physical infrastructure that you might need for availability requirements. If the customer demands four nines (99.99%), you will heavily rely on networks, power feeds and monitoring systems. You want to make assumptions that these services are available for at least the same number of nines.

The tricky thing with assumptions is that they (almost) always come with risks. In case of a supporting service failing, it will quite often mean that the VDI won't be available, either, so make sure that for every assumption, you figure out if there is an accompanying risk.

# USE CASES

I slightly touched use cases in the requirements section already, but let's dive a bit deeper into an essential part of your design; the end-user (as it is your most important stakeholder in a VDI project). Types of activities and functionality an end-user requires to perform their role are called *use cases*. Groups of end-users that have the same functional requirements can be consolidated into a single use case. Examples of use cases are:

- Road warriors
- Task users
- Knowledge workers
- Designers
- Developers

Defining a use case, starts with a story around the use case. For instance:

*Designers are users who could either be contracted or work as employees for the organization. They require graphically intensive applications to run on high-resolution monitors. They generally work from a fixed location in the main building of the organization and should also be able to work from home or a customer if necessary.*

The story describes the situation of the group of users with their critical characteristics that differentiates them from others – characteristics such as working locations and business hours, types of (business critical) applications, devices or other functional requirements.

The following table gives an overview of properties that define a use case.

| Attribute | Definition |
|---|---|
| User community/Business unit | Name of the user group or business community. |

| Attribute | Definition |
|---|---|
| Business justification for virtual desktop | A high-level overview of why this group will benefit from virtual desktops. |
| General use case | Name of general use case (for example, call center, or work from home). |
| Number of users | Outline the number of users, including initial number of concurrent users and any projected growth in number of concurrent users. |
| User classification | Task worker, knowledge worker, power user or developer. |
| Locations | The locations of where users will be connecting. |
| Time of use | The times and days when the desktop will (typically) be used. |
| Operating system | The operating system that will be used for the use case. |
| Language | The language of the operating system that will be used for the use case. |
| Core applications and datacenter kocation | List of the core applications required by the business unit and their primary back end datacenter locations. |
| Datacenter | The datacenter that will house the desktops for this user community. |
| Desktop class | Type of desktop standard that will be used (standard, powerful, graphical accelerated, etc). |
| Desktop type | Persistent or non-persistent. Full Clones, Linked Clones or Instant Clones. |
| Standard or custom image | Specifies whether the default desktop image is used, or a custom image will be required/added to the service catalog. |
| Active Directory Domain | The Active Directory Domain that this community will reside in. |
| Endpoint | The devices that users will access from (that is, third-party Windows machines, iPad, thin/zero clients) and the type of Horizon Clients that will be |

| Attribute | Definition |
|---|---|
| | leveraged (Horizon Client for Windows, Horizon Client for Mac, and so forth). |
| Elevated privileges required (install applications) | Yes/No. |
| Multimedia or video requirements | Yes/No. |
| Audio requirements (excludes VoIP) | Yes/No and Direction (one-way or bidirectional). |
| Accelerated graphics requirements (3D) | Yes/No. Further explanation required if the answer is Yes, such as a list of graphically accelerated applications or required API (like CUDA or OpenGL). More about these requirements in the *Graphics and Remote Protocols* section. |
| Printing and scanning | Yes/No and Type (network or redirection to client's printers). |
| Monitors | Number of monitors and maximum resolution. |
| PeripheraldDevices | Types of peripheral devices that will require USB redirection (excluding printers). |
| Authentication methods | Standard Windows login, smart card or other possible multi-factor authentication solution. |
| Connectivity | WAN, LAN or remote. |
| WAN bandwidth and WAN latency information | Identify the latency and bandwidth utilization for WAN users. |
| Specific requirements | Does this use case have specific requirements such as an increased availability? |
| Specific constraints | Does this use case have specific constraints such as specific peripherals? |
| Planned start date for pilot/test phase | When will this use case start testing or piloting the VDI? |
| Planned start date for production migration | When will this use case start working on the production VDI? |

Further in the book, I will go more into details on these individual properties of the use cases.

Next to creating several functional requirements (see the *Requirements* and *Constraints* sections for information), you can also see that this use case validates that your design goal "The solution must be available from external locations".

# ASSESSMENT

Assessing a customer should be part of every design project that one does. Because building something based on assumptions may work but will eventually end up not meeting the business requirements and the project may fail. But what should be assessed? A consultative answer would obviously be "It depends", and of course, it totally does. There are some questions you need to get answered before you can decide what to assess.

- Are you going to migrate from an old to a new VDI platform?
- Are you migrating physical endpoints to a VDI platform?
- Are you aiming for an operating system migration (i.e. Windows 7 to Windows 10)?
- Are you going to support Windows desktops only?
- Are you going to migrate specific use cases or everything?
- Which applications are used?

Depending on the answer to these questions, your assessment might look different in these scenarios. What isn't different is the duration of the assessment. On average, you should try to assess at least five weeks. Certain users might execute specific applications once a month for invoicing or other calculations. The longer the assessment, the higher your accuracy will be.

When you look at the types of goals of your design, the assessment might depend on them.

For instance, you might be migrating from an old to a new platform. Based on the current workload and possible complaints of users, you should have a good idea of what an average desktop should look like. But still, in this case it is wise to run an assessment in the current VDI to get the facts like resource usage, application usage and user experience (login times, application start times, etc.). Requirements might have changed since you deployed the first VDI solution. Also, operating system requirements might have changed (we all know that Windows 10 uses more resources and might even require a GPU to perform better).

If you are migrating physical endpoints to a new VDI platform, the assessment might look different. In this case, you basically assess all physical machines that you would like to centralize and consolidate on the VDI platform.

The assessment tool will collect data on a regular basis from every machine and send it to a central monitoring appliance. Again, try to collect data for at least five weeks. In the assessment application, you can see the collected information and run all sorts of queries and reports on that data. Things like performance data (CPU/MEM/Disk/Network/etc), application data (what applications are used and by whom) and user data (logon times including a breakdown, logon storms, etc.) provide essential data when you are preparing a migration or designing a new VDI environment.

The output of the assessment could serve multiple goals:

- Collect behavior from specific use cases (at what times are your road warriors working).
- Collect resource information which can be used for sizing the new infrastructure.
- Collect user experience information (what are the average logon times, is there a GPU required).
- Get insights in web-based and traditional applications that are being used by the organization and eliminate *shadow IT.*

To ensure that the assessment information is as specific as possible, it is wise to create a report set per use case. If you have an environment that contains 4,000 users of which 50 are graphical designers and create a single report set that shows averages of all of those 4,000 users, and will size based on those averages, you can be sure that the designers won't be happy if you migrate them to a pool with these settings. Therefore, run the reports on a per-use case basis to ensure the most specific numbers per use case.

When talking about tools, there are many of them. Examples are UberAgent, ControlUp and Lakeside Systrack. Liquidware Stratusphere is a tool that I would personally recommend. It's simple to deploy, not intrusive when the agent runs on a (virtual) desktop and querying the data is really simple. It offers out-of-the-box reports that are useful and has an API that is easy to use (even for non-developers).

Another excellent use case for assessment software is the elimination of shadow IT. In traditional workspace environments (Active Directory with GPOs, managed corporate Windows desktops/laptops and a fixed set of applications), the IT admin was in control over what and the end-user was doing. He knew what kind of software was used by the end-user and IT-services, like working from home was quite complicated to implement.

A few years later, software-companies invested heavily in SaaS-based applications. Solutions like Salesforce, Dropbox and Slack are good examples of applications that are easy to use, don't require an administrator to deploy and solve many user-experience issues that previously existed due to the traditional way of management.

*"If my IT Admin doesn't give me VPN access so I can work from home, I will just use Dropbox to solve that problem"*. This is one of the most common responses from end-users when they take a survey that I use during an assessment. Slack is a similar example. *"We use Slack as our primary collaboration tool because our own solutions lack ease-of-use and don't support mobile devices"*. Admins are entirely in the dark and security officers have challenges to keep intellectual property within the company premises. The last example presents another issue: Salesforce. Some of my bigger customers have teams

that are responsible for purchasing and invoicing and have a daily job of placing the right numbers in the cost center they belong to. Imagine what happens if someone from the sales team decides that the internal CRM system has lousy usability and uses his company credit card to purchase SaaS-based licenses from Salesforce? Again, a challenge to the customer and its governance.

This is what we call shadow IT: applications and services that seem to be unseen to responsible persons at the customer. And the main reason is that enterprise-IT hasn't evolved through the years while end-users have. Take the millennials for instance. They use their own device to work on during their college-years on high schools and universities. With the ease of use, they deploy software from an app store and when it is in need of a (sometimes daily) update, stuff just works. There is no need for a maintenance window, no service interruption and if the application they installed doesn't do as they like, they just download and install another one. It's that simple.

In my opinion, this is the main reason for shadow IT. If companies don't act, the problem will become even more significant.

But how should you act? I mean, this may sound like such a big problem that you might not know where to start. The first step in solving the shadow IT problem, is to become aware of what is happening in your workspace environment. To do that, assessing the environment is a great way to start.

As more and more applications are web-based, the solutions used to assess your environment must be able to analyze web sessions as well. That's where Liquidware Stratusphere is really helpful. Liquidware Stratusphere has a feature called the *Advanced Browser Inspector* which collects information on applications that run inside the browser of an end-user.

Assessing a customer or your own organization isn't complete with just technical details. Quite often, an end-user computing project comes along with a lot of changes to an organization. If you are going to implement VDI for the first time, you need to make sure the right stakeholders are involved to manage it when the project is completed. Would that be the current datacenter team? Or maybe the team that that manages the current physical desktops because a desktop is a desktop, right? Preparing a customer to a VDI journey takes more than just technical solutions. Talking to end-users and representatives of use cases is just as important. You as an architect have to know what the end-user is expecting and also have to set expectations for the end-user. I'm quite certain that for at least 50% of the customers I have worked for, the project had a bigger impact in a *people & processes* perspective than in a technical perspective. Of course, without technology, it would be impossible to help the customer, but you have to remember that most people who were born before the 1980's probably are more challenged in adapting to new situations (like a new desktop operating system, a new laptop and most certainly a complete new method of doing their job like VDI).

Be very sure to take the end-users seriously, because they are your best friends and the key to success. Designing a fast, stable and intuitive technology sounds like a surefire success, but I can assure you that the project will fail if the end-users are unsatisfied with the delivered solution. A use case assessment starts with asking questions and listening carefully to what the user has to say. With those questions, you need to find the answers to fill in the use case's definition from the *use cases* section. That definition together with technical details from the desktop and application assessment should be a great starting point.

# DESIGN DECISIONS

All the sections in this chapter have guided you in gathering as much information as possible. Based on all that information, the next thing you will do is create design decisions. You need these decisions because you need to justify why you used certain functionality.

For instance, if you need to design an architecture that requires four nines of availability, you need to decide to add a secondary datacenter and possibly a *Global Site Load Balancer (GSLB)* service to satisfy the requirement. Another example is the use of *Unified Access Gateways (UAG)*. If you have a requirement to provide external access, the chances are that you need to include UAGs in the design.

The next table is an example of how I use design decisions in a design.

| Design | Details |
|---|---|
| Number | DD001 |
| Decision | Unified Access Gateways will be used to provide secure remote access to the VDI |
| Quality | Security |
| Justification | Connecting to the Horizon Connection server and desktops directly from the internet is insecure and requires non-https network ports to be opened up in the firewall. UAGs are chosen since the customer doesn't have a VPN solution in place. |
| Impact | More resources are required to run UAGs in the management cluster |
| Risks | None |
| Risk mitigation | N/A |
| Requirements Met | The solution must be securely accessible from the internet |

As you can see, if there are any risks involved that can be mitigated, they can be justified in the table as well.

Design decision should be used throughout the whole architecture design process.

# DESIGN STRUCTURE

As you now know how the design process works, it's time to focus on architecture and what choices you have in which scenario. I will use examples of some of the most common scenarios to help you in making the right choices. There are many ways of structuring a design document and I believe that most of them are good.

During my VCDX project (which was a VMware Professional Services Organization engagement), I used the VMware Solution Enablement Toolkit, which includes a design template. The template is a fine tool if you need to design and deploy a straightforward Horizon infrastructure, but it lacks a structured storyline. There are stories of people submitting a VMware design template for their VCDX who almost always fail. When I did my first mock defense with that template-based design, I got utterly roasted. The design itself looked good, but it was quite hard to guide the group through my journey. That's when I decided to start over again entirely, but this time with a structured storyline. The first step I took, was to create a wireframe and use that as an index and guideline in taking the customer from specific topic to the next logical topic. The wireframe looks like this:

| Design section | Contains |
| --- | --- |
| Design overview | • Project background<br>• Scope and goals<br>• Guidelines on how to read the design |
| Conceptual design | • Requirements<br>• Constraints<br>• Risks<br>• Assumptions |
| Use cases and assessment framework | • Detailed information on different use cases<br>• Assessment outcome per use case<br>• Assessment information on application landscape |

| Design section | Contains |
|---|---|
| | • Endpoint standards |
| Conceptual architecture | • Use cases<br>• Conceptual architecture overview<br>• Connectivity overview<br>• Datacenter overview<br>• Delivery components<br>• Common solution elements |
| VMware Horizon logical architecture | • Solution overview<br>• Cloud Pod Architecture<br>• Local pods<br>• Management block |
| VMware Horizon physical architecture | • Broker components<br>• Databases<br>• Patch management<br>• Active Directory integration |
| Virtual desktop logical design | • Pool design |
| Virtual desktop physical design | • Virtual machine<br>• Operating System configuration |
| vSphere logical architecture | • vSphere virtual datacenter design<br>• vSphere Cluster design<br>• vCenter & PSC design |
| vSphere physical architecture | • Host design<br>• CPU, RAM and GPU design<br>• Host sizing<br>• Virtualization consolidation ratio virtual desktops<br>• Virtualization consolidation ratio Management VMs |
| Storage logical design | • Management storage logical architecture<br>• Management datastores<br>• Management sizing<br>• Desktop storage logical architecture<br>• Desktop datastores |

| Design section | Contains |
|---|---|
| | • Desktop sizing |
| Storage physical design | • Management physical architecture |
| | • Desktop physical architecture |
| Networking logical design | • Virtual networking |
| | • Load balancing |
| Networking physical design | • Switching |
| | • Host networking |
| | • VLAN design |
| | • Quality of Service |
| Graphical acceleration and connection protocol design | • Protocol choices |
| | • Encoding/decoding |
| | • Graphical acceleration |
| User environment management | • Active Directory |
| | • Profile strategy |
| | • UEM logical architecture |
| | • UEM ohysical architecture |
| | • Folder redirection |
| | • Policy settings |
| Application delivery | • Application landscape overview |
| | • Delivery strategy |
| | • App Volumes logical design |
| | • App Volumes physical design |
| | • ThinApp logical design |
| | • ThinApp physical design |
| Endpoints | • Endpoint strategy and design |
| Security | • Virtual desktop security |
| | • Endpoint security |
| | • Identity management |
| | • Role-based access |
| Monitoring and maintenance | • Monitoring critical services |
| | • User experience monitoring |
| Backup and recovery | • Backup strategy |
| | • Business continuity & disaster recovery |

This wireframe will make sure that you won't skip any topic that needs to be covered in the design document. Since the VCDX project, I continued using this wireframe and added or removed chapters based on the customer requirements. In the next sections, I will cover the essential details of a VMware VDI architecture. Not everything mentioned in the wireframe is going to be covered, as some parts are excellently documented in other books or whitepapers. I will refer to them, instead.

# DESIGN FRAMEWORK

To make sure you ask the right questions prior to/during the workshops with the customer and to gather as much information as possible, one of my community friends, Fabian Lenz, has developed a framework to achieve this goal. Fabian is like me, a VMware EUC Champion with tons of experience in the field of VDI. He is a blogger at https://vlenzker.net where you can find more information about the framework.

The framework will help you gather as much information as possible during the design phase. The framework consists of a lot of questions which can be answered in two ways. One is the actual answer to a question. The other one is the effort it takes to get a straight answer. If the answer is given straight away, the score is 5/5. If no answer can be given and you are expecting challenges along the way, the answer will be 1/5. Questions with a low score need more attention during the design phase than the ones with a high score. It's not that these will get a bigger focus during the design phase, it's more that it could take more effort or sessions with the customer to go through the subject.

Let run through an example:

*Which anti-virus/malware technology will be used?*

The answer could be a straight answer like "Palo Alto Traps". In that case, the score will be 5 because it doesn't require any additional effort to get it answered. If the answer needs discussions, design sessions and possibly vendors coming over, it's a 1. Everything else is between 1 and 5.

*Please note that you need to run the framework **before** the design phase, not during or after. Also, these questions can be used as an example. Additional questions can be added for your specific situation.*

# Service-definition

- Which services are delivered from the VDI platform? (management services, access services, desktop services)
- Which SLAs are defined for the specific services?
- How are the SLAs measured?
- Which reports are required for the services?
- How is the capacity for the VDI environment forecasted?
- How are service relevant tickets created?
- How can communication with the end-user take place?
- How will the maintenance window be communicated?
- How are service tickets evaluated after completion for efficiency, looking for duplicate instances, etc.?

# Hardware Layer

- Are there any constraints regarding a specific hardware vendor?
- How many availability zones/datacenters exist?
- What are the connectivity characteristics (redundancy, latency, etc.) between different availability zones and sites?
- Who is permitted to do racking and stacking?
- Who is responsible to get network connectivity
  - Layer 1 – cabling
  - Layer 2 - Ethernet/VLAN
  - Layer 3 - IP and ACL
  - Layer 4 - Firewall

- What constraints exist regarding networking (e.g. single VLANs only within a rack/row)?
- How are racks granted for future usage?
- What constraints exist regarding power/cooling/space/rack location?
- How can vendors get access to the datacenter facilities for support reasons?
- Are there any security policies regarding the access of the physical hardware?
- How much upfront time is required to get access to the datacenter?
- What network infrastructure is used for storage, management, vMotion and virtual machine traffic? (10G/40G)

## Virtualization & Management Layer

- Are there any requirements regarding a specific version of the management components?
- Are there any SSL certificate requirements for the management components?
- What, and how long is the process of signing certificates?
- Are there specific Windows Server versions / images that must be used?
- Which licenses are used for Horizon, Windows and other management relevant components?
- Which availability requirements exist for the management layer?
- How can the project/operations/support team access the environment?
- Are there any future security constraints regarding management of the environment? (transfer/usage of scripts or other useful tools to maintain the environment)
- How are the management operating system components maintained (patches, upgrades)?
- How can new operating/support people be onboarded to access the environment?
- How are Active Directory objects created?

- How are Active Directory OUs managed?
- How are service/technical users created (no expiry)?
- How are DNS entries maintained?
- Is there any additional system where components must be documented? (CMDB)
- Are there any existing security policies regarding VMware vSphere and Horizon?
- From which zones is access to the virtual desktop required? (internet, internal network, remote-office site, etc.)
- What are the maintenance windows for the management services?
- Are Microsoft Remote Desktop Session Hosts in place?
- In which of the corporate systems must the VDI platform be integrated?

## Virtual Desktop ILyer

- Which guest operating system is required for virtual desktops?
- What does the desktop operating system lifecycle look like (regarding patches, updates, upgrades)?
- Who is responsible for the guest operating system?
- How is software deployed in desktops?
- Is a user allowed to install applications? If so under which circumstances?
- Are there any security-relevant policies based on specific context (e.g. disallow printing, file exchange copy and paste while accessing via the internet)?
- How is the desktop ordered for a user?
- Which security policies exist for the desktops?
- Who is allowed to have support-access to the desktops?
- Which anti-virus/malware technology will be used?
- Who is responsible for the anti-virus/malware solution?
- Who defines security policies?
- Who defines firewall policies?
- Is it possible to optimize the virtual desktop for the usage within virtual environments?

- Is it possible to create dedicated GPOs with all Horizon and VDI relevant group policies?
- Who is responsible for packaging software?
- Who is responsible for packaging the user profile application config files
- How many applications are in use?
- Is there a list of applications?
- What is the lifecycle and QA process of applications?
- Has there been a use case analysis/assessment?
- How many users will be on the platform?
- Which percentage of the users are expected to use the platform concurrently?
- What is the expected growth rate?
- How many desktops will a user get?
- Which different workloads are required for the use cases?
- Do specific applications or use cases require graphical acceleration?
- Are there any legacy applications that might need to be virtualized?
- Which collaboration or communication tool will be used within the virtual desktops (Skype for business, Slack, Zoom)?
- Are there multiple releases of the same software package that need to be supported?
- Are there applications that are interdependent on other applications and perhaps even on certain releases/editions of other applications?

## Access Infrastructure Layer

- Which security requirements exist for the access to a virtual desktop (multi-factor)?
- What will be used as second factor?
- Is access via internet required?
- Who is responsible for the DMZ?
- Can VMware-based virtual appliance be deployed within the DMZ?
- Can the NSX load balancer be used?

- If not, which other load balancer will be used?
- Who is responsible for the load balancer?
- Shall events of users working on the VDI and Horizon itself be stored persistent (within a DB or a flat file via syslog)?
- Will any smartcards or other ancillary technologies be needed to control access and how compatible will these be with the current infrastructure?

## Endpoint Layer

- What security policies exist for the endpoint (where the Horizon Client is installed or embedded)?
- Which endpoints are used (Mobile devices, macOS, Windows, Linux, zero clients)?
- Which additional devices will be used (e.g. webcam, scanner, serial devices)?
- How many monitors and which resolution will be used?
- Are all endpoints managed or unmanaged devices?
- How is the Horizon Client installed and maintained on the endpoint devices?

The answers to these questions will both help you gather as much information as needed to do your design sessions with the customer, but they will also help you form your project. The project manager will be able to guide the team and assess all dependencies which will be beneficial.

# CONCEPTUAL ARCHITECTURE

The very first step in creating an architecture design is to create a conceptual design. This basically describes the VDI on a very high level. The conceptual design covers the design overview, conceptual design and conceptual architecture sections from the wireframe.

As we covered the design overview and conceptual design already in the previous chapter, let's dive into the conceptual architecture.

The conceptual architecture will be driven by the most essential requirements, that is to say, requirements that significantly impact your design if they are different. Examples of such requirements are:

- Availability (the higher the number, the more redundancy is needed)
- Accessibility (external, internal and/or Internet)
- Security (endpoint protection, firewalling and/or logging)
- The application landscape with its specifics (cloud, on-premises, mobile, etc.)

The conceptual design doesn't contain any products or specific solution, but the type of functionality that will be used.

Instead of describing that vSAN and ESXi will be used, it will be described as a *virtual infrastructure layer*. The same goes for vCenter. We will call it the management, instead.

The following diagram shows a conceptual architecture for a multi-datacenter VDI:

Use cases

**Management & Monitoring**

| Access layer | |
| Connection protocols | |
| Datacenter 1 | Datacenter 2 |
| User data | |
| Local Apps | Local Apps |
| Desktops | Desktops |
| Virtual Infra | Virtual Infra |
| Shared infrastructure | |

**Security & Zero-trust policies**

It's essential that every piece of functionality will be described in the conceptual design. In case of the figure above, users will connect from the internal network only. Which means it is essential to describe this in the conceptual design, as well as supporting components such as Active Directory (including DNS/DHCP), monitoring and logging.

Based on my experience, it is imperative to let the customer sign off the conceptual design before you start designing the logical and physical designs. The main reason is that customers need to be aware of consequences that (mainly) requirements and constraints bring to the table. It happened multiple times that a customer required four nines but didn't really know what (financial) impact it had (due to a wrong approach in creating a business case). I started designing the logical architecture. When I was almost finished, the customer decided that it was too expensive, and I had to design the whole thing again from scratch. Also, the conceptual part is the most critical part as the logical architecture (in most cases) will be based on deployment standards and reference architectures (such as the *Horizon multi-site reference architecture* created by the VMware EUC Technical Marketing team).

# LOGICAL ARCHITECTURE

The logical architecture contains your proposed solution including functionality. It also contains essential components such as connection brokers, desktop pools, application delivery components, profile solutions, monitoring solutions, etc. The level of detail of the logical architecture is limited to components only. The details of each individual component (such as the technical specs of a connection broker or a Microsoft SQL cluster) are typical examples of a physical architecture (and will be explained in the next section).

The following figure is an example of a multi-datacenter logical architecture:

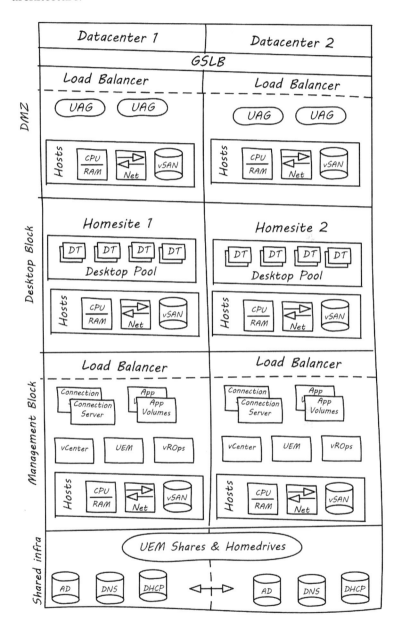

As you can see in the diagram, the architecture shows you some more detail on how the solution should be deployed. The individual components are shown in the middle along with the integration with the existing infrastructure. All components are described but limited to logical detail. If you look at the management block, you can see that it contains storage, but no additional details on the number of datastores or the path selection policy on the Host Bus Adapters (HBAs). The same for App Volumes. App Volumes Managers are used, but no details on the number or the individual App Volumes Managers (such as the number of CPUs or the version of Windows Server).

In the logical design, you also need to describe what the individual components will do for the solution. For instance, if VMware User Environment Manager (UEM) will be used to manage profiles, you need to describe what UEM's role will be in the entire solution as well. Typical examples of design decisions and topics that belong to a logical design:

- Is UEM deployed in one or both datacenters?
- Will it use mandatory profiles or default profiles for users?
- Are you going to manage applications as well?
- Do you need to create backups of the profiles?
- Is logging required?

These are typical things to describe and to include in the logical design as design decisions. The more detailed topics belong to the physical design such as:

- What permissions are required on UEM shares?
- What is the retention and level of logging of UEM?
- What GPOs will be used to configure UEM?

# PHYSICAL ARCHITECTURE

Like explained in the above section, the physical design is all about the details. And although the term "physical" is used, it's not directly paraphrasing something that can be physically touched or something like that. Every component (hardware or software) has a lot of parameters that need to be filled in before you are able to run a deployment of, for instance, VDI. All of those parameters belong to a physical design. In the logical design, we described what an individual component would do for the solution, in the physical design you will describe what an individual setting will do for the component.

Physical architectural diagrams contain more detail than the logical architecture diagrams and might even contain brand names or models of storage solutions, switches, etc. Basically, this contains every bit of information that impacts the solution in one way or another. You can describe what kind of network adapters or HBAs are used in a storage component. That's the deepest level of detail that you should describe. The color of the network cables in this case doesn't impact your design and shouldn't be described (in both diagrams or text).

The following diagram is an example of a multi-datacenter physical load balancing architecture.

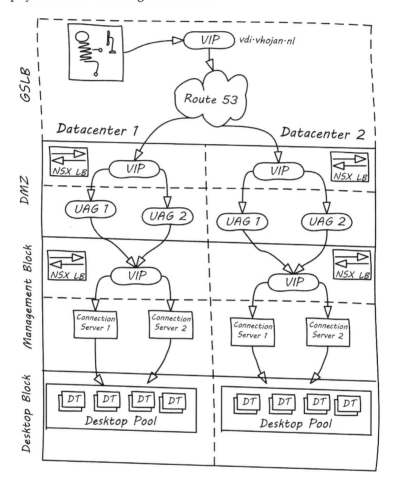

Typical examples of design decisions and topics that belong to a physical design:

- How many Connection servers will be used?
- What specifications will these Connection servers get?
- Number of CPUs
- Hard disk size
- Placement of the events database
- What kind of GPU profile will be used for my CAD users?

- What kind of disconnection timeout will be used for my task users' desktop pool?
- What Path Selection Policy will be used for my storage solution?

The physical design, together with a configuration workbook, are the two most critical guiding documents for a consultant or engineer to build a solution, so be sure to include all information that is required in order for them to successfully deploy the solution.

# INTERVIEW WITH SIMON LONG

In my journey in becoming a VCDX, but also in my daily life working as an architect, I find it very useful to read blog articles from fellow end-user computing architects. Designing architecture is fun and getting other people's opinion and view on certain topics (like design choices or requirements gathering) is what keeps me sharp and constantly critical to the work I deliver.

One of those blogs I was referring to, is The Slog (http://www.simonlong.co.uk) which belongs to Simon Long (End-User Computing Architect at Datrium). Simon is VCDX #105 (on Datacenter Virtualization and Desktop & Mobility) and has been a VCDX panelist for many years.

The first time I met Simon, was during VMworld in 2015. He was presenting on how to design a vSAN storage platform for Horizon (the VCDX way). That presentation was three days after I submitted my VCDX design. The next time I would meet him, was during my defense ☺.

In 2017, Simon has led a project in which he designed an EUC dogfood environment so employees at VMware are able to work on the latest and greatest version of any of the VMware EUC products. The project was called the OneDesk project for which he received a VMware CIO Innovation award.

Fun-fact about Simon: he is the co-founder of vBeers.org ☺.

Since to me, he is one of the best end-user computing architects around, I asked him some questions about architecture design.

Me: Why should people use the VMware design methodology to create and build a Horizon design?

Simon: As an architect, it's easy to get bogged down in the weeds during the design process. Following a sound methodology can help ensure you don't miss important aspects of the design that typically get overlooked.

Me: What is the most underestimated side of the design phase?

Simon: Monitoring and alerting. It's usually an afterthought. Most people understand the importance of platform security, performance and making sure the environment is available in the event of a failure. As such, the majority of time and focus is spent in these areas. But without sound monitoring and alerting, how do you know if the platform is performing adequately? How do you know if a component has stopped functioning? Usually, it's when someone calls the helpdesk to complain. Spending time to understand what metrics to capture and what thresholds to alert on can help your operations team identify issues before your users do.

Me: As a VCDX panelist, you have seen a lot of designs. What are the characteristics of a good design?

Simon: Simplicity. Usually the simplest designs end up being the most successful. Only include in your design what is actually needed to meet your customer's requirements. In my experience, as complex as a large Horizon design can be, ultimately customers end up having the most issues with the day-to-day operations of the environment. Keeping your design simple (where possible) will benefit the customer way more than utilizing all of the bells and whistles available to you.

Me: VMware Cloud Foundation has full support for the Horizon platform. What kind of impact does this have on the design phase of a project?

Simon: VMware Cloud Foundation is designed for performance, meaning, customers no longer have to spend time calculating how many hosts they'll need for X number of desktops. Just fill out the fields in the deployment wizard and let VCF do all of the sizing calculations for you.

Me: Why should people pursue the VCDX certification?

Simon: Embarking on the VCDX journey is not something that should not be taken lightly as it requires a lot of work and dedication. However, I can guarantee you, no matter how accomplished you think you are, you will learn far more than you expect, and you will come out the other end a much more rounded architect. It true! I've yet to be proven wrong ☺.

Me: What are the three key takeaways you have for readers regarding the design of a Horizon platform?

Simon: The first is to perform an assessment on the current desktop infrastructure <u>BEFORE</u> you begin the design process. If you do not understand the performance requirements of the desktops and applications, is it extremely difficult to design a Horizon environment that can offer performance adequately without being oversized.

The second would be Simplicity. By keeping your design simple, there should be fewer opportunities for issues to occur and it will also make it easier for the customer to manage.

And last, remember that the most important thing to your customers is usually the applications that their end-users need to perform their daily tasks. Not the desktop image, not vSAN, not DRS, not a vROps custom dashboard. If their end-users are unable to use their applications or the applications do not perform as expected, it doesn't matter how perfect your final design maybe, it will not be seen as a success. Don't lose sight of what is most important to your customer.

# ARCHITECTURE

Like I mentioned in the little bit of history at the beginning of the book, VMware Horizon once started off as Virtual Desktop Manager (VDM). The main reason for a new provisioning tool for desktop VMs is that desktops are utterly different from server VMs. Where a server VM is quite often treated as a pet, desktops VMs are like cattle. In case a pet gets ill, you go to the vet and try to make it better. In case of a cow (one of the thousands) becomes ill, a farmer probably replaces it with a new one.

To give you an idea of these differences, I summed up a couple of them.

**Operating System**

This is the obvious one; in most cases a desktop operating system (like Windows 10) is used in the VM. In some cases, a server operating system might be used because of license or application constraints (a DaaS provider had to use Windows Server 2016 dressed up like Windows 10 because licenses were cheaper).

## Licensing

The way a license is issued to a desktop differs from a server because desktops have in most cases a very short lifecycle. This means that a single user might use a different desktop every day and that the license for this desktop needs to be activated every day, as well. A Microsoft KMS server is required for this form of activation.

## Lifecycle

A server has in most cases a lifecycle that ends as soon as an operating system upgrade needs to be executed. In the worst case, this could take up to a couple of years. For a desktop, this could be a couple of years as well, but quite often it might be a month, a week, a day or a few hours even. This is due to the fact that desktops should be non-persistent (or stateless) where possible to reduce operations costs. Non-persistency has a direct impact on how user data, user settings, profiles, GPOs, etc. are handled. In case of a lifecycle change, these need to be persistent to avoid complaining users.

## Security

From a security perspective, desktops might be your worst nightmare. A server is in a typical situation only accessed by the IT admin. In case of a desktop, it is of course accessed by an end-user and through the console. It requires you to completely adjust the virtual desktop so end-users aren't able to pose a risk to your datacenter.

## User Experience

Because the user accesses the console of the desktop VM, he will notice it immediately when there is a performance issue. In case of a start menu that doesn't pop up when the start button is pushed, he will start to complain (and it might be to you). In short, ensuring enough compute resources, bandwidth and storage is essential for a great user experience. It is also crucial to monitor for user experience metrics, but more about that later.

## Applications

Everyone who has ever worked with VDI knows that this is the number one cause for a headache. Where a server generally has a specific purpose (mail server, file server, proxy server), a desktop doesn't. In an ideal situation, all of your desktops are non-persistent and are able to use all of the apps in your application landscape, all at the same time. See where this is going? A proper application provisioning strategy needs to be part of the VDI to reduce application issues and management overhead.

## Profiles

If applications are the number one cause for a headache, this is absolutely one of the runner-ups. Take a single virtual desktop. In cases this virtual desktop has a lifecycle of a week (because of update-Tuesdays) and is non-persistent, it means that a lot of different users might be using this single desktop. How are you going to retain their personal settings? If user Luke uses Desktop 1 today, he might be using Desktop 2 tomorrow. So, a proper profile solution is required, as well. If you are now thinking of using Roaming Profiles, please close this book, slap yourself with it as much as needed until you lose this idea. Roaming Profiles suck. Period. User Environment Management is the magic word. But more on that later.

## Accessibility

Servers are (except for web servers) not directly accessed from any location. A virtual desktop, however, is often accessible from any location and any device. Proper measures need to be taken to ensure secure access to a virtual desktop. Also, if a virtual desktop is accessed, quite often users will want to integrate with the filesystem or peripherals on their endpoints because they expect a similar user experience as when they still worked on their physical endpoint. To avoid security risks, be sure to control how the user accesses the desktop and what devices are allowed to be integrated into their session. Webcams, for example, are potentially less risky than USB flash drives.

Due to all of these differences, a dedicated provisioning and management solution is required to create, manage and delete desktop VMs. That's where Horizon comes into play. Horizon contains a broker service (since the acquisition of Propero) that was introduced with the first version of VDM. It provisions desktop VMs, handles entitlements, is able to distribute applications, is capable of tailoring the user experience and takes away the pain and suffering caused by Roaming Profiles with the use of VMware User Environment Manager.

# HORIZON COMPONENTS

VMware Horizon is a complete solution that contains different components that all have their own purpose in the solution.

## Pod and Block Architecture

The following definition of the Pod and Block architecture is taken from the VMware Horizon Enterprise reference architecture.

*One key concept in a Horizon 7 environment design is the use of pods and blocks, which gives us a repeatable and scalable approach.*

*A pod is made up of a group of interconnected Connection servers that broker desktops or published applications. A pod can broker up to 20,000 sessions (10,000 is recommended), including desktop and RDSH sessions. Multiple pods can be interconnected using Cloud Pod Architecture (CPA) for a maximum of 200,000 sessions (as of Horizon 7.5). For numbers above that, separate CPAs can be deployed.*

*A pod is divided into multiple blocks to provide scalability. Each block is made up of one or more resource vSphere clusters, and each block has its own VMware vCenter Server, Composer server (where Linked Clones are to be used), and VMware NSX Manager (where NSX is being used). The number of virtual machines (VMs) a block can typically host depends on the type of Horizon 7 VMs used:*

- *5,000 Instant Clone VMs (without App Volumes)*
- *4,000 Linked Clone or Full Clone VMs (without App Volumes)*
- *2,000 VMs if App Volumes AppStacks are attached*

## Connection Server

The Connection server is the main component of the Horizon solution. It contains the broker service, the (LDAP) database with all of your pools, settings and entitlements and the provisioning engine that creates Full Clone desktop and Instant Clone desktops. The Connection server can handle a maximum of 4,000 sessions in a single desktop block (2,000 is recommended). It can be deployed as a standard Connection server or a replica. The replica acts as a secondary server in case the primary fails. You can have a maximum of 7 Connection servers (including replicas) in a View Pod (which can contain 20,000 desktops in total per Pod). If multiple Connection servers are used in a single desktop block, they will automatically use the same LDAP database that was created with the first Connection server. The Connection server also contains the broker engine, which is based on a Java Messaging Bus (JMS). The JMS makes sure that is a user is requesting a desktop, it will be assigned to a session and redirected to a desktop. Unfortunately, the JMS is latency intolerant, but more on that in the Cloud Pod Architecture section.

## View Composer

Horizon has three different clone options: Full Clones, Linked Clones and Instant Clones. The View Composer was introduced for the purpose of creating Linked Clones only. It works like a project manager, assigning tasks to different project members to build desktops. It requests the creation of a VM from vCenter, customizes the VM according to the customization specification and adds the desktop to the domain. In case a user logs off, Composer will refresh the desktop and in case the desktop needs maintenance due to patch-Tuesdays, Composer will recompose the desktop. Composer is a service that requires a Windows-based machine, a Microsoft SQL database and is a single point of failure. Every vCenter that manages desktops is able to handle one View Composer. That means that in case of a desktop block of 2,000 desktops, a single View Composer must handle everything in that desktop block. If it fails, 2,000 desktops are like a headless snake. Or a project without a project manager; a challenge indeed.

## Enrollment Server

The Enrollment server was introduced in Horizon 7. Its primary purpose is to offer TrueSSO to end-users. TrueSSO is a feature that enables *Single Sign-On* for a virtual desktop and avoids asking for credentials in case a user starts a desktop session from VMware Identity Manager and uses multi-factor authentication (MFA). The Enrollment server is a service that requires a Windows-based VM and a Microsoft Certificate Authority to request short-lived certificates for logon purposes.

## JMP Server

Horizon 7.5 introduced the Just-in-Time Management Platform, also known as JMP. In the last couple of years, VMware acquired quite some different EUC solutions that, unfortunately, all came with their own interfaces and APIs. In terms of simplifying management and reduction if operational expenses, that wasn't really what customers were hoping for. Back in 2015, I got introduced to a new, universal API called Astro. *Astro* would become the new standard API where all (EUC) solutions were able to communicate through. Another cool project you might have noticed is the open-source UI solution called *Clarity*. Take a single

Clarity-based interface, let it talk to multiple different EUC solutions through the Astro API and what do you have?: Horizon JMP. In Horizon 7.5, JMP is able to deploy new Instant Clone desktop pools, add AppStacks to them and configure applications through User Environment Manager, all through a single wizard.

## Unified Access Gateway

The Unified Access Gateway (UAG) is one of the greatest additions to the Horizon architecture. It was introduced in Horizon 6.2 as the Horizon Access Point but has evolved into much more. The idea behind the UAG is simple. It acts as a reversed proxy in front of the Connection server and is the successor of the Horizon Security server. UAG tunnels all incoming sessions from end-users to their desktops or remote apps. In the later versions of UAG, more features were added. It is now capable of being a reverse proxy for Identity Manager and is able to act as an AirWatch tunnel appliance as well to provide secure access to mobile applications running in a datacenter. UAG is based on a hardened Linux appliance and (since version 3.3) running on Photon OS. With every new version of Horizon, a new UAG is accompanied. Instead of upgrading the UAG software, a new appliance must be deployed that includes the new UAG version. If you would use Mark Benson's PowerShell script (Same Mark Benson as from the Propero acquisition), deploying is done in a couple of minutes without the need for additional configuration steps.

# CLONES

As mentioned in the Composer section, Horizon has three different types of clones that can be used: Full Clones, Linked Clones and Instant Clones (next to the possibility to use physical desktops or vCenter VMs as a target desktop, as well). All of these clone types have their own advantages and disadvantages and can be used as persistent and non-persistent desktops.

## Persistent (or Dedicated) Desktops

There are two types of desktops that can be offered to a user, persistent (or dedicated) and non-persistent (or floating) desktops. A persistent desktop is a desktop that contains all of the changes that a user commits to the desktop. If a user logs off and on again, the changes are still there. It's quite comparable to a physical desktop. In most cases, a persistent desktop is used by a single user or maybe just a few users and profile information is quite often stored locally. Persistent desktops are quite often Full Clones as they are suitable of having a long lifecycle. In the case of a Linked Clone or Instant Clone used as a persistent desktop, the delta of that clone will grow until the desktop is refreshed or recomposed, which will break the persistence. That makes Linked Clones and Instant Clones less suitable as persistent desktops. Full Clones are usually backed up as they contain data that might be critical to the assigned user (such as developer or designer data and tools). In the event that a use case has a requirement to install software by itself in each virtual desktop, the persistent full clone is quite often your way to go. There are more options, and these will be discussed later in the book.

## Non-Persistent (or floating) Desktops

A non-persistent desktop is a desktop that is quite often shared by a lot of different users. Changes that are committed to the desktop, are saved in a delta. Non-persistent desktops are configured to be used by multiple users that belong to a similar use case. Changes they commit are saved to a user profile which is preferably managed with a solution like VMware User Environment Manager. As soon as a user logs off from a session, the profile is synchronized to a network location (including all user-related application changes). If the user requests a new session from the Connection server, the chances are that he will get a different desktop than the session before. During the logon process, the user settings will be synchronized with the new desktop, and the user has his old settings again. Elevated permissions and the requirement to install software within a non-persistent desktop are not very useful, as the delta with the changes is deleted as soon as the desktop undergoes maintenance (recompose or refresh) or when using Instant Clones (since the clone is decommissioned as soon as the user logs off).

## Full Clones

Full Clones are complete, customized copies of a template VM – basically, the same as when creating a new VM out of a VM template in vCenter. Full Clones are in most situations used for use cases that require persistent desktops like developers, designers or IT staff. A Full Clone, on average, has a lifecycle of more than a couple of months. Updating and maintaining a full clone is mostly done through the same tools that are used for updating and maintaining physical desktops. The process of creating Full Clones is the most time-consuming of the three and is quite often the least disk space efficient. A Full Clone requires the same amount of disk space as the VM template. I would highly recommend customers who are aiming to use Full Clones to also include a shared storage device that has great inline compression and deduplication functionality as this could save a lot of disk space capacity. Also, a storage device that supports VAAI*, will offload most of the cloning processes to the storage processors and vCenter will be less busy during cloning operations. Creating Full Clones can take from a couple of minutes up to even 15 minutes, depending on the size of the base image and the speed of the storage device.

The following diagram is an overview of the cloning process of a Full Clone:

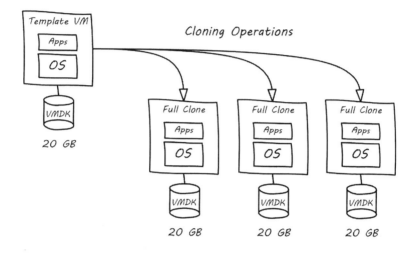

- A template VM is created.
- A pool will be created in VMware Horizon.
- VMware Horizon will instruct vCenter to start a cloning operation for the required number of Full Clones.
- Regular VM cloning operations will create a new VM and will customize it, based on VM customization specifications.

*VMware's description of VAAI:

*In a virtualized environment, storage operations traditionally have been expensive from a resource perspective. Functions such as cloning, and snapshots can be performed more efficiently by the storage device than by the host. VMware vSphere Storage APIs "Array Integration (VAAI), also referred to as hardware acceleration or hardware offload APIs, are a set of APIs to enable communication between VMware vSphere ESXi hosts and storage devices. The APIs define a set of storage primitives that enable the ESXi host to offload certain storage operations to the array, which reduces resource overhead on the ESXi hosts and can significantly improve performance for storage-intensive operations such as storage cloning, zeroing, and so on. The goal of VAAI is to help storage vendors provide hardware assistance to speed up VMware I/O operations that are more efficiently accomplished in the storage hardware.*

# Linked Clones

Until recently, Linked Clones were the best solution for most use cases that require non-persistency. A Linked Clone is a snapshot of a base image that is customized with a new name, SID and networking settings. In general, a Linked Clone will take up to 10% of the total size of a base image. So, a base image of 60GB will produce Linked Clones that are around 6GB each. The disk size of the Linked Clone (like a standard snapshot) depends on the lifecycle of a desktop. If a Linked Clone is running for a couple of months, the size is of course a lot bigger than when the Linked Clone is recomposed every week. Linked Clones require the View Composer in order to be built, refreshed or recomposed. That's where the biggest challenge is in terms of availability. What I will explain later is that when a customer has an availability requirement that forces you to avoid single points of failure (SPOFs), Linked Clones can become a challenge as View Composer isn't redundant. Creating a Linked Clone can take a couple of minutes, depending on the shared storage device. If it supports View Composer tasks that can be offloaded, it is very likely that you can run multiple composer tasks at the same time. Updating and maintaining Linked Clones is less time consuming as a Full Clone. In case of maintenance, the base image is updated, a snapshot is created and the new snapshot that contains the changes is selected in the desktop pool. View Composer will recompose all of the Linked Clones. The shared storage device will determine how long the operation will take. One of my customers has an XtremeIO box and completely recomposing 700 desktops by a single View Composer took up to 3,5 hours. Because this process is still quite time-consuming, it doesn't allow you to create Linked Clones upon request of an end-user. A batch of Linked Clones needs to be standby to accept user sessions and handle your possible boot storms.

The following diagram is an overview of the cloning process of a Linked Clone:

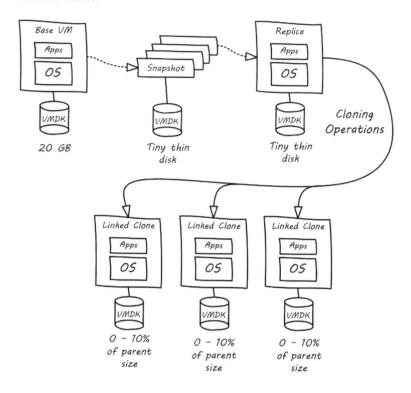

- A base image VM is created.
- A snapshot is created in vCenter.
- A pool will be created in VMware Horizon.
- VMware Horizon will instruct View Composer to start a cloning operation for the required number of Linked Clones.
- A Replica will be created on the datastore where the Linked Clones will be placed.
- Linked Cloning operations will create a new VM and will customize it, based on the specifications from the Pool creation wizard.

# Instant Clones

Ever heard of vmFork or Project Fargo? Instant Clones are the (relatively) new kid on the block. Instant Clones were first introduced in vSphere 6 with the vmFork feature. From a running VM, a snapshot is taken that runs in memory of the ESXi host. Taking the snapshot only takes a couple of seconds and the ClonePrep functionality will customize the Instant Clones desktop in just another couple of seconds. Because the complete process could be finished in under 10 seconds, Instant Clones are quite often created upon demand of an end-user. To avoid session queuing during boot storms, it still is a good idea to have a batch of Instant Clones ready to accept sessions. But this batch can be a lot smaller than in case of Linked Clones. Instant Clones are great for use cases that require non-persistency of the desktop. Instant Clones run in-memory, but still require some disk space on the shared storage device. On an average, 10% of the size of a base image can be used when sizing your storage and the same rules apply as when using Linked Clones in terms of the lifecycle. One of the most significant advantages of Instant Clones is in maintenance. Updating and maintaining the base image, which in case of Linked Clones can take hours to recompose, might only take a couple of minutes when using Instant Clones. From an OpEx perspective, using Instant Clones is a great idea. Instant Clones had some limitations in terms of feature parity comparing to Linked Clones in prior versions. Make sure to check if your required features are available before choosing Instant Clones (or any other type of clone).

The following diagram is an overview of the cloning process of an Instant Clone:

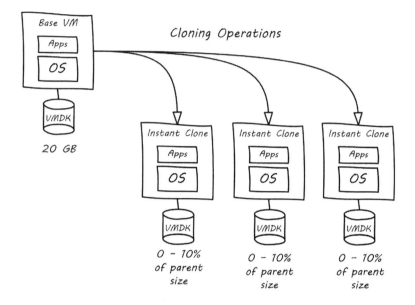

- A base image VM is created.
- A pool will be created in VMware Horizon.
- VMware Horizon will instruct vCenter to start a cloning operation for the required number of Instant Clones.
- Instant Cloning operations will create a new VM and will customize it, based on the specifications from the Pool creation wizard.

As VMware is adding more and more features into Instant Clones, my impression is that they will eventually replace Linked Clones with Instant Clones. When this happens, isn't clear, but it might happen sooner than expected.

If you would like to know more about the architecture of the Instant Cloning process, check William Lam's blog:

https://www.virtuallyghetto.com/2018/04/new-instant-clone-architecture-in-vsphere-6-7-part-1.html

If you would like to know more about the customization used in the different cloning technologies, check out this KB article:

https://kb.vmware.com/s/article/2003797

# POOLS

A collection of the cloned desktops, provisioned from the same source, is called a pool. Pools were created as a method to create and provide access to desktop VMs as a group rather than individually. A pool is set up to create one or more desktops from a single base image. During the pool creation, desktop clones are provisioned according to the pool settings. Things like the lifecycle of a desktop, startup/shutdown behavior and supported connection protocols are examples of settings that can be adjusted for a pool. There are different pools types that all have their own characteristics.

## Automated Pools

In an ideal IT world, everything would be automated. That includes your virtual desktops, as well. An automated pool is a pool that automatically provisions desktops, either with Full Clones, Linked Clones or Instant Clones. By creating the pool, you set up a number of desktops that need to be in standby mode and based on the type of desktop, the provisioning engine will do the rest. In most cases, the automated pool is recommended, because of the level of automation, expanding or maintaining the pool is relatively easy. In case of a Linked Clone pool, the base image gets updated. After the update, a new snapshot will be created and all the desktops in the pool can be recomposed. In most cases, you will use automated pools for non-persistent desktops.

# Manual Pools

Manual pools are your last resort when it comes to the type of desktop pools. Manual pools are pools where you have the ability to manually select VMs or physical machines that have a Horizon Agent installed. These desktops are available for the user to connect to from the Horizon Client and are quite often used by a single user or very view users. Like the Full Clones, desktops in a manual pool are usually managed with tools like SCCM. Use cases for manual pools are sometimes hardware related, such as hardware dongles. Another reason is that the desktop maybe running on a different platform or even in a cloud.

The reason why a manual pool is your last resort, is that they are managed in a different way without the standardization of Horizon. In case of a physical desktop, availability of the desktop is also a challenge as a physical desktop isn't capable of N+1.

# Base Image

Every automated pool is created with a base image. This can either be a VM template or a VM with a snapshot. In case of a Full Clone, this is a regular VM template. The template is configured to be used with Horizon (all Horizon specific agents are installed in the base image). After the cloning operation, the Full Clone doesn't share anything with the source template.

The base image of a linked clone or instant clone is based on a snapshot of a source machine. The snapshot is used to create new clones that are a customized copy of the snapshot. In case of a Linked Clone, it is linked to the source base image. This means that if the based image is deleted, the Linked Clone will be unable to start. An Instant Clone isn't depending on its base image anymore in order to run normally.

# CONNECTION PROTOCOLS

Horizon supports multiple desktop protocols that (depending on the use case) are either PCoIP or Blast Extreme.

## PCoIP (PC Over IP)

PCoIP was introduced in 2008 in version 4.0 of VMware View. It is a licensed protocol and owned by Teradici. The protocol can be encoded/decoded on both hardware and software levels. Mainly when using heavy graphical applications, hardware encoding/decoding can be used by leveraging Teradici Apex cards on ESXi host level and offloading chips on a client level. Many manufacturers like Dell, HP and Fujitsu build thin clients and zero clients that contain those chips.

For a long time, PCoIP was recommended when you were in need of graphically enhanced desktops or applications in a VDI solution. PCoIP has the ability to send lossless images to an endpoint which means that almost no compression is used. You can look at it as an MP3 vs WAV file. In case of a WAV file, no compression is used and what you hear is an (almost) exact dump of CD quality audio. The downside of this is that the protocol will use more bandwidth than possibly expected and in some cases even all bandwidth that it can use. So, proper tuning of the protocol is an absolute recommendation.

## Blast Extreme

This is the protocol formerly known as Blast. In the fall of 2013, VMware shipped the first version of Blast to customers. In the Horizon View 5.2 feature pack 1, it was possible to add the protocol to the Connection server and connect from an endpoint by using a web browser. Blast uses standardized encoding schemes for video (JPG/PNG and H.264) and audio (Opus). Unlike proprietary encoding schemes, these standard formats are supported in a wide variety of browsers and devices. In 2014, Blast became one of the standard protocols in Horizon 6 and in 2016 it even became a preferred protocol when it shipped with Horizon 7. Today, it seems to be the primary protocol that VMware is actively developing on and has a similar or better user experience while being more efficient on endpoints and handling network traffic (and latency) somewhat better.

In Horizon 7.1, VMware added additional innovations to the protocol, as Adaptive Transport was introduced. Adaptive Transport will automatically switch between TCP and UDP if the latency between the endpoint and the remote desktop increases and reaches a certain threshold (such as when working on a bad Wi-Fi network). Blast Extreme will try to give the user the best user experience possible, based on the network capabilities. As Blast Extreme uses standard encoding schemes and natively supports web browsers, this gives Blast Extreme an advantage over PCoIP as no separate client is needed to run desktops/applications. But, of course, this also has downsides. Browsers don't have that many options to integrate with an operating system on an endpoint. So, when looking for the ultimate user experience, HTML5 might not be your primary choice. But, as mentioned, Blast Extreme is much more network efficient than PCoIP. Especially when having bandwidth constraints or latency issues, Blast Extreme would be the way to go as it uses UDP instead of TCP when latency increases.

# CLOUD POD ARCHITECTURE

In 2014, VMware announced a new feature in Horizon 6 called Cloud Pod Architecture. This feature makes sure that you can run Horizon desktops/Remote Apps from multiple datacenters and that the maximum number of desktops can exceed 10,000 per Horizon implementation (by setting up multiple Pods with 10,000 desktops each). To use this feature, it is a best practice to set up load balancing and in case of geographically separated datacenters, a load balancer with support for a Global Traffic Manager, as well. F5 has such a module next to their Local Traffic Manager (LTM). More about technical details of Cloud Pod Architecture can be found in the *Availability and Disaster Recovery* section.

Cloud Pod Architecture consists of the following components:

## Sites

In a Cloud Pod Architecture environment, a site is a collection of well-connected pods in the same physical location, typically in a single datacenter. The Cloud Pod Architecture feature treats pods in the same site equally. When you initialize the Cloud Pod Architecture feature, it places all pods into a default site called Default First Site. If you have an extensive implementation, you might want to create additional sites and add pods to those sites.

The Cloud Pod Architecture feature assumes that pods within the same site are on the same LAN, and that pods in different sites are on different LANs. Because WAN-connected pods have slower network performance, the Cloud Pod Architecture feature gives preference to desktops that are in the local pod or site when it allocates desktops to users.

Sites can be a useful part of a disaster recovery solution. For example, you can assign pods in different datacenters to different sites and then entitle users and groups to desktop pools that span those sites. If a datacenter in one site becomes unavailable, you can use desktops from the available site to satisfy user desktop requests.

# Global Entitlements

In a Cloud Pod Architecture environment, you create global entitlements to entitle users or groups to multiple pools/desktops across multiple pods in the pod federation. When you use global entitlements, you do not need to configure and manage local entitlements. Global entitlements simplify administration, even in a pod federation that contains a single pod. Horizon stores global entitlements in the Global Data Layer. Because global entitlements are shared data, global entitlement information is available on all Connection server instances in the pod federation.

# Scope

During the creation of a global entitlement, you must specify its scope policy. The scope policy determines the scope of the search when the Cloud Pod Architecture feature looks for desktops to satisfy a desktop request from the global entitlement. You can set the scope-policy so that the Cloud Pod Architecture feature searches for desktops only on the pod to which the user is connected, only on pods within the same site as the user's pod, or across all pods in the pod federation.

# Home Site

A Home Site is an affinity between a user and a Cloud Pod Architecture site. With Home Sites, you can ensure that a user always receives desktops from a specific site rather than receiving desktops based on the user's current location. The Cloud Pod Architecture feature includes the following types of Home Site assignments.

# SIZING

Sizing is one of the hardest parts of the design phase. Why? Well, years back when most VDIs were based on hosts with a lot of CPU power and RAM and a shared storage device, it was a lot easier. You calculated the required cores, clock speed and RAM and the compute part was done. Sizing the storage based on IOPS requirements and disk space per desktop finalized the sizing. Nowadays, sizing is a lot more difficult due to the impact of graphical enhanced operating systems and applications. And don't forget Hyper-Converged Infrastructures (such as vSAN) that require a more precise sizing to ensure proper scalability and reduce waste of any of the sized components in a single host.

Because of all of these complexities, I'm wondering if sizing is essential. Wouldn't it be a lot more precise to order a small set of hosts and run a real-life proof of concept on a smaller scale? Add a number of sessions to a single host and just see when it becomes oversaturated and congestion occurs on one of the resources? The reality is that most projects I worked on had a time constraint. Running a proof of concept, unfortunately, takes time (time you might not have). My advice would be to run a proof of concept for your different use cases if possible. If you have a time constraint that doesn't let you, running a sizing exercise based on the assessment data is your second-best option.

An essential phase in sizing is of course a proper assessment. Like I explained in the assessment section, *the numbers tell the tale*. The more you measure, the more specific the assessment will turn out. Running the assessment on every use case is as essential, especially since not every use case might require the same (virtual) hardware specs. A task worker could be running fine on CPUs with a low clock speed, while knowledge workers might require CPUs with a high clock speed. And what about GPUs? They will have an impact, as well. So again, sizing does matter and as detailed as possible.

Where to start? Let's look at the assessment metrics that are required for a sizing calculation. The following metrics should be assessed from a single desktop.

| Metric | Description |
| --- | --- |
| Peak CPU usage (in MHz) | Clock speed at peak level |
| Average peak CPU usage (in MHz) | Clock speed at average peak level |
| Average CPU usage (in MHz) | Clock speed at average level |
| CPU core count | Number of used cores |
| Peak RAM usage (in MB) | Used RAM at peak level |
| Average peak RAM usage (in MB) | Used RAM at average peak level |
| Average RAM usage | Used RAM at average level |
| Storage capacity (in GB) | The required aggregated storage capacity (of all used disks) |
| Peak disk read IOPS | Aggregated read IOPS (of all used disks) at peak level |
| Average peak disk read IOPS | Aggregated read IOPS (of all used disks) at average peak level |
| Average disk read IOPS | Aggregated read IOPS (of all used disks) at average level |

| Metric | Description |
|---|---|
| Peak disk write IOPS | Aggregated write IOPS (of all used disks) at peak level |
| Average peak disk write IOPS | Aggregated write IOPS (of all used disks) at average peak level |
| Average disk write IOPS | Aggregated write IOPS (of all used disks) at average level |
| Peak network receive rate (in Mbps) | Network receive rate at peak level |
| Average peak network receive rate (in Mbps) | Network receive rate at average peak level |
| Average network receive rate (in Mbps) | Network receive rate at average level |
| Peak network send rate (in Mbps) | Network send rate at peak level |
| Average peak network send rate (in Mbps) | Network send rate at average peak level |
| Average network send rate (in Mbps) | Network send rate at average level |
| Framebuffer | The amount of video RAM in use |

In the above table, you can see different metrics from a single resource: peak, peak average and average. Why not just use the average, you might ask? It's mainly to discover anomalies. If a user during regular usage is running at 500 MHz and the peak is reached at 3200 MHz, it may be that physical CPUs with a lower clock speed could lead to performance issues. Also, the difference in average and peak average is essential when having performance-related requirements. Some customers have a requirement to size the VDI as conservatively as possible. In that case, you might size the VDI based on peak average. If the customer doesn't have a particular requirement, I tend to use a number between average and peak average. So, if the average is 500 MHz and peak Average is 600 MHz, I will use 550 MHz to calculate CPU sizing.

There are a couple of main resource types that need to be calculated: CPU, RAM, disk, network and GPU. They all bring different challenges to the table, so let's run through them.

# CPU

To me, CPU sizing is the hardest part of the sizing phase. CPU sizing is dependent on a lot of different factors. In most cases, the recorded metrics alone aren't sufficient to calculate the CPU sizing. Examples of these factors are:

- Applications (single or multi-threaded)
- Application layering (like App Volumes)
- Graphical workloads
- Number of displays
- Connection protocols (encoding/decoding)
- Users (user experience)

Years ago, when the ESX hypervisor was invented, the whole idea behind virtualization was to consolidate as many physical servers to virtual machines as possible and get the most out of a single ESX host in terms of resources. Some resources, like disks, could be over-provisioned with so-called *thin provisioned disks*. In theory, this could mean that a single GB of physical disk space can be used by multiple virtual disks that are all 1 GB as well. The risk in this is that if all virtual disks decide to grow, you will run out of physical disk space and end up in a shit storm. This is especially the case when using Linked Clones with aggressive sizing (but more about that topic later).

CPUs are another excellent example of resources that can be over-provisioned. When looking at the resources that are in use on your computer at home, you will probably see that your CPU on average isn't running at full capacity (100%). If a single physical quad-core CPU can run not only your own resources, but possible the resources of another machine like yours as well, your physical CPU will be used more efficiently. This is mainly how overprovisioning on a physical ESXi host works, as well. What you would like to do is to create an ideal number of virtual desktops that run on your physical host without oversaturating the physical CPU(s). If the physical CPU gets oversaturated, virtual CPUs need to get in line to get their resource requirements fulfilled (CPU scheduling). In IaaS (Infrastructure as a Service) environments, I see physical CPU to virtual CPU ratios that vary from 1:3 to 1:6. Of course, this totally depends on the type of applications. Database servers on average will require more resources than DHCP servers, for example.

In VDI, these numbers can be higher. With some projects which included Windows 7 and just task workers, I have seen ratios that varied from 1:5 to 1:12 even, but this entirely depends on the application workloads. With Windows 10, the demand for CPU resources increased, so these numbers are likely to be lower.

What the ideal ratio of over-commitment is, depends on your requirements. If the customer demands conservative sizing, you might want to aim for a lower over-commitment ratio. If, on the other hand, the customer is ok with a more aggressive approach, a higher number can be achieved.

*Important to know: On average, the lower the number, the more significant the investment. Because more hosts might be required if a lower number will be aimed for. If you have a budget constraint that doesn't allow for a low ratio, it might be somewhat easier to convince the customer to go for a higher number.*

The first step you should take, is to look at the recorded metrics.

In terms of CPU usage metrics, the one I use in general for calculating the required clock speed on a physical host is the *average peak CPU usage*. Average peak metrics will keep you on the conservative side of the required clock speed. When aiming for a lower over-commitment ratio, you might want to calculate with a number between the *average peak* and *peak* metrics. For a higher ratio, go for a number between *average* and *average peak*.

For now, I'll take the **average peak CPU usage** of a single use case and **multiply** this by the **number of desktops** for that specific use case that you would like to size for *et voila*: you have the required clock speed for the use case.

Another useful metric is the *peak CPU usage*. The main reason to use this metric is to determine which physical CPU to include in your ESXi hosts. If, for instance, your physical infrastructure has applications that require a high clock speed (such as single-threaded applications), this metric will tell this from your assessment. If you don't have any of these (poorly written) apps, you might want to go for CPUs with a lower clock speed (as these are much cheaper) and more cores. But, in case you require a high clock speed, I would suggest looking at the more expensive CPUs with high clock speeds and as many cores as you can afford.

The last metric that is important when sizing CPUs, is the core count. The higher the number of cores a single VM will require, the lower the consolidation ratio will be. This is due to the scheduling engine in a physical host. If a host has 16 physical cores, it will be able to schedule 16 virtual CPUs at the same time (cycle). In the cycle that a set of virtual CPUs are being scheduled, other virtual CPUs have to wait until it's their turn. If, in this case, you have 8 VMs with two virtual CPUs, 8 of these VMs can be scheduled at the same time. In an ideal situation, these scheduling queues should be as short as possible (try to keep the CPU %COSTOP metric below 3 on a per-VM basis as everything above 3 indicates the VM has too many vCPUs).

The ideal over-commitment ratio is hard to calculate. But, as mentioned on the previous page, as a rule of thumb you might want to start with 1:7 for task worker (light) desktops. For power user (heavy) desktops, I would start with an over-commitment ratio of 1:4.

In any case, I would recommend running load tests before the pilot phase to be sure that the physical resources won't be saturated, and contention occurs.

One should note when calculating the physical CPU to virtual CPU ratio, Hyperthreading (HT) can't be used as a full logical core. From my experience, HT is just a great 20% - 40% extra that may have a positive impact on your density, but the efficiency of

HT will depend on the type of workload that you are running inside the virtual desktops. With newer CPU architectures, HT might change in efficiency, as well. So, if you would like to stay safe, keep it out of your calculations and treat it as a bonus.

Another note here is that moving from 1 vCPU per desktop to 2 vCPUs per desktop won't cut the density in half. The CPU scheduler in the ESXi hypervisor is intelligent enough to schedule CPU cycles really fast so you might just drop 20/25% instead of 50%.

# RAM

RAM might be the simplest of all. One of the first questions you should ask yourself: Am I going to overprovision RAM and what would be the impact? I hope the answer is in most cases is *No*. Overprovisioning RAM is a huge risk. If the total amount of provisioned RAM on a single host, exceeds the RAM capacity of that ESXi host, the host will begin swapping on physical disks or shared storage. As physical disks (even SSDs) are much slower than RAM, this will have a direct impact on the performance of that host (and the user experience for the end-user). So, staying safe and calculating with rounded up peak usage is a good idea. RAM in a host is easily extendable. With that in mind, asking yourself the following question is important as well: Am I going to build hosts with a higher consolidation ratio or smaller consolidation ratio? The answer to that questions is harder to answer. If the customer has a budget constraint, it might be better to go for a higher consolidation ratio (as one big host is quite often cheaper than two smaller hosts). If, on the other hand, you would like to reduce the fault domain, more smaller hosts can be a better idea than less bigger hosts. One component might be game breaker though; the GPU (more about that later).

A virtual desktop has the ability to fully reserve its RAM on the host (something that's mandatory if you are using GPUs). The reservation guarantees the RAM is available for the virtual desktop (as vSphere High Availability Admission Control will ensure no RAM over commitment is applied). If a reservation is set for a virtual machine, no virtual machine swap file (vSWP) will be created (since the virtual desktop won't be swapping at all), which saves capacity on the datastore, as well. There are some requirements which would make you decide to enable reservations. The first example would be that the solution should be sized as conservative as possible. Another example is from a performance perspective. If the solution needs to guarantee performance as much as possible, reservations are a good idea.

If, on the other hand, you have to size aggressively because of a budget constraint, for instance, there is a solution to save some RAM. At the beginning of virtualization, when memory pages were only 4KB, VMs that ran the same operating system could benefit from a feature called *Transparent Page Sharing (TPS)*. TPS works a little bit like deduplication of storage. When a lot of desktops with the same operating system ran as a clone on the same host, all pages that were precisely the same as the first one written in RAM, the duplicates weren't placed in RAM. This saved some RAM. But, since VMs got more RAM, pages with a smaller block size created an overhead in performance which was solved by introducing pages with larger block size (2MB). The downside of that was, that the chances of having duplicate pages became small and thus had a low effect. It is possible to disable large pages so TPS could have a positive impact on your sizing.

*Please note that TPS might have a downside since it creates a minor possibility of a security risk. Check the Transparent Page Sharing section for more information.*

Planning for future RAM expansion is often a good idea. Even if buying memory modules twice as large as what you might currently need to save slots is sometimes a bit more expensive, it's cheaper than having to buy a whole new set of DIMMs or new servers if you run out of memory and cannot readily expand. Of course, at some point your other resources will run out, so expanding memory only will take you so far.

# DISK

Disk sizing metrics can be divided into disk size (capacity), I/O per second (IOPS) and throughput. Years ago, when flash was very expensive and not that common to shared storage systems, sizing your storage devices was important. Nowadays, it's still important, but less impactful as most shared storage devices contain flash storage and Hyper-Converged Infrastructures (HCIs) are based on SSDs as well and these can handle 50,000 to 100,000 IOPS, each. With NVMe being even faster with support up to 500,000 IOPS, this won't be an issue at all.

The average number of IOPS per desktop depends on the type of application being used. Web-based applications require fewer IOPS than applications for designers (like CAD apps). On an average for task users, the IOPS requirement is somewhere between 25 and 50 IOPS. You might think this is a low number, but task users aren't utilizing heavy apps.

If, hypothetically speaking, you still are sizing for IOPS, it's imperative to take boot storms into account. Even a task user will have a need for more IOPS during a boot storm. My rule of thumb is to add another 100 IOPS for a single user to stay on the conservative side. This makes a total of 150 IOPS per task user.

Power users are a different ballgame. Of course, not all power users are the same, but depending on the type of applications they are using, they might require more CPU, RAM, GPU or disk resources. In the case of disk requirements, it is (again) essential to use the assessment data as a baseline. End-users can either generate or consume data. For power users, that's no difference. But, the amount of data a power user generates or consumes can make a huge difference. Take graphical designers for example; if an application is for instance CAD or Adobe related, the output of these solutions will require a lot more disk resources from the desktop (because of bigger files, which can easily be multiple gigabytes).

Next to IOPS, is throughput, which is essential as well. But with 10 GbE being the standard for most IP-based and HCI storage systems and 16 Gbit for fiber channel-based systems, throughput becomes less of a bottleneck. Back in the days with 1 GbE NICs and 4 Gbit FC HBAs (Host Bus Adapter) you needed to make sure not to oversaturate the paths to the shared storage device. HCIs don't have the likelihood of getting oversaturated disk throughput because the disks (including caching) remain inside the host. You will most likely end up with compute-related resource issues before the throughput becomes oversaturated. If you are still sizing for traditional shared storage, take the peak throughput per desktop and make sure to size both for a maximum throughput of a single host, the shared storage device and the network switches.

The first component to be sized in terms of throughput is the shared storage device. If you are designing an infrastructure for 500 users that have a peak throughput of 10 Mb per second, per concurrent user, make sure that the shared storage device is able to handle the aggregated throughput. Again, if the connection becomes oversaturated, latency will increase on the fabric and this will result in poor performance. From a disk perspective, user experience is depending heavily on low latencies. To give you an idea: 0-5 ms latency is great, 5-10 ms is good, anything above 15 ms means: switch off your phone and hide; users will probably hunt you down.

Sizing a host for throughput is just as easy. Take the maximum number of desktops that will run on a single host and multiply it by the average peak throughput. The result is the minimum throughput on the HBA required.

If you take the number of the above sum, multiply it by the number of hosts you will attach to a switch and add the throughput for the shared storage device, you will have the minimum throughput required on a switch.

These numbers will quite often result in digits far lower than the throughputs a 2018 manufactured switch can produce. But still, I think it's important to know what to do in case of anomalies in the assessment.

The final component in sizing, is disk space. The required space is depending on the type of clone you will be using and the disk type. Like I explained in the previous chapter, Full Clones consume the total amount of assigned disk space. Linked Clones and Instant Clones only require 10% of the disk space of their base image.

Sizing for Full Clones might be the easiest. Take the average required storage capacity per desktop and add 10% for possible growth. The result is the total required net disk size for the use case.

Sizing Linked Clones and Instant Clones works a bit different. Take the size of the base image and add an additional 10% of that size per desktop that you will be adding to the VDI.

If you would like to calculate the required disk throughput on a per desktop-basis, the sizing rule I always use is:
IOPS x block size = disk throughput

*Please note that with all of the types of clones, it's important to take possible swap space into account. If no memory reservations are configured, every desktop will contain a vSWP file that has the same size as the configured RAM size.*

## Considerations

- To avoid excessive rebalance operations, make sure you included a 25% - 30% slack space in case you are going to use vSAN. More free space = faster rebuild

# NETWORK

Sizing for networking (from a host perspective) might not sound like an important thing anymore for most of the use cases, as hosts are being equipped with dual 10 Gbit network interfaces. It's true that it might be good enough for a great number of desktops. However, end-users aren't typically located within the datacenter next to the hosts, so when sizing networking for the VDI, you should think about other components such as firewalls and load balancers, as well.

Every session that is established to the VDI, requires capacity on all of the networking components until it reaches the VM. Imagine working from home and clicking on the Horizon desktop icon. If working over Wi-Fi, you will probably travel over the following devices:

- Wi-Fi access point
- Home router/firewall
- ISP infrastructure
- Datacenter firewall
- Datacenter load balancer
- Datacenter router
- Horizon Unified Access Gateway
- Datacenter switch(es)
- ESXi host
- Virtual desktop

These are just the devices that you are familiar with. The ISP has other devices through which your session is being routed. As every device might have different specifications and configuration maximums, it is essential to do your homework and get familiar with these individual components.

A vital starting point when sizing the network components is to know what kind of bandwidth you can expect. That's also the tricky part. In case of an existing VDI that you are going to migrate, it's simple. Take the recorded session metrics as a baseline and calculate the required bandwidth based on the number of sessions that the VDI needs to handle. This is quite often based on the scoped number of sessions.

If you are sizing VDI for the first time and migrating physical desktops to the new VDI, you are going to work with assumptions. This is because you can only make an estimate based on the type of applications, number of monitors (and resolution) and the protocol that you are going to use.

As a rule of thumb, these are some numbers I like to start with (based on field experience). The first two rows show the average bandwidth in use for single and dual monitor use. The rows that follow can be used as an addition to the first row. The standard user is defined as follows:

- A single monitor
- 1920 x 1080 resolution
- 20 frames a second
- No graphically intense applications and video
- Default image quality settings

| Use case | Estimated Bandwidth PCoIP | Estimated Bandwidth Blast Extreme |
|---|---|---|
| Standard user | 250 kbps - 500 kbps | 200 kbps - 450 kbps |
| Dual monitor | 450 kbps - 1 Mbps | 450 kbps - 1 Mbps |
| 30 FPS 720P video | + 5 Mbps - 20 Mbps per monitor | +5 Mbps - 10 Mbps per monitor |
| 60 FPS 720P video | + 5 Mbps - 20 Mbps per monitor | +10 Mbps - 25 Mbps per monitor |
| 4K single monitor without video playback | +1 Mbps - 25 Mbps | +0.6 Mbps - 5 Mbps |
| 4K single monitor with video playback | +25 Mbps - 90 Mbps | +10 Mbps - 40 Mbps |

## Considerations

In a default setting, both protocols are compressed and transmitted over the network. When running over a LAN, enough bandwidth is available and using PCoIP (as Blast Extreme doesn't support this feature), it is also possible to disable the "Turn off Build-to-Lossless feature". This feature will disable compression and transmits the images 1:1 to the endpoint. Mainly for use cases that require high-res image presentation on the endpoint, such as graphical designers and medical examiners, this is essential. There is one downside to this setting: It requires a lot of bandwidth. Especially with video playback or other applications that may have a high frame rate I have seen sessions that could easily utilize 120 Mbps, so be careful.

More about protocol choices and settings can be found in the *Graphics and Remote Protocols* section.

## Additional Network Traffic

The network traffic mentioned in the previous section is called the *Virtual Machine traffic*. It's simply all traffic transmitted and received from a VM-perspective. Next to VM traffic, a host has other traffic, as well, to take into account:

- Management traffic – All traffic required to manage a host from (for instance) a vCenter appliance or to collect syslog information.
- vMotion traffic – All traffic required to move a VM from one host to another.
- Storage traffic – All storage-related traffic between hosts and datastores.

Management traffic can easily run over just a 1 GbE connection. Most host hardware contains multiple 1 GbE network interfaces which are suitable for this type of traffic.

vMotion and storage traffic require a lot more bandwidth. Hypothetically, vMotion will work on a 1 GbE interface but as virtual desktops are getting more and more RAM, more bandwidth is always better. The more bandwidth is available for a vMotion, the faster a VM gets migrated to another host. Also, if a host is put into maintenance and VMs need to be evacuated, are there SLAs at the customer determining how long it should take?

Something also worth mentioning is that when vGPU vMotion becomes available, my assumption will be that 10 GbE will be minimally required as transferring large framebuffers from one host to another will for sure be bandwidth-consuming.

More information about storage traffic can be found in the *Hyper-Converged and Traditional Infrastructures* section.

# GPU

The Graphics Processing Unit (GPU) with the highest consolidation ratio, is an NVIDIA Tesla M10. It can allocate 64 (512 MB) profiles per card (although 1024 MB is recommended for Windows 10 use cases). Most 2U hosts, have the ability to include 2 of those cards (although the demand for more cards will slowly be filled in by OEMs). This means that 128 desktops using a light GPU profile is the max you are able to consolidate on a single host (including failure capacity). For now, it's important to know that the framebuffer of a GPU can't be overprovisioned and needs to be equally divided by a number of profiles.

More about sizing for GPUs can be found in the *Graphics and Remote Protocols* section.

# HOST SIZING

If you are sizing a single host, it is important to keep a couple of things in mind. First of all, you can't use all of the resources in a single host. There are processes that run on a host that require resources as well. Next to some hypervisor-related workloads, you need to reserve resources for solutions like vSAN, NSX and virus scanning appliances. Second, you want to avoid a host running out of its RAM, so be sure to reserve capacity to handle peaks as well. My rule of thumb is to reserve 50GB of RAM on a single host to handle peaks (so that's around 10% for 512GB sized hosts and 20% for 256GB sized hosts).

Be sure to include memory reservations for additional features. If you would like to know what reservations are required for vSAN, take a look at the following KB article:

https://kb.vmware.com/s/article/2113954

Another way to calculate the required memory overhead for vSAN, is to you use the calculator provided by Marco van Baggum on his blog:

https://www.vmbaggum.nl/2017/11/vsan-memory-consumption-calculator/

If NSX is going to be part of the solution, be sure to include between 23 GB and 38 GB of RAM required per host. More about NSX requirements in terms of resources, can be found here:

https://docs.vmware.com/en/VMware-NSX-for-vSphere/6.3/com.vmware.nsx.admin.doc/GUID-311BBB9F-32CC-4633-9F91-26A39296381A.html

If you are going to run vendor appliances for solutions like anti-virus integration, see the vendor's documentation for resource requirements.

# FAILOVER CAPACITY

Based on the availability requirements that you might need to work with, you have to include a failover margin. If you have a requirement to avoid single points of failure, you need to add at least one extra host to a cluster (N+1). If the customer has a requirement that they need to perform maintenance during business hours without the risk of failures, you need to add an additional host to the cluster (N+2).

If you have an availability or recoverability requirement that must be met by adding a second datacenter, the failover capacity might be 50%. Might be, because it depends on additional requirements.

What happens during a failure? Are you allowed to have a downgraded performance during a datacenter failure? Are you going to design an active/active or active/passive datacenter VDI? Are all of your use cases going to be running on both datacenters or are some of the use case less mission critical? More about these requirements and how to meet them the *Availability and Disaster Recovery* section.

# CONCURRENCY

Another requirement or assumption that impacts the sizing parameters, is the concurrency. Make sure to validate the concurrency with the customer. If you are sizing a solution that's going to replace an existing one, the current concurrency numbers can validate a concurrency requirement. If it's going to be a new VDI and concurrency can't be validated, make sure to define a risk (independent of whether concurrency is a requirement or an assumption in your design).

# SIZING EXAMPLE 1: SINGLE USE

# CASE

The following example is based on a customer project that I recently finished with a single task worker use case running on Instant Clones.

Recorded metrics during assessment:

| Metric | Value |
|---|---|
| Peak CPU usage (in MHz) | 2,143 |
| Average peak CPU usage (in MHz) | 887 |
| Average CPU usage (in MHz) | 513 |
| CPU core count | 2 |
| Peak RAM usage (in KB) | 3,829,265 |
| Average peak RAM usage (in KB) | 2,912860 |
| Average RAM usage (in KB) | 2,674,743 |
| Average storage capacity (in GB) | 90.2 |
| Peak disk read IOPs | 72 |
| Average peak disk read IOPs | 26 |
| Average disk read IOPs | 14 |
| Peak disk write IOPs | 62 |
| Average peak disk write IOPs | 23 |
| Average disk write IOPs | 12 |
| Peak network receive rate (in Mbps) | 1.2 |
| Average peak network receive rate (in Mbps) | 0.2 |
| Average network receive rate (in Mbps) | 0.1 |
| Peak network send rate (in Mbps) | 0.8 |
| Average peak network send rate (in Mbps) | 0.1 |
| Average network send rate (in Mbps) | 0.1 |
| GPU memory used (in MB) | 623 |

Furthermore, the use case had the following specifications:

| Item | Value |
|---|---|
| Number of users | 1,800 |
| User concurrency | 1,200 |
| Growth | 10% |
| Operating system | Windows 10 64 bit |
| Number of displays | 1 |
| Maximum resolution | 1920 x 1080 |

The customer was a call center company which had a maximum of 1,200 fixed desktops that could be used by any of the 1,800 users. It was a greenfield VDI environment. Most of these users worked during business hours, but some also in shifts, hence the lower concurrency number. Because of a budget constraint, the customer chose for a single datacenter VDI, but single points of failure needed to be avoided where possible.

The next thing to do is to start calculating all of the different required resource types. Let's start with the most difficult of them all: CPUs.

What we know, is that we are sizing for 1,200 concurrent users and that we need to anticipate for 10% growth:

10% growth (1,200 * 110% = **1,320**)

Next, we are going to calculate core speed. What I like to do, is stay on the conservative side and use the peak average numbers. Since we don't have single threaded apps to think about, using the peak average core speed is sufficient.

1,320 * 887 MHz = 1,170,840 MHz

Next, we are going to calculate the number of required cores:

1,320 * 2 vCPUs = 2,640 vCPUs

From a RAM perspective, I am again going to stay on the safe side. As you can see, the peak usage, peak average usage and average usage are quite close to each other. In this case, I convinced the customer that it is a good idea to size all desktops to a rounded number close to the peak usage. This because I believe that applications are becoming more RAM intense and reducing the number of different RAM configurations on the VDI (and reducing the number of pools), will ultimately save you in OpEx. So, let's use the peak RAM usage to calculate, but rounded up to 4GB.

1,320 * 4 GB = 5,280 GB RAM

The disk will be the next to calculate. From an IOPS perspective, I always use the highest of the peak numbers (read and write) and add an additional 100 IOPS to anticipate on boot storms (since they require some additional IOPS on a per-VM basis).

1,320 * (72 + 100) = 227,040 IOPS

The other disk metric, is the capacity. This is entirely depending on the type of clone that you will be using, but in this case Instant Clones (which take 10% of the base image size on average per clone). Please note that storage compression and deduplication are a bonus, so I don't take them into account.

1,320 * (90.2 GB * 10%) + 90.2 GB = 11,996.6 GB

The next topic is networking. I like to use the same calculation method as with disk throughput, so I use the highest peak number of either of the network metrics, in this case 1.2 Mbps
1,320 * 1.2 Mbps = 1,584 Mbps

The last one is the required GPU memory. As a GPU contains profiles that can be assigned to pools with a fixed memory size per profile, this calculation is straightforward. The smallest possible vGPU profile is 512 MB. In this case, that won't be sufficient, so I will use a 1024 MB profile to calculate the required GPU Memory size.

1,320 * 1,024 MB = 1,351,680 MB

To sum up, these are the aggregated numbers:

| Metric | Value |
| --- | --- |
| Users | 1,320 |
| CPU clock speed | 1,170,840 MHz |
| CPU cores | 2,640 |
| RAM | 5,280 GB |
| Disk IOPS | 227,040 IOPS |
| Disk capacity | 11,996.6 GB |
| Network throughput | 1,584 Mbps |
| GPU memory | 1,351,680 MB |

Now, we need to propose a type of host that is going to be used and the best physical CPU for the job. The type of CPU depends on the peak clock speed that is required. In our case, that was 2,143 MHz. This means that if we select a 3000 MHz CPU, 30% of the core won't be utilized. Since CPUs with higher clock speeds are also more expensive, it would be wise to go for a less fast CPU with more cores (as we are able to achieve a higher consolidation ratio).

From a RAM perspective, we used 320 GB as this turned out to be the sweet spot. More RAM was obviously possible, but as the bottleneck was a different resource, more RAM may have been a waste of money.

The specs of the host I used, were the following:

| Item | Value |
| --- | --- |
| CPU type | 2 x Intel Xeon E5-2690 v4 |
| CPU clock speed | 2.6GHz |
| CPU cores | 28 (56 with HT) |
| RAM | 320 GB |
| vSAN capacity (net per host) | 1,200 GB |
| vSAN IOPS | 50,000 |
| Network throughput | 2 x 10 Gbps |
| GPU memory* | 65,536 MB |

*The GPU which was chosen, was an NVIDIA Tesla M10 (2 cards), a card suitable for Windows 10 use without any applications with heavy graphical demands.

The next thing will be to calculate how many hosts are required from a RAM perspective. You need to take the total amount of required RAM and divide this by the net amount of RAM of a single host (raw RAM minus 50 GB):

320 GB – 50 GB = 280 GB net RAM per host

Now we take the required amount of RAM and divide it by the net RAM per host:

5,280 GB / 280 GB = 18.9 Hosts

As it is quite hard to buy 18,9 hosts, you need to round it up. So, the result is **19 hosts** (excluding failover capacity).

We will take the 19 hosts as a base number to check if the rest of the resources are sufficient.

Clock speed
19 hosts x 28 CPUs x 2,600 MHz = 1,383,200 MHz
1,170,840 MHz (required aggregated clock speed) / 1,383,200 MHz
= 0.85 (virtual cores that are allocated to a physical core, so 0.85:1)

Cores
19 hosts x 28 cores = 532 cores
2,640 cores (required aggregated cores) / 532 cores = 5.0 (virtual cores that are allocated to a physical core, so 5.0:1)

vSAN Capacity
19 hosts x 1,200 GB = 22,800 GB (net available) datastore capacity
22,800 GB is a lot more than the 11,996.6 GB required net capacity

vSAN IOPS
19 hosts x 50,000 IOPS = 950,000 IOPS
950,000 IOPS is a lot more than the 227,040 required IOPS

Network Throughput
19 hosts x 20,000 Mbps = 380,000 Mbps
380,000 Mbps is a lot more than the required 1,584 Mbps network throughput.

GPU Memory
19 hosts x 65,536 MB = 1,245,184 MB GPU Memory
1,245,184 is less than the required 1,351,680 MB. This means that two additional hosts are required to satisfy the required resources.

All these calculations are summed up in the following table (and based on the 21 required hosts:

| Metric | Required | Sized per 21 hosts |
|---|---|---|
| Users | 1,320 | |
| CPU Clock speed | 1,170,840 MHz | 1,528,800 MHz |
| CPU Cores | 2,640 | 588 |
| RAM | 5,280 GB | 6,720 MB |
| Disk IOPS | 227,040 IOPS | 1,050,000 IOPS |
| Disk capacity | 11,996.6 GB | 25,200 GB |
| Network Throughput | 1,584 Mbps | 420,000 Mbps |
| GPU Memory | 1,351,680 MB | 1,376,256 MB |

When running through the above numbers, there are some numbers that stand out.

Most of the values in the third column are higher than the values in the second column. As long as they are higher, the proposed sizing should be right (as in: no congestion on the accompanying resource).

If one of the values in the second column is higher, the sizing should be adjusted (in terms of adding more hosts or adding resources to the individual hosts, such as SSDs or RAM).

Two values are different though, the CPU clock speed and the cores. And like mentioned earlier, those are the ones in which we tolerate an over-commitment.

From a clock speed perspective, the 0.85 (virtual cores) to 1 (physical core) is excellent.

From a core count perspective, the 5.0 (virtual cores) to 1 (physical core) is also a good number to start with. A higher consolidation ratio might be possible, but this should be tested with either synthetic load testing (with tools like LoginVSI) or more preferably: pilot testing.

It's always a good idea to treat Hyper-Threading as a bonus, keep it in mind. The over-commitment numbers will in most cases positively be impacted by HT.

*Please note that there's one other thing to keep in mind which I mentioned earlier. The customer had a requirement to avoid single points of failure (N+1). So instead of building a cluster with 21 hosts, I had to build it with 22 hosts. Again, a positive impact on the CPU over-commitment. Keep in mind to do two things: set up vSphere HA Admission Control correctly (more about that later) and limit your Horizon Pools to the desktop limit which your cluster is sized for (so, in this case don't exceed the 1,320 desktop limit).*

**Result**

The result was like expected: a good performing VDI without any congestion on resources.

This first example was a real-life use case, but one to purely show you how to size in a conservative, but in-balance way. Unfortunately, I don't see a lot of those anymore. Use cases are becoming more diverse and may include more complex (and graphical intense) apps and users with high demands (like a lot of displays). Check the next example for more.

# SIZING EXAMPLE 2: MULTIPLE USE CASES

Sizing is always a challenge. When a customer has multiple use cases, it could become more complex. The next example is again a real-life example (although a little bit adjusted) and will show you how to size for multiple use cases. The reason for the adjustment is simple, it's the project I based my VCDX defense on.

The customer had two use cases:

- Knowledge workers
- Graphical designers

The customer had a couple of requirements which had an impact on the sizing. These are the ones that had the most significant impact:

- The VDI must have an availability of at least 99.9% uptime
- The Recovery Time Objective (RTO) of the VDI service must be 15 minutes or less
- Single points of failure must be avoided
- Sizing should be conservative

Also, I had a major constraint. One of the most used applications in both of the use cases was single threaded. You may notice this in the assessment data in the tables that follow shortly. The peak clock speed is almost 100% of the physical CPU. In this case, I'm going to use the average peak numbers, but when choosing physical CPUs, it's vital to use CPUs with a high clock speed that matches the peak speed of a single core. Applications that are used for 3D modeling, also require a CPU with a high clock speed, which you will see in the assessment data.

Like I explained in the assessment section, you should always run an assessment on all of the different use cases that need to run on the proposed VDI. The following tables present the assessment outcomes of the two different use cases.

Knowledge workers (800 users)

| Metric | Value |
|---|---|
| Peak CPU usage (in MHz) | 5,816 |
| Average peak CPU usage (in MHz) | 2,378 |
| Average CPU usage (in MHz) | 1,392 |
| CPU core count | 2 |
| Peak RAM usage (in KB) | 8,177,138 |
| Average peak RAM usage (in KB) | 6,421,769 |
| Average RAM usage (in KB) | 6,108,278 |
| Storage capacity (in GB) | 91.9 |
| Peak disk read IOPs | 67 |
| Average peak disk read IOPs | 16 |
| Average disk read IOPs | 7 |
| Peak disk write IOPs | 14 |
| Average peak disk write IOPs | 3 |
| Average disk write IOPs | 1 |
| Peak network receive rate (in Mbps) | 2.5 |
| Average peak network receive rate (in Mbps) | 0.3 |
| Average network receive rate (in Mbps) | 0.2 |
| Peak network send rate (in Mbps) | 0.3 |
| Average peak network send rate (in Mbps) | 0.1 |
| Average network send rate (in Mbps) | 0.1 |
| GPU memory used (in MB) | 812 |

All knowledge worker users were provided with a non-persistent desktop, based on Linked Clones, with Windows 10 64 bit and two 1920x1080 based displays.

Graphical Designers (150 users)

| Metric | Value |
|---|---|
| Peak CPU usage (in MHz) | 12,864 |
| Average peak CPU usage (in MHz) | 6,087 |
| Average CPU usage (in MHz) | 3,673 |
| CPU core count | 4 |
| Peak RAM usage (in KB) | 17,683,808 |
| Average peak RAM usage (in KB) | 14,112,752 |

| Metric | Value |
|---|---|
| Average RAM usage (in KB) | 13,338,788 |
| Storage capacity (in GB) | 287 |
| Peak disk read IOPs | 154 |
| Average peak disk read IOPs | 54 |
| Average disk read IOPs | 32 |
| Peak disk write IOPs | 34 |
| Average peak disk write IOPs | 10 |
| Average disk write IOPs | 6 |
| Peak network receive rate (in Mbps) | 5.8 |
| Average peak network receive rate (in Mbps) | 1.1 |
| Average network receive rate (in Mbps) | 0.5 |
| Peak network send rate (in Mbps) | 2.5 |
| Average peak network send rate (in Mbps) | 0.2 |
| Average network send rate (in Mbps) | 0.1 |
| GPU memory used (in MB) | 1954 |

All graphical designer users were provided with a persistent desktop, based on Full Clones. They worked with Windows 10 64 bit and two 1920x1080 based displays.

Similar to the calculation in the previous example, you need to calculate the required resources. Instead of writing them down in detail, I added them to a table in which the calculations are displayed.

Knowledge Worker required resources per datacenter (800 users)

| Metric | Value | Times | Required |
|---|---|---|---|
| CPU clock speed | 2,378 MHz | 800 users | 1,902,400 MHz |
| CPU cores | 2 cores | 800 users | 1,600 cores |
| RAM | 7 GB | 800 users | 5,600 GB |
| Disk IOPS | 167 IOPS | 800 users | 133,600 IOPS |
| Disk capacity | 91.1 GB | 800 users | 7,379.1 GB |
| Network throughput | 2.5 Mbps | 800 users | 2,000 Mbps |
| GPU memory | 1,024 MB profile (812 MB) | 800 users | 819,200 MB (800 profiles) |

Graphical Designers required resources per datacenter (150 users)

| Metric | Value | Times | Value |
|---|---|---|---|
| CPU clock speed | 6,087 MHz | 150 users | 913,050 MHz |
| CPU cores | 4 cores | 150 users | 600 cores |
| RAM | 18 GB | 150 users | 2,700 GB |
| Disk IOPS | 254 IOPS | 150 users | 38,100 IOPS |
| Disk capacity | 287 GB | 150 users | 43,050 GB |
| Network throughput | 5.8 Mbps | 150 users | 870 Mbps |
| GPU memory | 2,048 MB profile (1,954 MB) | 150 users | 307,200 MB (150 profiles) |

Depending on the number of desktops that belong to a use case, you need to figure out if you are going to deploy them on separate hosts or mix them with other use cases on the same hosts. There are a couple of reasons to split use cases to separate hosts (or clusters):

- A use case has a requirement to use different CPUs (such as a higher clock speed)
- A use case has a requirement to use (different) GPUs.
- A use case has a specific hardware dependency (like USB-directed dongles or pass-through linked devices).
- From a legal/security perspective, use cases must be running on wholly separated infrastructures.
- Different over-commitment ratios must be met to satisfy performance requirements.
- You might also need to restrict access to licenses for certain products to only specific hosts.

In this case, the reason for separation was based on two factors:

- The perfectly clear one is: different GPUs are required for graphical designers. More about why this is, can be found in the *Graphics and Remote Protocols* section.
- The second one is that on an average, use cases with a requirement to have graphical acceleration such as graphic designers or stockbrokers (with a vast amount of displays), have a much lower over-commitment ratio (1:4) than knowledge workers (1:7) to start with.

When choosing hardware for these use cases, we made the decision to build hosts with the same components (except the GPUs and the vSAN capacity). Because we had single-threaded apps that require a high clock speed, we choose the same CPUs for both use cases.

Knowledge worker hosts

| Item | Value |
| --- | --- |
| CPU type | 2 x Intel Xeon E5-2687 v4 |
| CPU clock speed | 3.0GHz |
| CPU cores | 24 (48 with HT) |
| RAM | 368 GB |
| vSAN capacity (net per host) | 1,200 GB |
| vSAN IOPS | 50,000 |
| Network throughput | 2 x 10 Gbps |
| GPU memory (NVIDIA Tesla M10) | 65,536 MB (64 profiles) |

Graphical designer hosts

| Item | Value |
| --- | --- |
| CPU type | 2 x Intel Xeon E5-2687 v4 |
| CPU clock speed | 3.0GHz |
| CPU cores | 24 (48 with HT) |
| RAM | 368 GB |
| vSAN capacity (net per host) | 6,000 GB |
| vSAN IOPS | 50,000 |
| Network throughput | 2 x 10 Gbps |

| Item | Value |
|------|-------|
| GPU memory (NVIDIA Tesla M60)* | 65,536 MB (16 profiles) |

*A single NVIDIA Tesla M60 GPU is able to support eight users with a 2GB profile. 2 of those cards could be placed in a single host we chose.

Based on the specs of the above hosts and the calculated required resources, the following tables display the required hosts per use case. Please note that for the knowledge worker use case, the same calculations were used as with the previous example.

**Knowledge Worker Results**

| Metric | Required | Host resources (net) | Result (rounded up) |
|--------|----------|----------------------|---------------------|
| RAM | 5,600 GB | 318 GB | 18 host required |
| CPU Clock speed | 1,902,400 MHz | 1,296,000 MHz | 1.5:1 (vCPU to pCPU ratio) |
| CPU Cores | 1,600 cores | 432 cores | 3.7:1(vCPU to pCPU ratio) |
| Disk IOPS | 133,600 IOPS | 900,000 IOPS | ✓ (enough resources) |
| Disk capacity | 7,379.1 GB | 21,600 GB | ✓ |
| Network Throughput | 2,000 Mbps | 360,000 Mbps | ✓ |
| GPU Memory | 649,600 MB | 819,200 MB (800 profiles) | ✓ (1,152 profiles available) |

**Graphical Designer Results**

When calculating the density on a single host for use cases that require a powerful GPU (such as NVIDIA Tesla M60 or Tesla P40 GPUs), the limiting factor on creating a similar density as the other use cases, is the actual GPU. A Tesla M10 GPU is purposely built for density and is able to support 64 profiles per card. A Tesla M60 or Tesla P40 is built for performance and has a limited number of profiles. Because of that reason, I started the sizing from the GPU density

| Metric | Required | Host resources (net) | Result (rounded up) |
|---|---|---|---|
| GPU Memory | 307,200 MB (150 profiles) | 655,360 (160 profiles) | 10 hosts |
| RAM | 2,700 GB | 3,180 GB | ✓ (enough resources) |
| CPU Clock speed | 913,050 MHz | 720,000 MHz | 1.3:1 (vCPU to pCPU ratio) |
| CPU Cores | 600 cores | 240 cores | 2.5:1 (vCPU to pCPU ratio) |
| Disk IOPS | 38,100 IOPS | 500,000 IOPS | ✓ |
| Disk capacity | 43,050 GB | 60,000 GB | ✓ |
| Network Throughput | 870 Mbps | 200,000 Mbps | ✓ |

As both use cases required the avoidance of single points of failure, an additional host was added to both cluster calculations.

- Knowledge Worker capacity:     19 hosts
- Graphical Designer capacity:     11 hosts

Due to an availability requirement of 99.9% and an RTO of 15 minutes, the decision was made to add an additional datacenter to the environment and implement Cloud Pod Architecture. As a result, the following hosts were required:

- Knowledge Worker capacity:     38 hosts (19 per datacenter)
- Graphical Designer capacity:     22 hosts (11 per datacenter)

These numbers might seem very high and it can be challenging to convince a customer to invest in such an infrastructure. Like mentioned in the Business Case section, high availability should be seen as an insurance policy. Insurance costs money, but it might be far more expensive if the customer has a datacenter failure and is unable to work for a couple of hours.

**Result**

Again, the result was as expected: a good performing VDI without any congestion on resources.

# AVAILABILITY AND

# DISASTER RECOVERY

If you ever have done requirements workshops with customers, you might know that availability and recoverability are one of the first requirements that need to be discussed. In my very first design project as a consultant, the availability requirements couldn't be filled in during the workshops because on the customer side, no one was available that was allowed to decide on the number of nines. Ten weeks later, the design was nearly finished when the guy turned up again. And guess what, the availability that was assumed, turned out to be a wrong number which led to a complete rework of the design.

Another thing I experienced in a different project, was that the customer decided to run VDI based on 99.99% availability (per month excluding maintenance) for 1,000 users. What the customer didn't think of, was the financial impact of that requirement. Back then, I wasn't experienced enough to be able to explain such an impact. 99.99% is quite impossible to achieve from a single datacenter, so when the customer found out they had to purchase twice the number of hosts, 99.99% uptime for just 25% of the use cases was enough. This is why finding out if the customer has a budget constraint is mandatory for every project. Every customer has a limited budget; the thing is that you need to find out if it mismatches the availability requirements. Please note that verifying the budget with someone who has a financial mandate is always a good plan. IT's plans and the CFO's budget quite often have mismatches. And don't forget that if the business case was solid, you wouldn't be having that discussion. So, see it as a validation.

Next to the number of nines, the Recovery Time Objective (RTO) and Recovery Point Objective (RPO) are just as important. These three different requirements will be your biggest cause for single-site or multi-site deployments.

The RTO determines the maximum time it may take before the service, application or component is available again after a failure. It may as well be set on the recovery of data. The RPO determines the maximum length of time that data might be lost in case of a disaster.

If you are looking at designing for availability and failure, it doesn't always have to mean you have to add a lot of Connection servers, load balancers, and metro clusters. A VDI could pretty much work with a single Connection server, without load balancers, and on a single site. The importance here is that the architecture is validated by the customer and that the decisions made, comply with your requirements.

# REQUIREMENTS

Any decision you make around components, sites, datacenters and Cloud Pod Architecture will be driven by requirements, so let's dive into these first.

## Availability

Availability is measured by calculating the percentage of the total time that a service or application is available to a use case. The total time is taken from either a month or a year and the requirement should specify if maintenance is included. Examples of availability requirements are:

*Desktops in the Basic Users pool should have a 99.9% uptime. The uptime is based on 24x7x52 availability (maintenance windows are not included).*

*The management services (such as Connection servers and App Volumes Managers) that support the infrastructure should have a 99.9% uptime. The uptime is based on 24x7x52 availability (maintenance windows are not included).*

*The management components that support the infrastructure should have a 99.8% uptime. The uptime is based on 24x7x52 availability (maintenance windows are not included).*

The percentages have a direct impact on the components, load balancers and sites. The following table shows an overview of availability percentages including the maximum downtime per month and per year.

| Percentage | Maximum downtime per month | Maximum downtime per year |
|---|---|---|
| 99% | 7 hours, 18 minutes and 17.5 seconds | 3 days, 15 hours, 39 minutes and 29.5 seconds |

| Percentage | Maximum downtime per month | Maximum downtime per year |
|---|---|---|
| 99.5% | 3 hours, 39 minutes and 8.7 seconds | 1 day, 19 hours, 49 minutes and 44.8 seconds |
| 99.6% | 2 hours, 55 minutes and 19 seconds | 1 day, 11 hours, 3 minutes and 47.8 seconds |
| 99.7% | 2 hours, 11 minutes and 29.2 seconds | 1 day, 2 hours, 17 minutes and 50.9 seconds |
| 99.8% | 1 hour, 27 minutes and 39.5 seconds | 17 hours, 31 minutes and 53.9 seconds |
| 99.9% | 43 minutes and 49.7 seconds | 8 hours, 45 minutes and 57 seconds |
| 99.95% | 21 minutes and 54.9 seconds | 4 hours, 22 minutes and 58.5 seconds |
| 99.99% | 4 minutes and 23 seconds | 52 minutes and 35.7 seconds |
| 99.995% | 2 minutes and 11.5 seconds | 26 minutes and 17.8 seconds |
| 99.999% | 26.3 seconds | 5 minutes and 15.6 seconds |

As you can see, the higher the percentage, the shorter the maximum downtime. Why not 100% you ask? It's simple, 100% uptime is something you can't guarantee because there is always a chance of something failing. Even the largest cloud-native applications such as Facebook or WhatsApp can't guarantee 100%. There are always dependencies for which you aren't 100% responsible. In May 2018, someone hijacked the CloudFlare DNS (1.1.1.1) which is used by millions of people for name resolution of websites and public applications. For a short time, the DNS requests were redirected to another provider (probably a Chinese telecom provider) for a short time. Check out this link to see a replay of the hijack and the effect it had to the redirected requests:

https://bgpstream.com/event/138295

In the end, nothing crucial was impacted by the hijack but imagine what happens if it did.

The higher the percentage, the more measures you need to take to design an architecture that is compliant with that percentage. The next thing would be to decide what kind of measures you would need in your case. If you have a hypothetical availability requirement of 99% per year, you will have a little bit over 3.5 days to recover from a failure. In that case, you would probably just need a single Connection server to broker the desktops. If it breaks, restoring it from a backup and making it available again can easily be done in that time. If you have an availability requirement of 99.99% per year, you need to recover from a similar failure within 52 minutes and 35.7 seconds. That would be significantly more challenging. If your SLA (and availability requirement) is based on a year, take the number of possible failures in a year into account, as well. You won't be the first assuming you will only have one failure a year ☺.

One of the first projects I ever did was to design a vSphere environment for a treatment plant. Although their primary business could impact millions of people if the water purification machines would stop, the availability requirement was just 99.5% because a vSphere failure didn't impact those machines at all. Proposing a vSphere architecture that is able to comply with even higher percentages doesn't add any value to the design. And so, keeping the design as simple as possible is recommended.

If the customer has done their homework, the percentage should be based on the maximum time they could tolerate a failure in the VDI without a direct financial/business impact. The higher the percentage, the higher the financial/business impact during a failure. The higher the percentage, the bigger the investment in a VDI architecture.

Another important part to discuss during a requirement workshop is the scope of a requirement. The Netherlands is famous for its height (or not, actually). I live in the coastal part of The Netherlands where my house is built at 15 meters below sea level. In case of a flood, I will probably be swimming to work. Imagine your datacenter being next to my house during a flood. That will be a challenge, right? What happens now if your hardware vendor of choice has around 1000 customers in the same datacenter, all being impacted by a disaster. Yep, don't think you will receive new hardware in time to restore your service in respect to the requirement. Another practical example would be if both of your datacenters are located in the Bay Area in San Francisco. It's an area which had quite a number of earthquakes in the past. If an earthquake would occur and your VDI becomes unavailable in both datacenters, you will have a similar challenge. My advice here is to open up the dialog with the customer to discuss what's realistic and take things like natural disasters or other events that might negatively impact your availability into account. Also, discuss the requirement for all use cases. In a hospital, people working in an emergency room would probably have a different requirement than the people working in the mail room. A full-blown multi-site solution for all use cases would probably be a bit of an overkill.

# RTO

The RTO is a recoverability requirement. The RTO requirement relates to the availability requirement in such a way that the time you would need to recover should always stay within the maximum downtime per required period. If your availability requirement is 99.9% per month and your RTO is 3 hours, you will probably violate the availability requirement during a recovery. The RTO should always be shorter than the maximum downtime.

If the customer has an RTO of 3 hours, it means that you have 3 hours to recover from a disaster. When designing your architecture, would it make sense if you included an active/active multi-site solution with 100% load per site? Or would an active/passive or even a single site with a DR site in a cloud be sufficient? I don't have a straight answer because it all depends on the rest of your requirements... ☺

Examples of RTO requirements:

*The RTO of the basic desktop should be 1 hour or less*

*The RTO of the VIP desktop should be 30 minutes or less*

*The RTO of the management components such as Horizon Connection servers and ThinApp and App Volumes services is 15 minutes or less.*

Filling in a low RTO (such as 15 minutes) in the design can be relatively easy. If your VDI consists of just non-persistent Instant Clones, recovering from a failure is simple. If, on the other hand, you have persistent full clones with 100GB+ worth of data which needs to be recovered from the backup, 15 minutes is quite undoable.

## RPO

The RPO, like the RTO, is also a recoverability requirement. The RPO requirement obviously also relates to the other two (availability and RTO). The RPO is basically your time between the failure and the restore point. Data that isn't altered that much such as App Volumes AppStacks might have a higher RPO than user data for instance. Like the RTO and availability, the value of the RPO says something about the business impact. It's the maximum data loss that a company could experience without any financial or business impact. There are different ways to achieve this. If the RPO of a desktop is 1 hour, this is again quite easily achievable by deploying non-persistent Instant Clones. A Full Clone would be somewhat more challenging as you need to ensure that the desktop is backed up every hour.

Examples of RPO requirements:

*The RPO of the basic desktop should be 15 minutes or less*

*The RPO of the VIP desktop should be 15 minutes or less*

*The RPO of the management components such as Horizon Connection servers and ThinApp and App Volumes services is 5 minutes or less*

# COMPONENT FAILURE

Based on the three types of requirements explained in the previous section, you need to design your architecture and include some form of component failure avoidance. I would say that from 99.5% and up, you need to design your VDI to avoid single points of failure because every single point of failure could possibly cause a violation of the availability requirement (since you probably won't recover in time).

I'm not going to explain how to avoid every type of component failure as every customer and situation is different. But, I think you should take the following components into account and verify with every single one if it poses a risk.

- Desktops
- Applications (including AppStacks and ThinApps)
- User data
- User profiles
- Horizon Connection servers
- View Composers
- App Volumes Managers
- Unified Access Gateways
- ESXi hosts
- Platform Services Controllers
- Network interfaces
- HBAs
- Blade/HCI enclosures
- (Fabric) Switches
- Storage hardware (either traditional shared storage or vSAN disk groups)
- Firewalls/routers
- Power feeds
- External connectivity (such as MPLS or internet connectivity)
- Datacenters

There are some components that could be offline for a while before you will have an issue. The following components are such:

- vCenter Appliances
- NSX Managers

Furthermore, be sure that the supporting infrastructure is going to be equally available (or assume this, but make sure to include risks, as well). Take the following components into account and verify with every single one if it poses a risk.

- DNS
- DHCP
- Active Directory
- NTP
- File shares
- Application backends
- SQL Servers

There might be more components you should include, but they depend on your situation. I think the above ones are a great starting point.

# REFERENCE ARCHITECTURE

VMware EUC Technical Marketing has released a great reference architecture for a Horizon Enterprise deployment. It's not a full design (as it doesn't contain requirements or design decisions). It simply describes the way a certain component should be designed when you require "High Availability" in your environment. The document is a great resource for your design questions. How many Connection servers should I use for a certain number of users? How many UAGs? And how should I implement App Volumes in terms of the number of App Volumes Managers and database placement?

The reference architecture can be found here:

https://www.vmware.com/content/dam/digitalmarketing/vmwar
e/en/pdf/techpaper/vmware-horizon-7-enterprise-validated-
integration-design-reference-architecture.pdf

# MULTI-SITE ARCHITECTURE

If the possible failure of a single site could cause your organization or customer a serious business or financial impact, you could decide to include a secondary site to your VDI. By using Cloud Pod Architecture, Horizon will able to federate entitlements between two or more Pods, which will be located in two geographically separated datacenters. Besides Horizon, the other solutions that are part of the architecture will need to become multi-site as well. Just like the reference architecture from the previous section, VMware has published a reference architecture which covers multi-site deployments. The multi-site reference architecture can be found here:

https://techzone.vmware.com/sites/default/files/vmware-
horizon-7-enterprise-edition-reference-architecture-multi-
site_0.pdf

## Cloud Pod Architecture Alternative

A couple of years ago, I worked on a project with a customer who already bought the complete Horizon Enterprise Suite during the design phase. The customer also brought some constraints to the table. The management components had to run in their existing management cluster and an F5 big IP with Local Traffic Management run in front of most of the management components to balance their load. The existing load balancer had to be used and because of both a budget constraint as well as a technical constraint, the customer wasn't able to add a Global Traffic Manager (GTM) module. Until then, the only way to properly run a Cloud Pod Architecture, was with a GTM acting as a Global Site

Load Balancer (GSLB) service to create site awareness. In our case, we had some additional requirements and constraints which we had to work with:

- The two datacenters we had to work with were situated 15 kilometers (9.3 miles) from each other with a dark fiber between them. Latencies were less than 3ms.
- Management virtual machines had to run on the existing management cluster which was based on a metro cluster with an IBM SVC for synchronous replication.

After a lot of research and meetings, conference calls with some of the brightest minds of both VMware as well as F5, we came up with a plan.

First, let's dive a little deeper into traditional Cloud Pod Architecture and take a look at the following diagram:

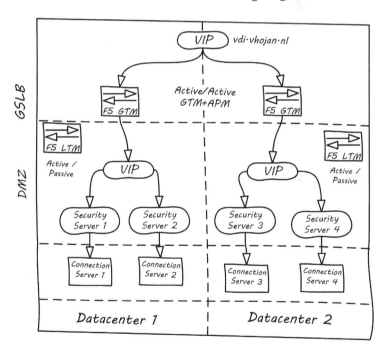

The top-level Virtual IP (VIP) is used (with an FQDN) for every external device to connect to an available desktop. A GTM is used to automatically balance the load between the two geographically separated Pods. F5's Access Policy Manager (APM) is used to create session persistence when users disconnect and reconnect their session and so aren't sent to the wrong Pod. Both Pods have F5's Local Traffic Manager modules to locally load balance the security servers for external connections. Connection servers can also be behind an F5 LTM to balance connections for internal users.

Since the release of Horizon 6, Cloud Pod Architecture has matured significantly, in addition to other features and capabilities such as the Unified Access Gateway and the development on the Blast Extreme connection protocol (which was released in Horizon 7). A lot has changed in the architecture.

Take a look at the following diagram:

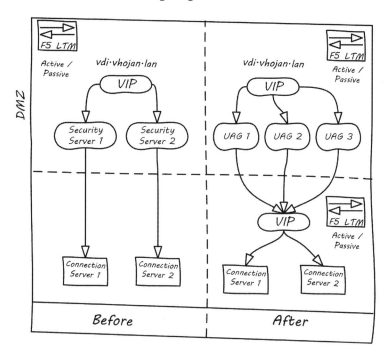

In this picture, we see a single Pod. On the left side, it is configured with LTM load balancing and traditional Security Servers. Each Security Server is directly paired with a Connection server. On the right side, LTM load balancing in combination with Horizon UAGs are used. UAGs aren't paired with a single Connection server but are linked to an FQDN. That's where the biggest added value was created because the FQDN could either be from a Connection server or a couple of Connection servers that are behind a virtual IP (VIP) of a load balancer as well.

Because the UAGs aren't paired to a Connection server, the Connection servers can be used for both internal and external connections (while dedicated Connection servers were needed for internal connections before the UAG was born).

The next feature that was added to Horizon 7 was the Blast Extreme protocol, which gave the user a similar user experience as PCoIP, but over the HTTPS protocol instead of a dedicated TCP/IP Port. This is an important part when looking at other possibilities for load balancing. F5's BIG IPs are a common practice with Cloud Pod Architecture, but is that still necessary? The answer (of course) is: it depends. When all the right factors are in place, it will be possible to use only LTM or maybe even NSX's edges as a load balancer with Cloud Pod Architecture.

To use a plain load balancer, the following prerequisites must be met:

- A minimum of 2 Pods
- Horizon 7 or newer
- Redundant hardware in each Pod (hosts, networking, storage, etc.)
- A stretched VLAN (over both datacenters) in which load balancers can be connected (based on VXLAN or Cisco's OTV)
- F5 LTM (or comparable load balancer) with an external VIP and an internal VIP
- A stretched management cluster
- Horizon 7 UAGs
- Blast Extreme (so no PCoIP)
- DRS Rules must be applied to make sure Connection servers remain in their datacenters
- Although 20,000 desktops are supported in a single Pod, you want to make sure to stay away from those

maximums. 10,000 is the maximum supported limit per Pod with multiple Pods

The architecture will look like this:

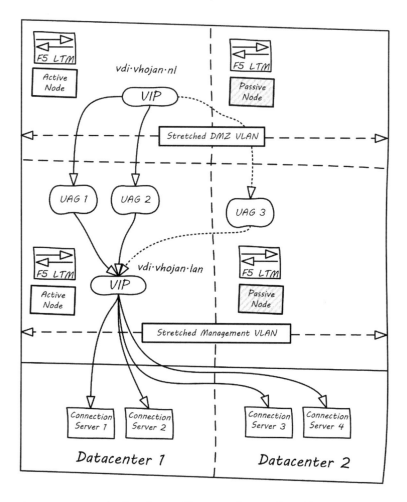

As you can see in the above diagram, the top-level load balancers are placed in a stretched layer 2 DMZ network. You could either choose active/passive or active/active load balancing. In my case, I have chosen active/passive to consolidate all incoming connections and reduce cross-site connections.

For an assumed number of 2,000 maximum connected sessions, we deployed 2 active UAGs and one passive UAG. The load balancer is set up with a pool containing the 3 UAGs, where 1 and 2 have a higher priority. In case datacenter 1 fails, UAG3 will accept incoming sessions and redirect them to their desktop. UAG1 and UAG2 will be restarted by vSphere HA in DC2 and within a couple of minutes, all UAGs will run from DC2. Make sure to add DRS anti-affinity groups in combination with DRS host groups. Also make sure to have storage DRS enabled with datastore groups and again, anti-affinity rules.

As mentioned earlier, in the pre-UAG architecture, Security servers were paired with Connection servers on a 1 to 1 basis. UAGs don't do that. In the case of a UAG, it is linked to a namespace. As you can see in the previous diagram, all UAGs are pointing to a VIP that is set on a secondary layer of load balancers that contain a pool with Connection servers. This will mean that the UAGs will tunnel an incoming connection to the VIP, which in its case balances the connection over a single Connection server in the pool. The Connection server will first check in its own Pod or eventually in the other Pod(s) if there is an available (or existing) desktop. If there is a desktop available, the incoming connection will be tunneled to the desktop and the user will be able to work.

In this case, no APM module is needed because all sessions are tunneled from one datacenter. Those sessions are known as long as they exist in either Pods. Please keep in mind that in the above situation only HTTPS (Blast Extreme) traffic is load balanced and tunneled.

The following diagram outlines the steps that are described in the above section.

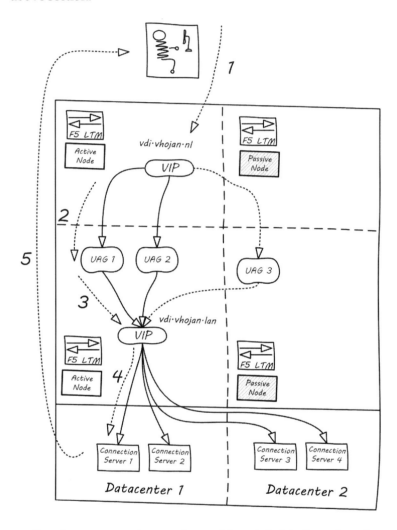

1. A user requests a session and is pointed to the external VIP of the UAGs
2. The active LTM LB sends the session to either of the UAGs in the pool
3. The UAGs forward the session to the VIP of the internal URL

4. The LTM LB sends the session to either of the Horizon Connection servers
5. The Connection server returns a desktop to the user from one of both Pods

## Failure Scenario

In case of a datacenter failure, there are certain steps that are automatically taken so traffic is routed and availability to the service is retained.

First of all, if the secondary datacenter is down, only active connections to the desktop will fail. If a user reconnects to Horizon, they will receive a desktop in the active datacenter. But, what happens if the primary datacenter fails? The following diagrams outline the steps that are automatically taken.

Step 1: The primary datacenter fails

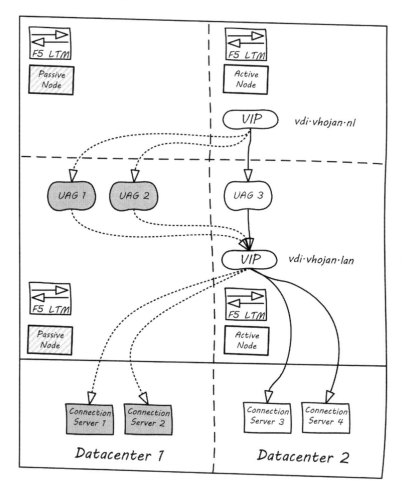

If the primary datacenter fails, the passive load balancer becomes active and automatically picks up new sessions. The existing sessions from the load balancer in Datacenter 1 are killed. The UAG in datacenter 2 directs the connections to the new active load balancer in front of the Connections servers and sends it to an available one.

## Step 2: vSphere HA boots up UAGs

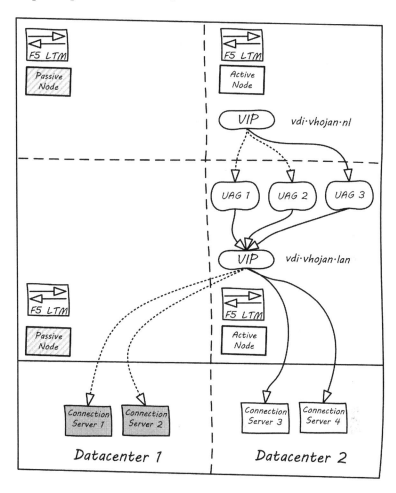

As the management cluster is stretched, UAGs that were running in Datacenter 1 are now booted in Datacenter 2. They will automatically pick up new connections as soon as the load balancer notices that they are online.

The Connection servers in the failed datacenter aren't being started up in the active datacenter since DRS won't allow this.

Step 3: Primary datacenter restores.

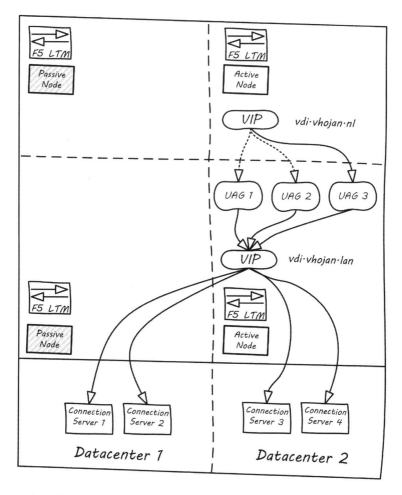

When the primary datacenter becomes available again, the Pod in that datacenter boots up and will accept incoming connections from the active load balancer in the secondary datacenter.

The above architecture is fully supported and will work with different load balancers. It's important to know that the external load balancer might tunnel all of the connections, so a load balancer that is able to support your user count is important. As mentioned, this architecture will also work with NSX. More about NSX can be found in the NSX section.

## Considerations

There are some considerations when looking at Cloud Pod Architecture for disaster recovery.

Cloud Pod Architecture will use twice the number of hosts for the use cases that require a higher availability (if other use cases don't require a multi-site VDI, just stick to a single Pod in for those users).

Cloud Pod Architecture only federates entitlements between Pods. Other data such as applications, profiles, and user data need to be synchronized by other methods described in the reference architecture.

This one might be a little from paranoid city but consider using different admin accounts/teams that manage the individual Pods. Imagine what happens if a single admin goes rogue and disables services in both Pods before leaving your organization.

# ALTERNATIVES

Cloud Pod Architecture is a great feature but might be expensive if just used for DR in an Active/Passive scenario. With cloud becoming cheaper and supporting an increasing number of use cases, desktops from the cloud are becoming more popular each year. Research has shown that many customers are thinking about moving to the cloud.

# Horizon 7 on VMC

In 2018, VMware announced Horizon 7 on VMC (VMware Cloud on AWS). VMC is VMware's Software-Defined Datacenter Cloud service, which runs on top of Amazon bare-metal hosts. VMC can be used as an extension from the on-premises datacenter or as an Infrastructure-as-a-Service (IaaS) without an on-premises datacenter. As the SDDC is the basis of most of the Horizon deployment, the logical step of VMware was to extend Horizon towards the VMC service, which is available in the US and Europe and will probably expand to other regions.

VMC requires at least 1 host but is easily and quickly expandable if you require more hosts. The initial bringing-up of a VMC instance might take a couple of hours. Additional hosts can be brought up in 10 minutes, with a number of desktops being available within a couple of minutes after. Like in a conventional CPA, the Horizon 7 on VMC service requires a load balancer to balance the load between the on-premises Pod and the Horizon 7 on VMC Pod.

The following diagram shows the Horizon 7 on VMC Cloud Pod Architecture.

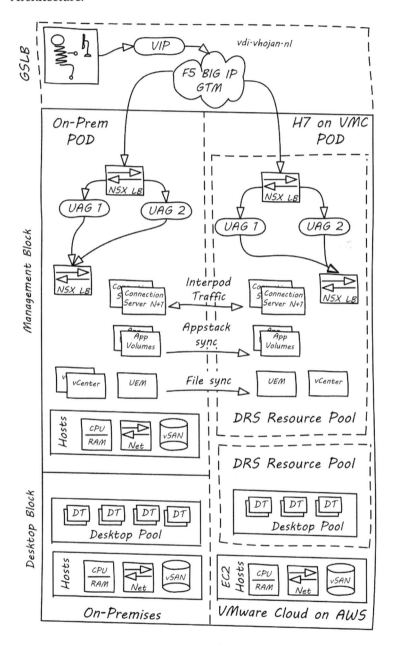

Please note that as of this writing, an F5 Big IP with GTM is the only supported load balancer. I know Amazon's own load balancing service *Route 53* was tested as well but wasn't available yet when this book was released.

In my opinion, Cloud Pod Architecture with Horizon 7 on VMC is a great alternative to the conventional one, especially if applications and datacenter workloads are already working on VMC. If your organization is already consuming native services on AWS, these can be integrated, as well (which can be another consideration). Some vendors are already offering to store profile data in S3 buckets. Imagine what would be possible if you could store your content library, AppStacks and User Environment Manager profiles in an S3 bucket so you don't have to constantly run lots of VMs running those services.

## Considerations

There are some risks involved, though. VMC has a pay-as-you-go model. This means that if you spin up 50 hosts to run desktops on them, you will be billed for those resources. If you keep them powered on while not using them, you might burn money. So, be aware of this and keep track of your resource usage.

As of this writing, GPUs aren't available yet on VMC. Applications might not require a GPU, and a reduced user experience might be acceptable in case of a disaster. Add this as a risk to the design or include it in the SLA.

A positive consideration could be AWS' native services. How awesome would it be if you would be able to create a backup of your entire on-premises Pod to services using an S3 bucket and restore it on VMC as soon as it spins up? Sounds like a next project ☺.

Especially if your organization is located in Europe, it might be mandatory for you to keep your data in specific regions/countries. VMC is available in multiple Amazon datacenters but check first if you are allowed to run your applications and host your data in a specific region.

This consideration might be one from a conspiracy theory, but Amazon is expanding and extending its services, and not only in IT. In 2017, they began to offer insurances and mortgages. If your business is focusing on these services, you might want to think twice before you host your services at a competitor.

## Horizon DaaS

VMware announced on October 15, 2013, that it had acquired Desktone. Desktone was one of the pioneers in the field of Desktops as a Service (DaaS), delivering desktops and applications as a cloud service. Desktone provided a desktop virtualization platform that enabled the deployment of Windows desktops and applications from the cloud to any user, anywhere, on any device. Built from the ground up for cloud delivery and service providers to offer DaaS, the Desktone platform was selected by the world's largest cloud providers including Dell, Fujitsu, NEC, Dimension Data, and Navisite to deliver desktops from the cloud.

The Horizon DaaS architecture is a lot different from Horizon 7. Most of Horizon 7's components are based on Windows services while the Horizon DaaS architecture is based on Linux appliances. Feature parity-wise, Horizon 7 and Horizon DaaS are quite comparable. GPU support, Blast Extreme, HTML access and Horizon Client access are all available. From an application and profile standpoint, App Volumes, ThinApp, and User Environment Manager are all supported as well. Horizon DaaS is offered by VMware partners and is multi-tenant by nature as its biggest value to cloud providers.

## Considerations

Horizon DaaS can be used as an alternative to DR, but certain measures need to be taken. Horizon DaaS itself can't be integrated with Horizon 7. In case of a failure, users need to switch to a different Horizon connection or URL in the browser to connect to the DaaS tenant. An alternative (which provides a better user experience), is to integrate both solutions with Identity Manager (vIDM). By entitling users to both Horizon 7-based pools and Horizon DaaS-based tenants, an end-user is able to connect to both within the same interface (which can either be with the Workspace ONE app or HTML5 portal).

If your datacenter workloads or applications are already running at an IaaS provider that offers Horizon DaaS as well, the choice to move towards Horizon DaaS for DR might be easier.

Like Cloud Pod Architecture, no data is synchronized between the Horizon 7 on-premises and Horizon DaaS services. You need additional services to make sure user profiles, applications, and user data are synchronized.

# Horizon Cloud

In 2015, Project Enzo was announced. Project Enzo (a solution which stemmed from Project Marvin; VMware's answer to Nutanix's HCI solutions) brought several technologies together:

- Automated provisioning of desktops based on Just-In-Time Desktops (JIT)/VMware Instant Clones
- Automated application provisioning based on App Volumes
- Customization of the user environment with User Environment Manager
- A new UI, based on the early stages of the Clarity framework
- A centralized control plane to manage both cloud-based desktops as well as on-premises desktops

The base architecture for all individual components is basically forked from the Horizon DaaS architecture. As time went by, VMware rebranded the solution to Horizon Cloud and opened the door for global VMware partners to offer Cloud Desktops as well. There are currently two major partners offering the cloud desktops; Microsoft (with its Horizon Cloud on Azure) and IBM (with its VMware Horizon on IBM Cloud). Horizon Cloud services have a similar feature set as Horizon 7 and Horizon DaaS. Microsoft and IBM both offer GPU support, as well, if this is required.

## Considerations

The considerations for Horizon Cloud are quite comparable to Horizon DaaS. Horizon Cloud can be used as an alternative to DR (in conjunction with an on-premises VDI solution), but not out of the box. Like Horizon DaaS, Horizon Cloud can't be integrated with Horizon 7, either. Using vIDM or Workspace ONE as a primary portal can integrate on-premises and cloud services for the best user experience possible.

Also similar to Horizon DaaS, if your datacenter workloads or applications are already running at IBM or Microsoft, the choice to move towards Horizon Cloud for DR might be easier.

Like Horizon DaaS, Horizon Cloud doesn't offer a built-in feature to synchronize data between the on-premises VDI and the Horizon Cloud backend. Additional services are required to make sure profiles, user data and applications are synchronized.

# SINGLE SITE DR

Is a secondary datacenter out of scope? Or is it just a waste of money because of lower availability or recoverability requirements? Backing up your data with a backup (or data management solution as backup vendors are calling themselves nowadays), can be considered, as well. There are multiple solutions which can offer RPOs/RTOs varying between 15 minutes and multiple hours or days. Choosing the proper solution depends on your RTO/RPO requirements. There are a gazillion backup vendors to choose from, so do your homework and choose wisely.

## Considerations

It is quite useless to create a backup of your non-persistent desktops. Only create backups of the services that create a persistent user experience, instead (such as your profiles). User data is one of the components that makes a user experience persistent. Make sure to create a backup of your user data in respect to the RPO and RTO requirements.

Make sure all management virtual machines and things like base images are being backed up and automate the process of adding a VM to a group of backed up VMs as much as possible. You won't be the first who creates new VMs but forgets to add them to the backup resulting into a very, very bad day when the virtual infrastructure breaks down.

Create a backup of all supporting infrastructure such as Domain Controllers, DNS services, NTP servers, etc.

# VSPHERE

The one solution that made VMware what it is today is of course, the hypervisor ESXi that comes in a bundle with vCenter and its features. This bundle is called vSphere. This section describes some of the features and architecture components that are included in vSphere and will share some design common practices and considerations when using them with VDI.

## ESXI

The first hypervisor VMware released, was called VMware ESX (Elastic Sky X). VMware ESX was a solution which had to be installed on top of an existing Linux operating system and was able to run virtual machines with shared resources. VMware ESXi was born in 2010, which was an integrated bundle of a Linux operating system and all components to run the hypervisor. Up until today, the VMware ESXi hypervisor is the most popular one in VDI deployments (according to research from the EUC State of the Union survey).

## Considerations

In terms of design considerations, there are some things that can be decided around VMware ESXi itself. There are some common practices in terms of deployment and maintenance which I will share. The following considerations are an overview of the considerations applicable for VDI, shared through the *Performance Best Practices for VMware vSphere 6.5 guide* from VMware and my own best practices.

- Plan your deployment by allocating enough resources for all the virtual machines you will run, as well as those needed by ESXi itself.

- Use the installation media from the hardware vendor of choice to automatically include all required device drivers and agents required for monitoring your physical host (in some cases, firewall rules required for the vendor are automatically applied).

- Change the location of your scratch partition to a datastore if you are using SD cards or USB flash drives as the installation location. These media aren't really suitable for a lot of small writes and will eventually break.

- Make sure to enable all performance-related and virtualization-related settings in the BIOS of your host (such as power settings) as well as in the ESXi power configuration after the installation is finished (set everything to *High Performance*).

- In terms of consistency, my advice would be to use host profiles. Host profiles will make sure that a single set of configuration items (such as logging settings or NTP settings) can be pushed to an entire cluster.

- Make sure DNS and NTP are working properly to avoid issues.

- Apply the appropriate Non-Uniform Memory Access (NUMA) configuration. More information can be found on either Frank Denneman's blog (http://frankdenneman.nl) or the book he and Niels Hagoort wrote called the *Host Resources Deep Dive*).

- Configure syslog to export the ESXi logs and use a solution like vRealize LogInsight to monitor the logs for anomalies.

The full guide can be downloaded here:

https://www.vmware.com/content/dam/digitalmarketing/vmware/en/pdf/techpaper/performance/Perf_Best_Practices_vSphere65.pdf

# VCENTER & PLATFORM SERVICES

# CONTROLLER

The management platform to manage your ESXi hosts, is called vCenter (Virtual Center). vCenter once originated as a service that could be ran on top of Windows Server. The bigger the virtual datacenter, the bigger the vCenter Server. Back in the day, the biggest monster VMs we saw at customers were quite often the Windows-based vCenter Server and accompanied Microsoft SQL Server (because back then, the vCenter database had to run on an external database server). During VMware Partner Exchange in 2012, I attended a session where I saw the vCenter Appliance for the first time: a single Linux-based VM, containing all vCenter services and integrated database. My mind was blown. It totally made sense to run vCenter with all of its services inside a black box (that was somewhat harder to break by unintended use).

Six years later, the Windows-based vCenter Server is rare sighting at customers; vCenter 6.7 is the last version to support the Windows-service and the migration utility to convert your existing vCenter inventory to the vCenter appliance is really simple and included in the deployment. A big shout out goes to Emad Younis (Staff Technical Marketing Architect at VMware) for all of the content he has created around the vCenter Appliance (VCSA). You can find the content here: http://emadyounis.com

When vSphere 6.0 was released, a new feature called the *Platform Services Controller* (PSC) was introduced. It was a new role of the vCenter architecture that handled specific services such as:

- Licensing Service
- Certificate Authority (VMCA)
- Certificate Store (VECS)
- Lookup Service for Component Registrations

The PSC has a key role in creating a *Single Sign-On (SSO) domain*. The SSO domain will let you manage all of your objects in the different vCenter inventories with the use of a single account that has permissions on all of the individual inventories. Linking different vCenter appliances to each other (called enhanced linked mode) required external PSC appliances in which the role ran in a dedicated virtual appliance. For smaller deployments, the PSC could run as an embedded role on the vCenter appliance, but for an enterprise-scale deployment, the PSC was deployed as a separate appliance (as the internal PSC deployment didn't support Enhanced Linked Mode). In case of high availability requirements, it was deployed as a pair with a load balancer in front of them. In vSphere 6.7, the architecture of the PSCs has changed. Enhanced linked mode doesn't require an external PSC anymore. This means that even for enterprise deployments, an embedded PSC can be deployed which makes the design a lot simpler and reduces external components for a high available SSO domain.

## Considerations

There are some considerations that might impact your deployment of vCenter.

- Instead of designing a single big vCenter (in case of a multi-cluster deployment), consider using multiple smaller vCenters. Every cluster needs a vCenter to manage it. By using multiple, smaller vCenters, you are able to run maintenance operations simultaneously. The fault domain will be reduced as well as during a failure of a single vCenter, other vCenters with their own clusters (and pools) will still be manageable.

- In case of a vCenter failure, all processes that require the vCenter (like the creation of new clones) will not run. Existing desktops will still be usable. If you have a requirement that lets you reduce the number of single points of failure, you might want to consider using vCenter High Availability. Since vSphere 6.7, vCenter HA can include your embedded PSC role, which makes your SSO domain highly available, as well. Please note that this option will require additional resources for the active, passive and mirror nodes.

- I would highly recommend using separate vCenter appliances for your management cluster(s) and payload cluster(s) (like the Horizon Enterprise reference architecture describes). Although this will require more hosts and more resources, separating your management workloads from your desktops will increase the availability of your management components since no desktop will be able to act as a "noisy neighbor" to your management virtual machines.

# VIRTUAL DATACENTER

Every Pod consists of one or more virtual datacenters. A virtual datacenter is the boundary of a vCenter and the clusters it manages. It's the highest level in your vCenter inventory. If you start designing your virtual datacenter(s), you should consider the following things:

- Separate your desktops' workloads from your management workloads and run them in their own clusters, managed by their own vCenters. This consideration is completely in line with the Horizon Enterprise reference architecture and the pod and block architecture.
- VMware publishes new configuration maximums with every new release of a solution. An example is the

maximum number of desktops in a single block, which is 4,000 in case of vSphere 6.7 and Horizon 7.5. The important consideration here is: just because you can run 4,000 desktops in a single block, doesn't mean you should. Reducing the number of desktops in a single block (and thus reducing the cluster size) reduces your fault domain and is in line with the consideration to use multiple, smaller vCenters instead of a single, big one.

The following diagram is an example of a multi-site VDI environment with separated management clusters and desktop clusters (also called blocks):

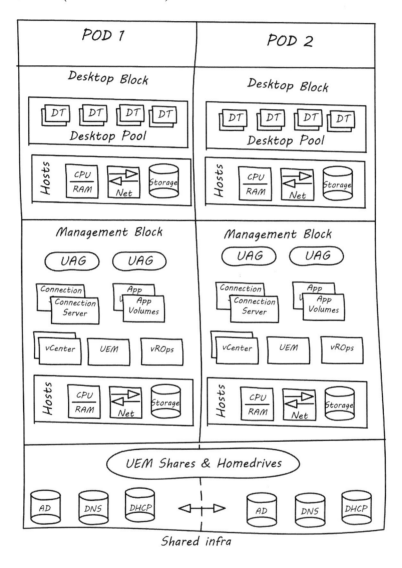

# VSPHERE HIGH AVAILABILITY

vSphere High Availability (HA) provides easy-to-use, cost-effective high availability for applications running in virtual machines. In the event of server failure, affected virtual machines are automatically restarted on other production servers with spare capacity.

Each cluster can be configured for vSphere HA to automatically restart virtual machines in the event of ESXi host failure or individual virtual machine failure. A host is declared as failed if the other hosts in the cluster cannot communicate with the host. A virtual machine is declared failed if a heartbeat inside the guest operating system can no longer be received. vSphere HA can be designed in several ways. A great resource for vSphere HA, is Duncan Epping's blog (http://www.yellow-bricks.com), which contains a lot of information about vSphere HA in general and some of the design considerations. Another great resource is the vSphere Availability guide, which can be found here:

https://docs.vmware.com/en/VMware-vSphere/6.7/vsphere-esxi-vcenter-server-67-availability-guide.pdf

## Considerations

This is an overview of some of the considerations mentioned in the previously named resources, but also from my own best-practices.

- The first question would be if you would need vSphere HA for your desktop workloads. If your desktops are non-persistent clones, it is very likely a user will receive a new desktop on a different host in case of a host. Non-persistent clones don't require vSphere HA from an availability perspective, but can benefit from functions from vSphere HA (such as *Admission Control*). Admission Control will calculate the maximum number of desktops that can run in a cluster, including failover capacity. It will ensure you don't over-allocate resources and end up in an oversaturated vSphere cluster in case of a host failure.

- vSphere HA can restart virtual desktops in case of a host failure or network isolation. Especially when using persistent clones, vSphere HA is essential to increase the availability of your desktops.
- Properly configuring the heartbeat is required for vSphere HA to work. You could use network or datastore heartbeat settings or preferably a combination.
- Admission Control can be designed differently for desktop clusters and management clusters. Design choices and values depend on your cluster size, availability requirements and the number of datacenters. Check Duncan Epping's blog for more detailed information.
- If vDGA is used, vSphere HA won't be able to restart a virtual desktop on a different host in case of a host failure since the GPU in the host is linked to that specific virtual desktop. Consider adding a risk to your design if vDGA is required.

# VSPHERE DISTRIBUTED RESOURCE

# SCHEDULING

vSphere Distributed Resource Scheduling (DRS) can be enabled for dynamically balancing compute capacity across a collection of hardware resources aggregated into logical resource pools, continuously monitoring utilization across resource pools and intelligently allocating available resources among the virtual machines based on pre-defined rules that reflect business needs and changing priorities. When a virtual machine experiences an increased load, DRS can automatically allocate additional resources by redistributing virtual machines among the physical servers in the resource pool.

It is possible to create so-called affinity and anti-affinity rules. These rules force a VM to run on a specific host (until a failure occurs with that host) or to separate two VMs and run them on different hosts. These rules are intended for VMs where high availability is handled by the application, such as two Connection servers or two App Volumes Managers.

## Considerations

Like vSphere HA, vSphere DRS is a great feature for a virtual infrastructure but will require additional considerations in order for it to work.

- For the ESXi management clusters housing the Connection server virtual machines, DRS anti-affinity rules should be enabled to prevent any of the Connection servers from running on the same ESXi host; this prevents multiple virtual machine failures if these Connection server virtual machines exist on the same physical ESXi host.
- vSphere DRS can be configured in 5 different modes from conservative to aggressive. As a best practice for management clusters, I always set up vSphere DRS in the middle of these options. Setting it up too aggressive will increase the number of vMotions between hosts (which is unnecessary). Setting it up too conservative will do nothing unless really necessary. Noisy neighbors will not be avoided in that case. If you don't have any specific requirements that will force you into adjusting the vSphere DRS mode, just keep it set to the default. Without vSphere DRS, you won't be able to put a host in *Maintenance Mode* without shutting down virtual machines, which is another consideration to make use of it. Please note that you should absolutely monitor how VMs behave and change the DRS settings, if needed.
- vSphere DRS is supported with Instant Clones since vSphere 6.7. All other clone types already supported it before. The main question would be if you would really need vSphere DRS on a cluster only containing desktops. In my opinion, the only benefit will be that you are able to put a host in maintenance mode without shutting down virtual desktops. Would you really want vSphere DRS to

move around virtual desktops from one host to another when users are working? Please note that a vMotion has a certain penalty on the user experience as it creates a small lag during the final execution of the vMotion. That lag will become bigger if a virtual desktop is using vGPU. Users will notice the lag immediately and might start complaining. When a new session is brokered, the Connection server will balance sessions across different hosts, depending on the resources' availability, which in general avoids resources congestion, anyway. My advice here would be to enable vSphere DRS on a cluster containing desktops but set it up very conservative.

# TRANSPARENT PAGE SHARING

Transparent page sharing (TPS) is a technology which eliminates redundant copies of memory pages on a single host. This helps to free memory that a virtual desktop would otherwise be using.

The following section is taken from the VMware KB site to explain a little bit more about TPS. The complete article can be found here: https://kb.vmware.com/s/article/1021095

*In ESXi, a 4KB page backing any guest page with content identical to another 4KB guest page can be shared regardless of when, where, and how those contents are generated. ESXi periodically scans the content of guest physical memory for sharing opportunities. For each candidate page, a hash value is computed based on its content. The hash value is then used as a key to look up a global hash table, in which each entry records a hash value and the physical page number of a shared page. If the hash value matches an existing entry, a full bit-by-bit comparison of the page contents between the candidate page and the shared page is performed to exclude a false match. After a successful content match, the guest-physical to host-physical mapping of the candidate page is changed to the shared host-physical page, and the redundant host memory copy is reclaimed.*

*In hardware-assisted memory virtualization systems, ESXi will preferentially back guest physical pages with large host physical pages*

*(2MB contiguous memory region instead of 4KB for regular pages) for better performance. If there is not a sufficient 2MB contiguous memory region in the host (for example, due to memory over-commitment or fragmentation), ESXi will still back guest memory using small pages (4KB). ESX will not share large physical pages because:*

- *The probability of finding two large pages that are identical is very low.*
- *The overhead of performing a bit-by-bit comparison for a 2MB page is much higher than for a 4KB page.*

*However, ESXi still generates hashes for the 4KB pages within each large page during page scanning.*

*In the cases where host memory is overcommitted, ESXi may have to swap out pages. Since ESXi will not swap out large pages, during host swapping, a large page will be broken into small pages. ESXi tries to share those small pages using the pre-generated hashes before they are swapped out. The motivation of doing this is that the overhead of breaking a shared page is much smaller than the overhead of swapping in a page if the page is accessed again in the future.*

If you are using non-persistent clones (especially Instant Clones), TPS could have a positive impact on memory resources, since Instant Clones are similar to each other and the parent machine (which might have a higher density as a result). In 2017, some considered TPS to pose a security risk. The following text (which also is also taken from the VMware KB site explains something about TPS, Instant Clones, and the possible risk involved).

*The InstantClone feature operates identically when Transparent Page Sharing is enabled or disabled. InstantClone will always generate new VMs sharing physical memory pages with the source VM.*
*At the time of creation of a new cloned VM, InstantClone relies on the ability of the generated VM to share pages of the source VM. This One-time operation enables rapid creation of Instant Clones, which inherit the exact state of the source VM. Any changes with the source VM pages aren't visible to the new VM or vice-versa, after the InstantClone operation.*

*Published academic papers have demonstrated that by forcing a flush and reload of cache memory, it is possible to measure memory timings to try and determine an AES encryption key in use on another virtual machine running on the same physical processor of the host server if Transparent Page Sharing is enabled between the two virtual machines. This technique works only in a highly controlled system configured in a non-standard way that VMware believes would not be recreated in a production environment.*

*Currently, VMware believes that the risk of information disclosure described in the recent academic papers leveraging TPS between Virtual Machines is very small in real-world conditions. The conditions under which the researchers were able to extract AES encryption keys are very specific and are unlikely to be present in a real-world deployment.*

## Considerations

The only consideration I could come up with to decide whether to use TPS or not, is security related. Some customers accept the security risk (as it can be considered as small and unlikely to happen). Others may have strict security requirements and can't be exposed to even the slightest risk (like banks). If no specific requirement exists that forces you to disable TPS, I would always enable it as it might have a positive impact on your density.

# ENHANCED VMOTION CAPABILITIES

Enhanced vMotion Capabilities (EVC) is a vSphere feature that enables you to vMotion virtual machines between hosts with different CPU architectures (such as Intel's *Broadwell* and *Skylake* architectures). It masks certain unsupported features and presents a homogeneous processor feature set to any host in a cluster. Prior to vSphere 6.7, EVC had to be enabled at cluster-level, so that all hosts running in a cluster were compatible with each other. Since vSphere 6.7, EVC can be configured at VM level, which is very useful when migrating VMs to other datacenters.

## Considerations

There are a couple of considerations regarding the use of EVC.

- Always enable EVC on the latest level available. The features of that level will be exposed to a VM running on the cluster. If you need to expand your cluster and only hosts are available with a newer architecture, the newer hosts will be able to run in the cluster, but with the feature set of the older hosts.
- If you really need to expand a cluster, try to avoid doing so with different hosts. Keeping your cluster as consistent as possible will make performance predictable and will make it easier to manage (less host profile configs, different hosts might use different hardware and use different drivers).

# HYPER-CONVERGED

# AND TRADITIONAL

# INFRASTRUCTURES

To me, this is always a fun topic to discuss with customers. The most important question that needs to be answered: *What kind of iron are you going to run underneath the Horizon infrastructure?* In the end, it's all about resources: CPUs, RAM, storage, networking and possibly GPUs in one big package called a host. These packages come in different shapes and sizes and every shape and size brings different challenges to the table. For instance, if you choose to go with blades, you could possibly have some extensibility challenges if you also would like to go for vSAN (since the combination is possible, but with limited options). If you'd like to go for 2U hosts, but you have a rack space constraint, you would probably end up with a lower density of desktops per rack. What about building a custom host versus going for a preconfigured one or even a full stack like VMware Cloud Foundation? Building and designing a custom host yourself may sound fun and exciting, but when you end up with compatibility issues, you will wish that you went for a preconfigured and prebuild host like a VxRail appliance. Before we end up in a deeper discussion, let's first start with the different options.

# CUSTOM BUILD OR PREBUILD?

The first question that needs to be answered here is: *Are we going to build hosts ourselves?* It is a difficult question to answer. Not that the question is complex, but every type of answer has an impact on the budget. If you are going to design and build hosts yourselves, chances are they will be cheaper than prebuild packages such as VxRail or HP Synergy. But what to do if the hosts exhibit compatibility issues? Most of the time, everything works great. We all know Murphy's Law and sooner or later we all get to experience it, including myself. I was designing an RDSH environment for a big customer in the Netherlands and we were customizing and building the hardware ourselves. The challenge here was that we were assured by the hardware distributor that everything was compatible. First of all, it took a couple of months before all hardware was delivered. After the building had started, we found out that there was a compatibility issue between the onboard NICs and the top of rack switches. Both the NIC vendor as well as the switch vendor were pointing to each other as the root cause of the issues (which did not help to solve it). It the end, we had to order additional 10 GbE NICs for the entire infrastructure which cost an additional 26,000 euros (about 30,000 dollars). The worst part for the customer was that the project was delayed for three months, which cost even more and those are conversations you most definitely would like to avoid. If you are going for the custom build option, be sure to cross check everything to the different Hardware Compatibility Lists (HCLs) from the vendors you have to work with.

The second option that you have here is to buy preconfigured systems that are completely designed for your specific use case (such as VDI). The systems are configurable to include the CPUs, RAM, disks and, GPUs, based on your sizing needs. And best of all, some vendors bring out a list of models every month (called vSAN-ready nodes) which are completely supported/compatible by the VMware HCL. This is obviously essential as no one would like to run hardware that is not supported. On average, the preconfigured systems can be compared to customized systems from the same vendors. Not all vendors have preconfigured systems, so you are somewhat more limited in your choice of vendor.

The last option is to buy a complete stack like Dell EMC's VxRail or HPE's Synergy platforms. These are completely preconfigured and prebuild including hosts, switches (management and top-of-rack) and supported versions of VMware vSphere and Horizon. A full stack like this is called VMware Cloud Foundation (VCF). VCF includes all components that are required to run a Hyper-Converged Infrastructure that is completely software-defined based on the VMware SDDC stack. This includes vSphere, vSAN, NSX, vROps and vRLI for operations and maintenance. From a supportability perspective, VCF is great, but it has some challenges, as well. If a new VCF version is released, it includes specific versions of the individual components which have been tested thoroughly to guarantee supportability. This means that on an average, the versions of the individual components (like vSAN and NSX) might be a little behind. When VCF 2.3 came out, Horizon 7.2 was included while 7.4 was already released. You have to accept that fact and possibly add that as a risk to your design.

The likelihood of you being a technical person is high. I am one, too. It's always fun to look at different hardware models and completely customize them. When I built my current home lab, it took me over 2 months before I ordered the hardware and another month to completely install it. I love to do it all, but it takes a lot of time. This is time you might not have in a project because of deadlines or tight budgets to build the hardware. At first, it may seem cheaper to build those hosts yourself, but from experience I can tell you that quite often it's not. Ordering, waiting for all components to arrive, building, testing, sending back DOA SFPs, waiting for new ones, rebuilding hosts, solving performance issues, etcetera, etcetera. This is not an exception, especially when building large environments with 20+ hosts.

I believe you should completely take this into account when choosing your infrastructure.

## Considerations

- Try to find out if preconfigured hosts exist which fit your requirements (or most of your requirements). It's easier to select an existing compatible model and in case it's almost what you are looking for, just add more resources (such as bigger SSDs or more RAM). If they exist, this would always be my pick as they are quite often less expensive.
- Be sure your hardware is validated. Take things like power and GPUs configurations into account (besides the obvious components like CPU type and RAM size).
- In some cases, I have seen huge differences in prices between vendors with the same host configurations. If you don't have a vendor constraint, it might be good to compare and request multiple offers from different vendors.

# FORM FACTORS

The choice to go for a custom build infrastructure, preconfigured infrastructure or complete stack, is quite often influenced by a form factor. Rack space constraints will limit you in your choices, as well as requirements such as graphical acceleration. If you choose a form factor that suits your needs, as always, you need to take all of the information in the conceptual design into account.

Do you have specific requirements that forces you into a specific form factor? Any possible constraints that do the same?

When looking at the possible form factors, there are typically 4 different ones that I come across at customers:

- 1U hosts
- 2U hosts
- Multi-node 2U systems (there isn't a real naming standard for these types of systems as HPE, Super Micro and Nutanix all call them differently)
- Blades

The ones I use most are 2U hosts, basically, because they are the most versatile of all. They are the biggest in terms of size, but the advantage of that is that they have a lot of expansion possibilities: dual CPU sockets, enough memory banks to easily scale up to 1 TB of RAM, enough external bays to create multiple vSAN disk groups and please don't forget about the ability to add multiple GPU cards to a single host. Almost every hardware vendor sells these models, which can be an advantage as you have a lot of models to compare with.

1U hosts are versatile as well, but obviously not as much as 2U hosts. They have fewer drive bays at the front and PCIe slots at the back, so they might be less suitable for (bigger) vSAN datastore deployments and hosts with a bigger GPU density. Like the 2U hosts, a lot of vendors sell these. Clearly, there are more than enough models to compare.

Multi-node 2U systems and blades should be handled pretty much the same in terms of compute power, if you ask me. Both are great if you are aiming for a lot of power in less space. But they offer fewer expansion options compared to the other hardware models. Smaller vSAN deployments will work on a multi-node 2U model, but as you have a limited number of drive bays (6 per host on average), be sure to take growth into account before purchasing.

Blades are even worse in terms of vSAN capabilities, as they aren't typically built for local storage. Most of them are limited to two disk bays, so running vSAN might not be your best option (but absolutely possible, if necessary). Both have limited support for GPUs, as well. For blades, there are specific GPU models that fit in a mezzanine slot, but they have limited density (more about GPU models can be found in the *Graphics and Remote Protocols section*). Most multi-node 2U systems have low profile PCIe slots, but only fit single slot expansion cards. The only GPU model currently able to fit is a Tesla P4. If your form factor of choice is a multi-node 2U system, be sure to contact the vendor so see if GPUs are supported.

# TRADITIONAL SHARED STORAGE

Until so far, I have mentioned vSAN quite a lot. This is mostly due to the fact that I am an advocate for Software-Defined Storage. We live in a software-defined world and more and more components are being moved into it. Software-Defined Networking is another great example. In a complete Software-Defined Datacenter (SDDC), you are able to manage everything through software. Things like firewall rules, VLANs, storage availability, cache tiering, etcetera can all be defined through policies. This makes the SDDC highly scalable and suitable to automate as much as possible (which has a positive impact on operational expenses and is less prone to error).

Is there still a future for traditional infrastructures? I do think so, but it all depends on your use cases and requirements. Take VMware Horizon DaaS for instance. VMware Horizon DaaS is a multi-tenant VDI solution that VMware offers, but uses a completely different architecture based on Linux appliances. For a long time, Full Clones were the only type of clone supported in VMware Horizon DaaS. When using non-persistent desktops in Horizon DaaS, storage operations are executed to build, customize and remove Full Clones. vSAN has been tested with these types of workloads but was less performant as some traditional shared storage solutions that are more suitable for this type of use cases (as you can offload these tasks to a storage box and some have penalty-free inline deduplication and compression).

Are there any other reasons to choose traditional storage over HCI? The number one reason I encounter with customers is a hardware constraint. If a customer still has a storage team that manages the storage part for everything in the datacenter, it will be a challenge to convince them to go for HCI. Other reasons might be:

- Hardware purchasing contracts with a specific vendor (which is still a hardware constraint).
- Existing storage hardware needs to be reused (which is also a hardware constraint).
- Different storage performance requirements between workloads. vSAN doesn't have the option to have some VMs on Flash, others on spinning disks.

# VMWARE VSAN FOR HORIZON

In terms of scalability, ease of deployment and simplicity, vSAN is a true value-add to VDI. I'm not going to explain here how to deploy vSAN, what kind of SSDs or controllers to use as a lot of vendors have specific vSAN-ready nodes for VDI and VMware delivers a lot of documentation and how-to guides. There are some things to take into account when going for vSAN as your primary storage solution for VDI though.

vSAN is an object-based storage platform. This means that virtual desktops (and VMs in general) can be seen as objects and each copy and witness of an object can be seen as a component. This means that the intelligence and disaster avoidance technology is handled from the software layer instead of hardware. vSAN doesn't require any form of RAID on controller level, just a bunch of disks (configured as JBOD or in pass-through mode on an appropriate storage controller).

If a VMDK of a virtual desktop lives on a specific disk on Host 1, vSAN will automatically make sure that a copy is present on Host 2 and a witness (which can be seen as the parity or quorum) on Host 3. Well, this is all dependent on the type of policy that is set on the virtual machine. Next, in being an object-based storage platform, vSAN is also policy-driven. Every virtual desktop or pool will automatically be assigned to a storage policy that contains the storage settings for that virtual desktop or pool of virtual desktops. Things like the number of failures to tolerate (FTT) and the failure tolerance method can be configured. This way of management simplifies your daily operations a lot and saves time which might be required to manage your user experience. Using the default vSAN policies for your virtual desktops and Horizon management components (such as Connection servers and UAGs) might be sufficient, but this all depends on your requirements.

Avoiding a single component failure in a vSphere cluster that has vSAN configured is by default enabled. Horizon handles the policies somewhat differently, though. When you use vSAN with Horizon, the broker component in the Connection server defines virtual desktop storage settings, such as capacity, performance, and availability, in the form of Horizon default storage policies. These policies are automatically deployed onto virtual desktops which are managed by vCenter. The policies are automatically and individually applied per disk (vSAN objects) and maintained throughout the life cycle of the virtual desktop. Storage is provisioned and automatically configured according to the assigned policies. You can modify these policies in vCenter. Horizon creates vSAN policies for Linked Clone desktop pools, Instant Clone desktop pools, Full Clone desktop pools, or an automated farm per Horizon cluster.
The most important part of designing vSAN for your Horizon-based VDI solution is to design your policy definitions based on your requirements.

## All-Flash or Hybrid?

The first thing to determine is the type of vSAN platform you are going to deploy. You have two options here: All-Flash or Hybrid. All-Flash is (like you might be guessing) based on a flash-only configuration. Both the cache tier as well as the capacity tier only consists of non-spinning disks. These can be SSDs, PCIe flash solutions or NVMe (as long as they are on the VMware HCL). In case of a Hybrid vSAN deployment, the cache tier obviously is based on a flash drive and the capacity tier consists of spinning disks. The choice for either one of them depends on performance, availability and security requirements and outcomes of the desktop assessment. The following table displays the differences between the two options.

| Feature | All-Flash | Hybrid |
|---|---|---|
| IOPS | Up to 100K per host | Up to 40K per host |
| Failure tolerance method | RAID 1, RAID 5 and RAID 6 | RAID 1 |
| Dedup and compression | Yes | No |
| Cache tier | Cache tier is used for write cache | 70% used for reads, 30% for writes |
| Cache size | It depends* | 10% of consumed capacity |
| Required network | 10 GbE | 1 GbE |

As a vSAN Hybrid deployment has different types of performing tiers, it's very important to configure the Flash Read Cache Reservation option in the storage policy for Horizon. The recommended setting is 10%.

* In 2017, VMware published some information about how the vSAN All-Flash cache should be calculated. They published the following table to show what the recommended cache size is for the different read/write profiles and disk group sizes.

| Read/Write profile | AF-8 80K IOPS cache size | AF-6 50K IOPS cache size | AF-4 25K IOPS cache size |
|---|---|---|---|
| 70/30 read/write *Random* | 800 GB | 400 GB | 200 GB |
| >30% write *Random* | 1.2 TB | 800 GB | 400 GB |
| 100% write *Sequential* | 1.6 TB | 1.2 TB | 600 GB |

Check the original post for more information:

https://blogs.vmware.com/virtualblocks/2017/01/18/designing-vsan-disk-groups-cache-ratio-revisited/

Desktop workloads running on a VDI platform behave totally differently from server workloads. Where a server workload on average has a 70/30 Read/Write profile, a desktop has it the other way around. A 30/70 Read/Write profile (or more writes) is quite common. Because of this, my recommendation would be to go for a fixed cache with the values stated in the middle row.

## Considerations

- On an average, Hybrid vSAN deployments should be delivering enough resources for an average task worker use case. But, it totally depends on the rest of your requirements. Running a lot of App Volumes AppStacks might change that (as it will require more IOPS and throughput).
- With the decreasing price of flash storage, I think it will become less and less attractive to go for Hybrid vSAN deployments.
- Although not available yet, you can imagine that another reason to go for All-Flash, is the possibility to use vMotion for vGPU-enabled virtual desktops. The bigger the framebuffer is, the more resources it might require from your infrastructure, so my suggestion, in this case, would be to go for All-Flash, as well.

# Disk Groups

As you read in the previous sections, a disk group consists of a single flash drive for caching and a minimum of one flash or hard drive for capacity purposes. vSAN also has the ability to use multiple disk groups in a single cluster. Multiple disk groups will not only expand your capacity but will also increase the performance of your datastore. Next to that, it will also reduce the failure domain. If in a disk group, a flash device for caching fails, the whole disk group will be marked as degraded or absent which could make your host useless if you just have one disk group. From a performance perspective, it might be a bit overkill, but this obviously depends on your requirements.

## vSAN Configuration Maximums

Always take the configuration maximums for vSAN into account if you start designing and sizing your vSAN datastores. Please find the vSAN configuration maximums for vSAN 6.7 in the following table.

| Item | Description | Maximum |
|------|-------------|---------|
| vSAN Cluster | Number of datastores per cluster | 1 |
| vSAN Cluster | Number of vSAN hosts in a cluster | 64 |
| vSAN ESXi host | Cache tier maximum devices per host | 5 |
| vSAN ESXi host | Capacity tier maximum devices | 35 |
| vSAN ESXi host | Capacity tier maximum devices per disk group | 7 |
| vSAN ESXi host | Components per vSAN host | 9,000 |
| vSAN ESXi host | Spinning disks in all disk groups per host | 35 |
| vSAN ESXi host | SSD disks per disk group | 1 |
| vSAN ESXi host | vSAN disk groups per host | 5 |
| vSAN iSCSI Target | iSCSI IO queue depth per Node | 4,096 |
| vSAN iSCSI Target | Max iSCSI LUN size | 62 TB |
| vSAN iSCSI Target | Number of initiators who register PR key for an iSCSI LUN | 64 |

| Item | Description | Maximum |
|------|-------------|---------|
| vSAN iSCSI Target | Number of iSCSI LUNs per Cluster | 1,024 |
| vSAN iSCSI Target | Number of iSCSI LUNs per Target | 256 |
| vSAN iSCSI Target | Number of iSCSI sessions per Node | 128 |
| vSAN iSCSI Target | Number of iSCSI Targets per Cluster | 128 |
| vSAN iSCSI Target | Number of outstanding IOs per iSCSI LUN | 256 |
| vSAN iSCSI Target | Number of outstanding writes per iSCSI LUN | 128 |
| vSAN virtual machines | Disk stripes per object | 12 |
| vSAN virtual machines | Percentage of flash read cache reservation | 100 |
| vSAN virtual machines | Percentage of object space reservation | 100 |
| vSAN virtual machines | Virtual machine virtual disk size | 62 TB |
| vSAN virtual machines | Virtual machines per host | 200 |
| vSAN virtual machines | vSAN networks/physical network fabrics | 2 |

The above configuration maximums were taken from the online configuration maximums portal. It is updated on a regular basis and can be found here: https://configmax.vmware.com/

## Storage Policy Adjustments

As mentioned earlier, Horizon deploys a default storage policy. But, this policy possibly requires adjustments based on the type of pools that you deploy. Every type of clone is different and consists of different storage components. The following text is taken from Cormac Hogan's site and explains the different policy settings that should be taken into account when designing vSAN for Horizon deployments.

The full article can be found here:

https://cormachogan.com/2013/09/10/vsan-part-7-capabilities-and-vm-storage-policies/

## Number of Failures to Tolerate (FTT)

This capability sets a requirement on the storage object to tolerate at least 'Number of Failures To Tolerate'. This is the number of concurrent host, network or disk failures that may occur in the cluster and still ensuring the availability of the object. If this property is populated, it specifies that configurations must contain at least Number of Failures To Tolerate + 1 replicas and may also contain an additional number of witnesses to ensure that the object's data are available (maintain quorum) even in the presence of up to Number of Failures To Tolerate concurrent host failures. Witness disks provide a quorum when failures occur in the cluster or a decision has to be made when a split-brain situation arises.

## Number of Disk Stripes per Object (Stripes)

This defines the number of physical disks across which each replica of a storage object is striped. To understand the impact of stripe width, let us examine in first in the context of write operations and then in the context of read operations.
Since all writes go to SSD (write buffer), the value of an increased stripe width may or may not improve performance. This is because there is no guarantee that the new stripe will use a different SSD; the new stripe may be placed on an HDD in the same disk group and thus the new stripe will use the same SSD. The only occasion where an increased stripe width could add value is when there are many, many writes to destage from SSD to HDD. In this case, having a stripe could improve destage performance.

From a read perspective, an increased stripe width will help when you are experiencing many read cache misses. If one takes the example of a virtual machine consuming 2,000 read operations per second and experiencing a hit rate of 90%, then there are 200 read operations that need to be serviced from HDD. In this case, a single HDD which can provide 150 IOPS is not able to service all of those read operations, so an increase in stripe width would help on this occasion to meet the virtual machine I/O requirements.

## Object Space Reservation

All objects deployed on vSAN are thinly provisioned. This capability defines the percentage of the logical size of the storage object that may be reserved during initialization. The *Object Space Reservation* is the amount of space to reserve specified as a percentage of the total object address space. This is a property used for specifying a thick provisioned storage object. If *Object Space Reservation* is set to 100%, all of the storage capacity requirements of the VM are offered up front (thick). This will be Lazy Zeroed Thick (LZT) format and not Eager Zeroed Thick (EZT).

## Flash Read Cache Reservation

This is the amount of flash capacity reserved on the SSD as read cache for the storage object. It is specified as a percentage of the logical size of the storage object (i.e. VMDK). This is specified as a percentage value (%) with up to 4 decimal places. This fine granular unit size is needed so that administrators can express sub 1% units. Take the example of a 1TB disk. If we limited the read cache reservation to 1% increments, this would mean cache reservations in increments of 10 GB, which in most cases is far too much for a single virtual machine.

## Horizon Common Practices

Like mentioned, Horizon might require different values, depending on the type of clone/virtual desktop.

The following table displays the recommended settings per type of clone.

| Clone type | FTT | Stripes | Space reservation | Flash Read Cache reservation |
|---|---|---|---|---|
| Linked Clone Parent | 1 | 1 | 0% | 0% |
| Linked Clone VM | 1 | 1 | 0% | 0% |
| Instant Clone Parent | 1 | 1 | 0% | 0% |
| Instant Clone VM | 1 | 1 | 0% | 0% |
| Full Clone | 1 | 1 | 100% | 0% |
| Replica | 2 | 1 | 0 | 10% in case of Hybrid |
| Persistent Disk | 1 | 1 | 100% | 0% |
| Base image | 2 | 1 | 0% | 0% |
| Management VMs | 2 | 1 | 0% | 0% |

The value that might stand out, is the FTT for replicas, base images and management VMs (such as the Connection server). The main reason for these deviations is that you want to ensure that these objects stay protected at all costs. If one of these objects is completely unavailable, chances are that an entire VDI or desktop pool could be unavailable. So, make sure to adjust the FTT for those objects.

*Please note that when using vSAN, a 20% - 30% spare capacity on your datastore is recommended. In case of a host (or multiple hosts) failing, you want to make sure enough capacity exists to rebuild the objects.*

# FABRIC CHOICES

I think the choice for a fabric depends on the type of architecture you will be using. If you are going to start in a greenfield situation, chances are the biggest that an HCI will be your platform of choice. In that case, ethernet with at least 10 GbE is required if you are running an All-Flash vSAN. To reduce the complexity, I would just go for plain ethernet. There are options to run different kinds of fabrics such as InfiniBand, but they will only increase the complexity of your infrastructure and probably costs. You also need to make sure the fabric of choice is supported on all hardware platforms (InfiniBand has limited support since not all vendors offer it as a fabric).

If you are going for traditional shared storage, you will have three different choices of the type of connectivity to the datastores: NFS, iSCSI, and Fiber Channel. Quite often, the type of protocol will be a constraint given by the storage vendor. In case of an existing shared storage, the protocol choice will be limited due to the fact that you would probably be connecting your hosts through an existing network to the shared storage.

# HOST CONSIDERATIONS

I gave you a brief overview of the different options that exist. Of course, there might be other options out there that could be more suitable to your needs, but at the end, it will be all driven by requirements and constraints.

# Free Choice

*What to do when nothing limits you in your choice of infrastructure?*

Let's start with the easiest situation there is: there aren't any requirements and constraints that force you into a certain type of infrastructure. If it would be up to me, I would certainly go for HCI. Software-Defined Storage is able to handle most of the task user, knowledge worker and power user use cases. If the customer already has Horizon Advanced or above, vSAN is included in the bundle, so why not use it? The second choice would be to go for a complete stack or just vSAN-ready nodes (since I wouldn't recommend to you to build your own hosts). Both have advantages. A full stack would probably cost more but saves you time in deploying and in second-day operations like updates/upgrades. It will also limit you in your choices of software versions but has a bigger supportability including networking components.

In terms of the form factor, 2u hosts offer the best expansion options for the smaller rack footprint when compared to larger host form factors. As explained, 2U hosts have the best expansion options for multiple vSAN disk groups or GPUs. Most big OEMs sell complete vSAN-ready nodes including GPUs and the proper CPUs. Some of them also sell them as VCF-compatible if you would like to go for a full stack.

## Budget Constraint

*What to do when on a tight budget?*

In case of a budget constraint, it might make sense to still go for vSAN-ready nodes instead of a full stack, such as VMware Cloud Foundation. By leveraging Horizon Advanced or greater, you will have everything you need to set up VDI based on an HCI, but without the additional costs of items you might want to skip, like NSX.

In terms of choosing the appropriate form factor, blades or multi-node 2U hosts will probably be a bad choice since (in many cases) these are quite often more expensive compared to 1U or 2U hosts with the same specs. Depending on your scalability or expandability requirements, you could either go for 1U or 2U hosts.

## Rack Space Constraint

*What to do when your datacenter has limited room for hosts?*

This is a tough one to answer. In my opinion, you have two possible options here. One would be to go for blades or multi-node 2U hosts since you could stack a lot of hosts in a limited rack space. Another option is to go for 1U or 2U hosts but increase the desktop density on a single host. The last option isn't without risks though.

Option 1: Blades or multi-node 2U hosts

When going for this option, you will be able to rack and stack hosts with similar CPU and RAM specs as 1U/2U hosts. If your design has a preference for multi-node 2U hosts, you will also have the ability to create a vSAN disk group containing a single flash disk and around 5-7 additional capacity disks (which might be fine for the number of desktops you would like to run on a single host). When choosing blades, this would be more challenging since they could only handle 2 disks. It's still possible to run vSAN, but just a single disk for capacity purposes. In both cases, if a disk fails, the host will be unavailable for vSAN (and thus aren't able to avoid component failure).

Another challenge with blades and multi-node 2U hosts is with GPUs. Running vGPUs on a large scale will be challenging, as well. Be sure to take these risks into account when going for option 1 (more about GPUs can be found in the *Graphics and Remoting Protocols* section). Blade enclosures have a high power-consumption. Be sure to check your datacenter's power capacity to avoid a low desktop density (as some datacenters only deliver enough power for one or two blade enclosures).

Option 2: Increase the desktop density on a single host

This might be the less interesting and riskier option, but I do see customers that go for it. The advantages in terms of scalability and expandability are still there, and so, you can still use graphical acceleration on bigger scale compared to blades or multi-node 2U hosts, but it does come with a cost. Increasing the number of desktops will mean that in case of a host failure, a bigger group of end-users will be unable to work (or will be required to set up a new connection). With more hosts that contain fewer desktops, you will have a smaller risk which we call a *failure domain*. Another challenge with bigger hosts, is that you need to align all individual resources, so they match and are able to handle the bigger scale without a single bottleneck. Since RAM and GPU profiles can't be overprovisioned, the ones to especially look out for are storage and CPUs. In terms of disks, be sure to calculate the proper (vSAN) datastore size. In terms of CPUs, be sure to size them conservatively (so you are able to handle peaks). In all cases, monitoring your resources with solutions like vRealize Operations for View, Liquidware Stratusphere UX or Goliath Performance Monitor is essential to avoid performance issues.

## Scalability

*What to do when you need to be able to quickly and easily scale* the number of desktops up (or down)?

In theory, all types of hosts are capable of being scalable. But, the size of the building blocks will be different. If you would like to scale one host at a time, 1U or 2U hosts most likely will be your way to go. This is mainly due to the fact that in the case of Multi-node 2U hosts or blades, an enclosure is also needed. If your last enclosure is fully occupied, a new enclosure needs to be added first before you are able to scale up with another host. This might bring additional costs, time and complexity to a project. Please note that some multi-node 2U OEMs offer additional enclosures for free.

Make sure to find out the scale size if a customer has a scalability requirement. If they would like to scale 50 desktops at the time, the way of scaling out will be different compared to 500 desktops (as you might scale an almost fully occupied blade enclosure at a time). So, be sure to know what to scale for.

## Graphical Acceleration

*What to do when you need to use GPUs in a host?*

If your use cases require GPUs, you need to determine the number of profiles you would like to offer on a single host. If the number is quite low (and possibly just for a couple of users), a single GPU which might even fit in a blade server, multi-node 2U host or 1U host, you could go for those type of hosts. You will be limited to specific GPUs though, without any chance of scaling out on a single host. If you are looking to achieve a high density of graphical accelerated desktops on a single host, 2U hosts (or bigger) which can handle at least two NVIDIA Tesla M10 cards, is the way to go (or possibly your only choice).

Also, mixing and matching different types of GPUs on a single host isn't supported (yet). So, if you have different use cases with different graphical needs, I would suggest building separate clusters with different hosts to fill in those use cases.

# OPERATING SYSTEMS

Like many who were born in the late 70's or early 80's, my first computer was a Commodore 64. It contained an *Operating System* called BASIC V2. It was quite simple. You typed in some commands and an application or game started. I had a floppy drive with it on which I could save data such as homework for school. Back then, things were really simple if you knew how to operate a Commodore 64. The Commodore 64 has been listed in the Guinness World Records as the highest-selling single computer model of all time, with independent estimates placing the number sold between 10 and 17 million units. In the early 90's, my good old Commodore 64 got replaced by my first x86 computer containing Microsoft Windows 3.1. Windows 3.1 to me was the first operating system which could use a mouse as a UI control device. It also had the ability to view content in different containers called *Windows* (hence the name). Although the computer itself and Windows 3.1 were nice and were able to run all kinds of awesome games like Commander Keen, SimCity and Lemmings, I wasn't going to use it as long as I used the Commodore 64.

Late 1995, my father bought my family the first Compaq computer containing Windows 95. In terms of user experience, Windows 95 was the first to raise the bar to a whole new level. Many of the UI features that were introduced in Windows 95, such as the Start Menu, the Windows Explorer and Control Panel, are still part of the Windows operating systems of modern times (except for a short while, when Microsoft decided to remove the start menu out of Windows 8 and brought it back in 8.1 because of bad publicity). Of course, a lot of other things have changed, especially under the hood.

The first couple of versions of Windows, were primarily built for single user usage. Everything that happened in the operating system, happened in kernel mode and wasn't user agnostic. That changed rapidly when Citrix decided to bring out the first version of WinFrame, the very first successful attempt of a technology we nowadays know as either Remote Desktop Services (by Microsoft) or XenApp/Virtual Apps (by Citrix). WinFrame was based on the Windows 3.51 architecture from Microsoft. Citrix developed a multi-user operating system engine called MultiWin based on the licensed Windows 3.51 code. I think the great success of the solution made Microsoft think again before they licensed any of their future operating systems to others. From Microsoft's side, the answer to WinFrame came in 1998 when they released Windows NT4 Terminal Server Edition. A fun fact here is that NT4 Terminal Server Edition was relying on the MultiWin engine from Citrix to build this competing solution. Some of the DLLs in NT4 Terminal Server Edition carried a Citrix copyright instead of a Microsoft one. Microsoft's first attempt of a multi-user operating system was a success, as well. The RDP protocol wasn't as good as Citrix' ICA protocol in terms of bandwidth and usability, but in some use case it was good enough to be used on an enterprise scale.

Since Windows XP, the Terminal Services engine (which is the Remote Desktop Services engine nowadays) is still part of every operating system that Microsoft developed for x86 and x64 based devices.

The multi-user mode created opportunities for a lot of use cases. One of them led to a multi-user mode on a single desktop machine that enables you to sign out and sign in as a different user and have your own context in the operating system with features like a different desktop background, my documents folder and browser favorites. These settings are stored in a so-called *Profile*. More about profiles can be found in the *Persistency and Non-persistency* section.

In this section I would like to guide you through the operating system possibilities you have and the challenges you could be facing for a VDI deployment.

# SERVER VS DESKTOP OPERATING SYSTEM

The first Microsoft operating systems that enabled multi-user mode were Microsoft's Server operating systems. Starting with Windows NT4 Terminal Services Edition, the multi-user mode was a core part of the operating system and gained in features with every version that was released. Since Windows 2000, the client operating system and the server operating system shared the same UI, which made it somewhat easier for an end-user to navigate through the operating system when it was published as a remote desktop. The client versions of the operating systems underwent the same development, with Windows 7 being the first operating system that (personally) felt stable enough to actually run inside a virtual desktop. But as the server operating systems are stable enough for heavy use, contain the multi-user mode and are built with the same UI, you might ask yourself why you shouldn't use a server operating system inside VDI. The answer is twofold. The footprint of a server operating system is somewhat bigger, which you will notice when you are deploying at scale. The second answer to the question is licensing, a topic on which Brian Madden has written some content. On the cover of his 2014 version of the *Desktops as s Service* book, he states that *Microsoft Licensing still sucks* and I do think, although a few years have passed, he is still right about that.

For quite some time now, I have been wondering if there would be any other requirement/constraint for using Windows Server 2016 as a VDI operating system, other than a licensing constraint. Service providers who offer a Desktop as a Service (DaaS) to their customers, have been constrained in using server operating systems as Microsoft didn't offer any client operating system licenses for multi-tenant infrastructures. By the time you read this section, I hope Microsoft will have updated their Service Providers Use Rights (SPUR) to offer client operating systems to multi-tenant infrastructures as well. If not, you are still screwed...

So, if you don't have any licensing constraints, you don't have any client-side applications that require Windows Server 2016 as a client operating system or you aren't a service provider, I won't bother running a Windows Server operating system inside a virtual desktop.

# CLIENT OPERATING SYSTEMS

Microsoft has ruled the desktop operating system world for quite some time now. I do see an increase in Linux operating systems, but as mainstream applications are not compatible with Linux (since they are made for Windows), I'm not seeing this becoming very popular within the next couple of years. And as Apple is only releasing macOS on proprietary hardware, you will be stuck with the products of our friends in Redmond for as long as your applications will require it. Is this a bad thing? The obvious answer is of course: *it depends*. For a long, long time, Window 7 has been a great desktop operating system to run inside a virtual desktop. But as you all know, all good things end.

Research from both myself as well as other publicly available surveys (like the State of EUC surveys) have told us that there is still a big percentage of customers running Windows 7 as an operating system inside the virtual desktops. Windows 7 has been announced as end-of-support, starting from the 14th of January 2020. As there is a lot of great content and documentation around the deployment of Windows 7, I won't be focusing on this operating system in the book.

After Windows 7 came Windows 8 and 8.1. Although support for 8.1 is active until the 10th of January 2023, I think running Windows 8.1 inside VDI is a bad plan. Windows 8.1 came out because Windows 8 was probably Microsoft's biggest mistake after Windows Millennium Edition (ME). Windows 8 contained a new version of the start menu that was hidden in the top corner. Gestures to open up the menu didn't really have a great user experience and as people in general hate changes, Windows 8.1 was released within a year that included the good-old start menu again.

I personally think that the majority of customers still running on Windows 7 do so because Windows 8.X has been so disappointing from the start. Sure, there are some early adopters that ran Windows 8.1, but they upgraded to Windows 10 because of the same reason.

# WINDOWS 10

On the 1st of October 2014, Microsoft announced the very first technical preview version of their latest flagship product: Windows 10.

Windows 10 is Microsoft's first attempt of creating a universal platform for basically all types of x86/x64 devices, tablets, phones, wearable devices and even ARM devices like Raspberry Pis. With the new operating system, Microsoft also released a framework for developers to create *Universal Apps*. As the name might give the surprise away, the idea is to create an application that could run on basically every device that supports Windows 10. Microsoft has also created an App Store model, similar to Apple's App Store for iPhone and iPad, to distribute the Universal Applications to devices.

Microsoft also introduced some new native applications, as well as a new Start Menu interface that combined both the traditional look-and-feel from Windows 7 and tiles from Windows 8.X.

Since the very first Windows operating system that was released, every successor came with tons of changes. This included changes like new architectures (16 bit, 32 bit and 64 bit), new profile types, new folder locations, new device drivers requirements, etc. This means that with every new operating system, a migration had to be executed (which became more complex as the time went by). With the migration towards Windows 10, it's no different, but it looks like there is a light at the end of the tunnel.

The new philosophy behind Windows 10 was to bring out a new version of Windows 10 every 6 months that can be applied to the current installed version. Since I have been using Apple products (my first Mac was a 13-inch MacBook with OS X Tiger), upgrading OS X to a newer version was easy, took just a little bit of time and was finished without any big application compatibility issues.

While Microsoft has supported in-place upgrades for years, the length of time between Windows releases and the significant changes between versions have made in-place upgrades a risky proposition at best. Starting with Windows 10, however, Microsoft has put more effort into their in-place upgrade technology as seamless upgrades are required to support the frequent release cycle. Sounds like an awesome idea if your virtual desktops could be upgraded in a same way, right? Sorry to spoil the fun here, but while this sounds awesome, it is a bad idea. Windows 10 in-place upgrades are not supported by VMware.

Check the following KB article for more information:

https://kb.vmware.com/s/article/2148176

## Base Image Creation and Lifecycle Management

How should you act in case of so many updates? Let's first look at the base image creation. The base image is where it all starts when creating virtual desktops. The base image is the reference machine that all the virtual desktops are created from.

When building a new base image, I still see a lot of customers doing this by hand. Create a VM, install the operating system, add drivers, agents and possibly apps, run Windows Updates, and the base image is finished.

The question I always ask these customers: *How often do you create a new base image?* Unfortunately, in most cases the answer is somewhere between "once every year" and "when a new operating system is released." (luckily in most cases this doesn't mean the customers don't update the base image, though). When I think of these two facts (manual installs and the times it happens), I wonder why that is. The average customer I visit, is (for Northern European standards) an enterprise customer with 1,000+ end-users. Another question pops up. *Would a customer of that size deploy fat clients manually too?* Of course not. Then why would they deploy base images manually?

The base-image creation process can be easily automated without the use of expensive tools. Microsoft provides two free tools that can be deployed in any enterprise shop. Microsoft Deployment Toolkit (MDT) is a free tool that can automate the installation and configuration of Windows and desktop applications. MDT can also integrate with Microsoft Systems Center Configuration Manager (SCCM) to deploy existing application packages. Windows Deployment Services is another tool for deploying Windows, and it is a Windows Server feature for deploying images to unprovisioned machines over the network. Windows Deployment Services, Microsoft Deployment Toolkit, and Systems Center Configuration Manager (SCCM) are often used together to create and manage both virtual desktop and physical desktop images.

There are other options for deploying virtual desktop images. Free tools like Hashicorp Packer, Boxstarter, and the Chocolately package manager provide non-Microsoft options for building desktop images.

With a little use of PowerShell scripting, the image building process can be finished.

There are a couple of reasons to automate the deployment of the base image:

- Automated deployments are repeatable
- Automated deployments create consistent base images
- Automated deployments reduce the number of mistakes that could lead to errors
- Automated deployments reduce the time required to create a base image

Although somewhat more complicated, automation can even help you create automated test sequences to validate if everything still works after creation of the base image.

These reasons alone should be enough to dive into automated base image creation. There is another reason, though, and it might be the biggest of all. The thing here is that hypothetically, a base image could be created once and updated/patched until eternity. Once created, this image may never need to have a major change or rebuild because it keeps working.

Like I mentioned in the previous section, Microsoft is releasing a new version of Windows 10 every 6 months. On a fat client, you would probably push the upgrade through automation tools or choose to defer or skip specific releases. As this may sound like a solid process to apply on your VDI as well, it is in fact not. There are two issues with using the current image as a starting point for *Lifecycle Management*. The first is that you create a potential risk for breaking key applications or agents during the upgrade process. Base images are widely used, so any applications and agents would need to be validated to ensure that they were not broken during the upgrade process. The second is that you create a potential risk of a base image containing tons of garbage you don't need (such as update files and backups, older DLLs or even executables). To reduce the size of the base image and increase the quality, automating the base image creation process is essential. In fact, I would even consider creating a new base image with every set of updates you might be running. Instead of applying patches/updates/upgrades on an existing base image, my suggestion would be to create a fresh base image every time including the updated content (which could also be components like a Horizon Agent or NVIDIA GRID Drivers).

## Windows 10 Builds

As we all know, Microsoft's licensing structure is somewhat complex and, to quote Brian Madden again, *licensing itself still sucks*. With Windows 10, that's no different. Windows 10 (for VDI) is available in two main flavors; Windows 10 Enterprise Semi-Annual Channel (SAC) and Windows 10 Enterprise LTSC (Long Term Service Channel).

The Windows 10 Enterprise SAC is a feature-enhanced version of Windows 10 Home or Windows 10 Pro. These are the Windows 10 versions you might run at home. Like the non-Enterprise SAC versions, the Enterprise SAC includes access to the Windows App Store, Edge browser, Windows Modern Apps, and the twice-per-year update cadence. The main feature differences between Enterprise SAC and the other two is that the Enterprise SAC contains tools such as an embedded App-V client and an enhanced version of Windows Defender.

There are use cases where frequent Windows feature updates would be extremely disruptive or cause the introduction of potential issues into the environment. Windows 10 LTSC, or Long-Term Servicing Channel, was created for these situations. Windows 10 LTSC is a stripped-down version of Windows 10 Enterprise that received a feature update every two to three years. Each release of Windows 10 LTSC receives support for ten years, and during that time Microsoft provides security fixes. Unlike the SAC releases, the LTSC releases do not contain the Windows Store, Edge Browser, or Modern Apps. Some Modern Apps, like Calculator, are replaced with their legacy Windows 7 version.

Choosing between the Windows 10 Enterprise SAC and LTSC versions depends on your requirements and constraints. If no requirements or constraints force you into using LTSC, I would just go for Enterprise SAC. The reasons for this are:

- You will be able to run the latest and greatest version of Windows 10, but also have the freedom to use a previous version if your use cases require that.
- Every new version of Windows 10 has support for current hardware/chipsets. If your choice will be LTSC, it might be that features in your chipset will be supported in a next release that could be due in 2/3 years.
- New SAC releases may contain valuable features for your VDI deployments or use cases. For example, the 1709 release brought OneDrive Files On-Demand, which is very useful when OneDrive is required in non-persistent desktops because it does not require OneDrive files to be cached locally.
- Your users will have the same user experience as their home computer, which is beneficial in terms of adoption and usability.
- Office 365 click-to-run isn't available on LTSC.
- Some applications may not be supported on LTSC. For example, Microsoft Visual Studio is not supported on LTSC.

Your requirements might dictate additional reasons beyond the ones listed above.

Windows 10 LTSC is primarily created for devices that require extended support of an operating system. Examples include ATMs, Point-of-Sale devices, factory control equipment, or medical devices. Such solutions require stability and are quite often also run on hardware that is serviced with long-term support. You might have good reasons to use LTSC in your VDI as well. Possible requirements or constraints which would force you into using LTSC include:

- Applications that will require a certain long-term version of Windows 10.
- Your industry might require a long-term operating system from a supportability perspective.

LTSC could possibly create some risks though:

- The feature set used in LTSC is minimal compared to SAC as it lacks apps like the Edge browser.
- Security patches will be released for LTSC, but improvements to the Windows 10 kernel that enhance security will not be included in the current or previous LTSC releases.

## OPERATING SYSTEM OPTIMIZATION

Windows 10, like all versions of Windows, is optimized to run on physical hardware. This includes extra services, scheduled tasks, and how the operating system is configured. When Windows 10 is deployed in a virtual environment, it has to share access to the hardware with other virtual machines. The default, out-of-box Windows 10 experience has many unnecessary services running that impact user experience.

Part of the process of building a base image is operating system optimization. In theory, you could install Windows 10 and deploy virtual desktops but a little bit of optimization to make it "VDI Ready" is essential. If you don't optimize your Windows 10 base image, more physical host resources will be required. By optimizing, you will also increase the available density of your environment.

Another example is the removal of native apps. Native apps are installed on a per-user basis, and they can cause issues with Windows 10 deployments. The only method to update them is through the Windows App Store. Do you really want your end-users to be able to play games or install apps through the App Store? Operating system optimization can remove features and apps you don't require, and it will also set specific settings that will optimize your use of resources.

Optimizing an operating system is something that is an essential task, but it can be so extensive due to the number of configurable options that you could fill a complete book with on the topic. In this section, I'm not explaining every detail on optimization, but I will highlight some of the tools used and some of the major settings, apps, and features that you might want to optimize.

## VMware Operating System Optimization Tool

There are a couple of ways to optimize your operating system. The one most used by VDI admins is the VMware Operating System Optimization Tool (OSOT). The OSOT is a VMware Fling, or unsupported tool developed by VMware engineers as a side project and released by VMware. Sometimes, Flings are officially incorporated into a product. If you want to learn more about Flings, check out the site at https://labs.vmware.com/flings. OSOT has been one of the most popular Flings.

The OSOT Fling analyzes the system on which it is running and checks on a couple of hundred different settings that can be optimized. These include registry keys, services, apps, and other

Windows Settings. After analysis is completed, you have the option to disable specific settings before applying the recommended optimizations to the template. When optimizations are applied, it updates the system configuration, such as changing registry keys, disabling services, and removing apps.

The OSOT includes settings profiles that contain the list of settings and the recommended configuration. VMware has developed a default set of settings profiles, and they have included a settings editor so that other vendors like LoginVSI or even the community can create their own.

I think this is where the real power of the OSOT lies. You can create your own customized settings profile to fit your base image building process, your environment, and your use cases.

However, there is one big risk in using OSOT. A couple of years ago (when OSOT wasn't born yet), optimization was done manually or with scripts. Back then, VDI admins knew exactly what optimizations were being applied to the base image, and thus the outcome was mostly predictable. With OSOT, it is really simple to apply all of the optimization settings and end up with a bad user experience or increased administrative overhead because key settings or features were disabled. It is important to understand exactly what settings are being changed when running the OSOT and tweak it to meet your requirements. I had some issues in the past regarding scaling of monitors. The profile I used limited the maximum resolution of a single monitor and thus I wasn't able to run my desktop on Ultra-Wide monitors with near-4K resolutions. After a while, we found out it was caused by a specific setting manipulated by OSOT. So, OSOT is great, but use it with care and know what you are doing.

## PowerShell

PowerShell has become one of the most powerful scripting languages. I've seen customers that were able to script basically everything from the deployment of VMs to complete DTA (Development/Test/Acceptance) architectures. PowerShell has tons of extensions, called modules, from Microsoft, other vendors and the community. It's also easy to learn, even if you don't have prior experience with other scripting languages.

Microsoft, VMware, and other vendors do not make any "official" optimization scripts available. If you search for "Windows 10 VDI Optimization PowerShell" you will find examples from the community which you could use as a starting point for your own optimization script. Like the OSOT, it's important to understand what you are going to optimize instead of just running a script that might break required application features or negatively impact user experience.

## Optimization Details

It's important to understand what tools are available for optimizing a base image. But those tools are only effective if you understand how they work and what changes they make. Windows contains thousands of options that can be adjusted and making the wrong changes can negatively impact user experience, reduce desktop performance, or increase administrative overhead. It is important to understand what changes are beneficial for your use cases and environment, and this may require some testing during the image creation process.

Microsoft provides some guidance around optimizing Windows 10 for VDI environments. You can find these recommendations at:

https://docs.microsoft.com/en-us/windows-server/remote/remote-desktop-services/rds-vdi-recommendations

The next section will cover some more about optimization, but from a profile and User Environment Manager point of view.

# PERSISTENCY AND NON-

# PERSISTENCY

Like mentioned earlier, desktop persistence reflects the state of the desktop. Persistent desktops are desktops that retain their state when the user logs out or the desktop is shut down. Non-persistent desktops are desktops that revert to a known good state at logoff or shutdown. When these desktops are reverted, any changes that were made are lost.

Persistency can be a challenging discussion during the design phase, but it's one that can have a substantial positive impact on your VDI. In the eye of a customer, non-persistency means that they are unable to use a virtual desktop like they use their home computer or company issued physical machine. This includes tasks like installing software, changing their desktop wallpaper, filling their desktop with shortcuts, or customizing their Outlook signature.

The trick here is to ask the right questions, so you can find the source of their misconception.

- What requirements are driving the need for persistent desktops?
- Do users require applications that are licensed by some hardware attribute such as MAC address or UUID?
- Would users like to customize their desktop environment (such as shortcuts, wallpapers, etc.)?
- Do users need elevated permissions in order to properly run an application?
- Do they need to install software?

If users "believe" they can alter things like their desktop wallpaper or Outlook signature and have those settings load each time they log into their desktop, it should be enough to satisfy their needs. You shouldn't have to depend on a persistent Full Clone to satisfy their persistent user experience requirements.

However, not all applications support a non-persistent model. Some older applications as well as applications in some high-end engineering or science fields utilize some component of the machine for licensing. This could be the hostname, MAC address, or a hardware key.

If you are in the process of deciding what type of persistence model you're going to use, it is essential to define a proper use case including specific functional requirements. What should the user be doing on the proposed VDI? Not *how*, but just *what*. The *how* is something you are going to decide in the design.

Functional requirements that can be filled in from within the user world are in most cases solved by setting up a proper profile solution. Changing a wallpaper, creating shortcuts and favorites, drive mappings, connected printers, language settings for well-developed apps, and other settings can be covered by using a profile management solution such as VMware User Environment Manager (UEM). By letting VMware UEM manage these settings for users, you take one of the biggest reasons for persistent desktops out of the design.

Another tool that can be used to solve some of the persistence issues is VMware App Volumes. App Volumes is an application layering tool, and it can insert applications into a virtual desktop without having to install them in the image. When attached, these applications appear to be installed natively, and they run in the context of the user. However, they can be detached and replaced almost seamlessly at login and logoff.

App Volumes provides two types of application layers. The first are AppStacks. AppStacks are application volumes where the application has been installed and configured. These can be attached to a VM during boot or on a per-user basis when the user signs in. AppStacks are read-only VMDKs and use a one-to-many deployment model. Because of this, users are unable to make changes to the applications installed in the AppStacks.

The second type of application layer is a Writable Volume. A Writable Volume is a persistent VMDK file that is attached to a user's virtual desktop in a one-to-one deployment model during login. A Writable Volume acts like a hidden writable layer on top of a non-persistent machine. When something is written to the local disk of the non-persistent machine, a filter driver redirects it to the Writable Volume. If you sign out of the desktop, the Writable Volume is detached and ready for use on a different desktop. So, as soon as you connect to a new (fresh) desktop, your Writable Volume is attached again, and it seems like you connected to the same desktop again.

Windows requires administrative rights to allow users to install applications. When using administrative rights in combination with Writeable Volumes, it allows for the user to install applications, but limits the damage that they can do to the virtual desktop. With Instant Clones for example, if the user signs out, the desktop is decommissioned and a new one is created. Any changes are committed in the Writable Volumes, which doesn't contain operating system adjustments. This is an excellent way to achieve a persistent user experience and managing user-installed applications without the need of deploying persistent clones.

There are some limitations to these tools. Large and/or complex applications, such as those that require Windows Services, hook deeply into the Operating System, or run a database engine, are not a good fit for Writeable Volumes or application layering in general. A Writable Volume is attached during the user login process after authentication, and therefore a Writeable Volume is not a solution for applications that require this level of interaction with the operating system.

Another challenge or limitation is that App Volumes leverages a Microsoft filter driver. All changes that are committed to the Writable Volume are handled by the filter driver. If an application commits a high number of changes, the filter driver will be heavily utilized. This can have a negative impact on the performance.

Multi-datacenter VDI is another challenge. Writeable Volumes are VMware virtual disks, or VMDKs, sitting on VMware datastores. VMware does not provide any mechanism to replicate virtual disk files that are not attached to VMs to another location. Writeable Volume replication has to be handled at the storage layer, and this can add significant cost and complexity to an infrastructure design.

More information about App Volumes can be found in the *Applications* section.

From a UEM perspective, that limitation comes from how Microsoft is handling profiles in conjunction with filter drivers. The one thing to remember here is that a profile can only exist in one location at a time. If you run an active/active multi-datacenter VDI, that's going to be a challenge (but solvable). More about profiles in the next section.

The same goes for persistent desktops. If the customer has a requirement for a highly available VDI or a low RTO that forces you to add a secondary datacenter, you should ask yourself if you are able to comply with these requirements. Running cloned virtual desktops on a metro cluster isn't supported and making persistent Full Clone desktops highly available in a secondary datacenter is challenging. Be sure to have an open discussion with your customer on the possibilities and limitations of the requirements and the proposed technologies.

Not all use cases are suitable for non-persistent clones. Applications are the primary constraint that forces the adoption of persistent full clones. There are some applications, especially older Windows applications, that can't be virtualized or don't allow you to save settings to a user context. Other applications don't have a network licensing solution or have licensing that is tied to some attribute of the virtual machine such as the MAC Address or host name.

As mentioned in the assessment section, a desktop assessment can help discover applications that might not be suited to a non-persistent environment. Tools like Liquidware Stratusphere have the ability to do an application assessment that predicts the likelihood of the virtualization capabilities of an application. This is another reason to run a proper assessment prior to the design phase of VDI.

From an operational and administrative perspective, persistent desktops lack the ease of management that non-persistent desktops have. Patching, updating, deploying software, upgrading operating systems and other management tasks require a lot more effort with persistent desktops because these desktops must be managed like physical machines. Additional tools like System Center Configuration Manager (SCCM) or Workspace ONE are required to manage them.

If you look at applying a security patch to 1,000 Instant Clone desktops, a single admin could execute the update by applying it to a few machines and then redeploying the desktop pools. This could possibly be completed in a couple of hours. Now imagine having to apply that same patch to 1,000 persistent Full Clones. In addition to having to install the update, you also must coordinate the reboots of 1,000 machines and remediate any machines where the install did not complete successfully. This can result in significant user disruption. What happens if a new version of Windows 10 is released? See where this is going?

Using persistent Full Clones does not preclude the use of user environment management software like VMware UEM. These solutions can still be implemented to manage user data and user application settings for compatible applications. This can be part of the disaster recovery strategy for the environment.

The use of persistent full clones comes with some significant trade-offs. It's important to understand these trade-offs and how they can impact the management of the environment.

# CONSIDERATIONS

- Use persistent Full Clones only when your applications aren't suitable for non-persistent desktops.
- If you are going to use persistent Full Clones, be sure to validate if they can be designed with respect to your availability, RTO and RPO requirements.
- Make sure you choose a proper solution to manage Full Clones (like SCCM).

Examples of requirements or constraints in which you would decide to use persistent Full Clones instead of non-persistent clones in your design:

- Specific applications must be able to do things to your file system (which can't be handled through layering or application virtualization).
- Users must be able to use hardware connected devices to a virtual desktop that can't be connected through PCoIP or Blast Extreme (such as specific network cards or dedicated GPUs through vDGA).

# PROFILE STRATEGY

Achieving non-persistency without a proper profile strategy is nearly impossible. This is yet again another topic which can have a substantial positive impact on user experience. Starting with Windows NT 3.51, Microsoft invented in a feature called *profiles* that would let you alter user settings in their own context. When signing off and on as a different user, the context of the other user was loaded including shortcuts, wallpapers, printers, file shares, favorites, etc. Great stuff if you ask me! But, after Citrix built WinFrame and Microsoft decided to do the same trick with Windows NT 4.0 Terminal Services Edition, we had a challenge regarding the profiles. This is because a farm of Terminal Servers on average consists of more than one machine. If I'm working on Terminal Server 1 today and Terminal Server 2 tomorrow, I would like my profile to be available to both machines. Hence, the Roaming Profile was born. The profile that is synchronized locally from a network drive as soon as I sign on to Windows. When signing off, the profile is synchronized again to the network drive. So, in theory, the profile is available on all machines that have access to the network drive.

Non-persistent desktops require a similar solution if you would like to achieve a persistent user experience. Today I could be working on Desktop 1, but the chance is huge that I will be working on a Desktop 2 the next time I sign on. So, the first VDIs that were built years ago used a lot of roaming profiles to achieve non-persistency. It worked, but as it turned out, not very consistently and a bad, bad idea.

Roaming profiles have a few major downsides when it comes to user experience. If a roaming profile gets too big, starting from around 50MB, loading the profile might take too long. Depending on performance requirements you might have (presenting a desktop shouldn't take longer than 30 seconds), this can become a challenge. This problem can be solved by setting a quota on roaming profiles. But, if you sign off and the profile is unable to sync because the maximum quota is reached, you are quite sure to get a corrupted profile.

Users are impatient and on average don't wait if logging off from a desktop takes a lot of time (let's say more than 30 seconds). I've seen users just powering off thin clients or closing the lid of a notebook instead of waiting. This behavior can cause Windows to not fully sync the roaming profile or even cause profile corruption.

If profile corruption occurs, restoring the previous version of the profile from backup is quite often the only solution. If for some reason, there is no backup, it will mean that all user-defined settings are lost and need to be set again by the end-user.

When a new version of the Windows architecture is released (Windows XP/2003 to Windows 7/2008 to Windows 8.1/2012 to Windows 10/2016 or Windows 10 to a newer Windows 10), the structure of a roaming profile gets updated and a new profile is required. The old profile isn't exchangeable. This means that operating system migrations from a profile perspective require extra attention to keep a user happy.

Are there anything positive to mention about roaming profiles? To be honest (and from a personal perspective), not really. My opinion: *Friends don't let friends use roaming profiles.*

If you are serious about designing a non-persistent VDI, be sure to incorporate a proper profile management (or User Environment Management) solution. As this book is all about my ideal way of designing a Horizon Enterprise based VDI, I will explain some more about VMware UEM (which is included in the license).

A User Environment Management solution, in general, is excellent for doing two things. The first being that you are able to avoid profile corruption. The second being that a user context is quite powerful and that you are able to manipulate a lot of settings within this context.

Let's start with the first one, profile corruption. With a User Environment Management solution, you are able to create a zero-profile or hybrid profile strategy. When the user signs into a desktop, the default (or mandatory) profile will be loaded. After the user is presented with a desktop, all kinds of settings will be loaded such as personal settings (shortcuts, wallpaper), forced settings (such as security policies) and protocol settings (such as a maximum bandwidth). All this happens while the user is already able to work (which shortens the logon process to seconds instead of maybe minutes). As soon as the user starts an application, the application settings are injected into the application part of the profile. Because these settings aren't loaded during logon, the logon process is again shortened. Something else to consider is that the application settings that a user might change will be saved to the *Hybrid Profile* as soon as the user shuts down the app. The same happens if a user signs out: the changed settings are saved to the hybrid profile.

So, what is a Hybrid Profile? It's quite simple. It might not surprise you that it consists out of two parts (hence the name Hybrid). One part is still the local profile of the system on which the user signs in. The other part consists out of small compressed files that contain the minimum data required to let the user roam between different desktops. So, instead of copying all kinds of files, directories, and entire registry trees, it contains the specific data to achieve a consistent user experience between desktops and sessions. This has many advantages.

Every application and desktop setting has its own little container with its own data. This means that you are able to recover a backup of a specific moment in time for a user -- a little bit like how Apple time machine works. It's even possible for users to do this themselves instead of harassing IT with such things.
Hybrid Profiles are great for non-persistent desktops. Have you ever experienced a desktop that had challenges loading the default user profile because someone broke something? Well, imagine you are using Instant Clones with a Hybrid Profile. A new desktop is generated and a user signs in. The Hybrid Profile is loaded, and the user is happy. If he or she breaks the default user profile and signs out, it doesn't matter because the desktop is decommissioned anyway after the user signs out. As soon as the user signs in again, a brand-new desktop will be created that includes a new default user profile resulting in a happy user. Another great benefit is that in case the UEM settings aren't available because of a fileserver outage, the user is still able to sign in and work on a new desktop because the default user profile is still available. Ever tried signing in to a desktop when your roaming profile isn't available? Exactly.

From a Lifecycle Management (LCM) perspective, a UEM solution is also great. In most cases, the application containers are interchangeable between operating systems, but also between different versions of a single app. Be sure to check this on a per-application basis.

Examples of requirements or constraints in which you would decide to add a UEM solution to your design:

- The solution must provide a consistent user experience between devices and sessions.
- Users must be able to manage as much as possible through Self-Service.
- The RPO of the user's application and profile settings must be as short as possible (which you are able to set through GPOs).
- The RTO of the solution must be 15 minutes or less.
- The logon process of the user should be 30 seconds or less.

# FOLDER REDIRECTION

Creating a Hybrid Profile is a great first step but doesn't solve all issues. There are certain parts of the profile which need a different approach to make them non-persistent as well. Things like the desktop folder, the downloads folder and possibly the documents folder need a different methodology to make sure the user is able to access those files independent of the virtual desktops that are in use. Saving them in the same way you would with application data (through UEM zip files) is a little bit better compared to using Roaming Profiles, but still a very bad plan. Users can easily store data in folders you would like to keep as clean as possible (such as the desktop). Ever walked by a user that had a physical machine with desktop full of files and folders so the wallpaper is sort-of useless? This is basically what users do. You can tell them to save everything in a file share or in a solution like Microsoft SharePoint (which are protected from disasters), but they won't listen. I still remember those conversations with users that demanded you to do everything you can because of the excel file that they worked on is on their desktop, and the desktop died. Or what about the developer that loses two months of code because of a malware infection that couldn't be fixed. These are perfect examples of data that need to become persistent through a technology called *Folder Redirection*.

Why just not redirect the entire profile you might ask? It's quite simple, folder redirection comes with a penalty in terms of performance. Not every folder is suitable to be redirected, especially ones that contain files and folders that are accessed on a large scale. The favorites folder is an example. Every time the user starts typing a URL in Internet Explorer, the favorites folder is accessed and thus could cause performance issues. For one user it might work, but having 5,000 users doing this, you are sure to have issues.

There are multiple ways to implement folder redirection but the one I would recommend, is through VMware UEM. Through UEM you are able to setup folder direction in the same way as you would configure other settings. All of the folders that can be redirected through a GPO, can also be redirected with UEM. The following folders can be redirected without any performance issues:

- Documents
- Downloads
- Music
- Pictures
- Videos

## Considerations

Not all folders have the ability or need to be redirected. When designing folder redirection, take the following into account:

- If you would really like to persist the favorites of a user, your best pick would be to do this through a different browser (such as Chrome or Firefox). These will store their favorites on a different location that UEM could synchronize in the Hybrid Profile. Redirecting your Internet Explorer favorites is possible but be warned that it could cause performance issues when using the browser.

- Although the possibility exists to redirect the AppData folder, I would highly recommend to **NOT** do this. AppData redirection could cause applications to stop working or perform very badly.
- Just because you can redirect everything doesn't mean you should. If certain folders (like the desktop) aren't required, you should avoid users from saving data there. The less data needs to be redirected, the better.
- The desktop folder can be redirected. Although this folder is considered as one that can be impacted in terms of performance, the benefits could weigh more. Ever walked into a user that created a smiley on their desktop by moving all sorts of icons in that shape? These users need folder redirection too ☺.
- When using UEM to configure folder redirection, data won't be moved if a user will use it for the first time. This might impact the migration scenario (from a non-redirected solution to a redirected solution), so keep this in mind.

# WINDOWS 10 ENHANCEMENTS

If you follow the latest developments for Windows 10, you will have heard that setting up a mandatory profile for your non-persistent use cases is something you need to repeat with every major release. Microsoft is adding new features in every release, chances are quite high that the user section of for instance the registry or the profile directory are being impacted by it. The biggest example of this is the Start Menu.

VMware User Environment Manager can help you with this. With VMware UEM, it is possible to roam user settings between Windows 10 desktops, but there are some measures you need to take before it will work. For versions 1703 and up, you can do so by configuring a UEM config file. For versions older than 1703, it works a bit different. VMware UEM specialist Pim van de Vis wrote a great article on how to accomplish this. You can check the article here:

https://blogs.vmware.com/euc/2016/11/managing-windows-10-vmware-user-environment-manager.html

*Please note that the methodology to create a UEM profile for Windows 10 may vary with every new version of Windows 10 that is released. Contacting your local partner or the VMware EUC community is a great way to find out what the best practices for your current Windows 10 release are. Another great resource is the UEM Deployment Considerations Guide, which can be found here:*

https://www.vmware.com/content/dam/digitalmarketing/vmwar e/en/pdf/techpaper/vmware-user-environment-manager-deployment-considerations.pdf

# APPLICATIONS

The number one reason why companies would consider VDI is related to applications. If your complete application landscape would consist out of web-based applications, would you still consider VDI? Me personally, I won't. I would probably try to consolidate all web-based applications in a *Digital Workspace* solution such as Workspace ONE so everyone is able to run their web-based applications without the need for an expensive VDI.

Unfortunately, the reality is that there might be just a handful of companies that completely run on applications that run in the cloud. Most of them are start-ups since they don't have to cope with legacy or (somewhat more friendly) *traditional* applications. Companies that have existed for more than 10 years, will for sure have applications which can be considered a traditional application. If not, their CIO did an awesome job! This section will help you in your quest to design your VDI, so it will run your applications in the most efficient way.

# TYPES OF APPLICATIONS

There are lots of different types of applications: SaaS and web-based apps, mobile apps, traditional apps, apps that run from a network, monolithic apps, etc. There might be a lot more, but let's focus on the apps that you might be deploying on VDI.

## Traditional Apps

What is a traditional app you might ask? Every app that needs to be installed on a (virtual) desktop can be considered to be a traditional app, it's that simple. Even a recent suite of applications like Office 2016 can be considered as traditional apps. The reason why we call them traditional is because you need "traditional" ways to deploy the app to an endpoint, such as VDI. There are multiple ways to deploy such an app to a virtual desktop, more about that in the *deployment strategies* section. Traditional apps have a couple of other characteristics, as well. They heavily rely on the operating system they're running on. Traditional apps aren't just built to run on any operating system. Apps built for macOS probably won't run on Windows 10 and vice versa. Traditional apps also have dependencies with things like DLLs, quite often are installed in folders that won't tolerate any deviation, quite often require elevated permissions and from a manageability perspective, basically just suck.

## SaaS and Web-based Apps

SaaS and web-based apps are the future, right? From an endpoint perspective that might be true. But if you look at the type of endpoint we are using, I believe that apps which are purposely built for and endpoint (such as iPad apps) are the real future (since they are capable of leveraging the power of the endpoint and provide the best user experience possible). Unfortunately, mobile apps are out-of-scope when you purely talk VDI (as you would manage these with a Unified Endpoint Management solution like

VMware AirWatch). The next best things are SaaS and web-based apps in terms of deployment or distribution. Like the name might give away, these apps run in a cloud and can be run as a service. Perfect examples are Salesforce, Dropbox and Concur. Most of those apps just run in your browser and possibly only require a plug-in. Some (like Dropbox) also have a client, but it runs in the user context and doesn't require any elevated permissions. Getting those apps is a lot simpler as well. Some are free and just simply require a registration. Others will require a credit card. Because of the ease of implementation, these apps were one of the reasons why shadow IT was born. If you need an app for working from home and your IT team is not able to offer it, installing drop box (from a user perspective) is a perfect solution. Obviously, IT doesn't feel the same.

# APPLICATION ASSESSMENT

As explained in the Assessment section, starting your journey in designing VDI all begins with knowing what to design for. As your applications are the most important driver behind sizing, architecture and deployment methodologies, it's clear that application assessment is essential. When looking at an assessment outcome, it's not the user that demands a certain number of resources, it's the applications used by the user. Making sure you start with a complete list of used applications is the best way to start your design. The hardest part might be to take all of the applications into account. If it's over five hundred applications and you end up with five applications not running on the VDI, would that mean you are canceling your project? It might if those five apps are the most crucial in your application landscape. My lesson learned here is to scope a certain number of apps. Let's say the top 25 of applications in use by all of the use cases. Or something like the top 10 of applications in use by the individual use cases. The rest of the applications would hopefully still work, but don't pose a risk for a successful project.

Another lesson learned was to exclude the other applications from your design project. Imagine you have to migrate 500 apps from MSI deployments to App Volumes AppStacks. If hypothetically speaking all documentation is perfect for every single app (which isn't, I guarantee you) you might be able to convert one app every 2 days on average. It will take you 2 years' worth of FTEs to complete the initial migration. But wait, what about upgrades of an app you already migrated? Get the point?

When designing an application strategy, it's important to think about the following topics:

- Number of applications
- User count per application
- Operating system dependencies (such as versions, builds, etc.)
- Hardware requirements (does it require any dongles, printers, GPUs, etc)
- Is it single or multi-threaded?
- Is an app considered mission-critical?
- Does an app require a high clock speed?
- Does an app require any drivers?
- Does an app require services?
- Does the app have to run before a user signs in?
- Does an app require a full installation?
- Are elevated permissions required?
- Is middleware (such as Java or .NET framework) required to run?
- Is a specific version of that middleware required?
- Does the app require shell or UI integration?
- Does the app have a backend (such as a database)?
- Are there multiple versions of an app currently delivered that could be consolidated (such as multiple version of a PDF reader)?
- Could the app be phased out?

Although it seems those questions could steer you in all sorts of directions, the outcome is quite often the same. To be able to run all of those apps inside your virtual desktop, you need a delivery strategy.

# DELIVERY STRATEGIES

Getting an app to the end-user is what a delivery strategy is all about and doing it in a way, so it is beneficial for all stakeholders is key to a successful project. In an ideal situation, every app that is being delivered to an end-user undergoes a development, test and acceptance phase before actually delivered to the end-user. In realistic situations, the testing phase is the bare minimum I include in the delivery strategy. Without any application tests and especially with large application landscapes, I have had some really bad experiences. Apps will work by themselves, but as soon as you combine them with others in an App Volumes AppStack or implement them together in a base image, strange stuff might happen. Apps might not run that well or basically conflict with each other's middleware. So, testing them is essential!

There are multiple ways to deliver a traditional application to an end-user. If you have a small set of applications and no growth in the landscape is expected, you might completely design your delivery methodology based on that set. These customers are quite rare, unfortunately. In the projects I have worked on, the app count varied between 50 and 500. Some had even more but were consolidated as much as possible. This means you might need all of the options offered in the Horizon Enterprise Suite to successfully deliver the complete landscape. The following options are included:

- Installing in the base image
- App Volumes AppStacks
- App Volumes Writable Volumes (user installed apps)
- ThinApp
- Regular deployment (through MSIs)
- User Environment Managemer (UEM)
- Creating shortcuts

The following sections describe the individual components before we dig into the complete delivery methodology.

## Installing in the Base Image

This is delivery as we know it. Basically, just install the app in the VM you created as a base image and create clones. Nothing more, nothing less. Although considered by many to avoid this as much as possible, I disagree. Some applications must be installed in the base image because of a variety of reasons:

- The application needs to be started before a user logs on (such as anti-virus solutions or management agents)
- The application includes system services
- The application uses specific hardware to run (like dongles or Point-of-Sales components)

Installing apps in the base image might be a good idea depending on your requirements. There are some things to consider.

### Considerations

- As explained in the operating system section, building a base image should be as automated as possible. When deploying apps through your base image, you need to make sure that your automation solution includes the deployment of these apps.
- Microsoft Office is a great example of an application that is better suited to run in the base image. The biggest reason being that the update cycle and methodology are the same as your OS. As everyone within your organization would probably use Microsoft Office as a primary app (especially Outlook), it makes sense to add it to your base image.

## App Volumes AppStacks

In 2014, VMware acquired a company called CloudVolumes. CloudVolumes built a solution that we now know as App Volumes. Like explained in the *Persistency and Non-persistency* section, App Volumes is a layering technology which enables you to deliver applications to virtual desktops. Within an instant, you are able to deliver a gazillion applications to a desktop. That's what the marketing slides tell you, at least. This is partly true. App Volumes is capable of attaching a volume containing a lot of apps within a couple of seconds to a large number of desktops. It comes with a cost though.

In order for App Volumes to work from a functional level, you need to create AppStacks in a logical way. Every AppStack is filled with applications that belong to a business unit. It starts very generic and ends very specific. When talking about layers, the following diagram shows what it should look like.

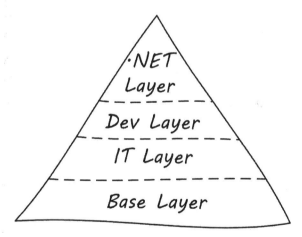

- Base layer: containing all apps that all users use (such as Adobe Reader, 7zip and Paint dotNet).
- IT layer: containing all generic apps that the IT department uses (such as a time tracker, a bug tracker and remote assistance software).

- Dev layer: contains all generic dev apps (such as Notepad++, Atom, and Slack).
- .NET Dev layer: containing specific apps for the .NET/Dev/IT team (such as Visual Studio).

In this simple example, you have 4 layers for a .NET Developer. The same applies to all other teams like Finance, Sales, and HR. In a more complex example with over 500 apps, you will likely end up with a lot more layers.

App Volumes attaches an AppStack (which like a Writable Volume is a VMDK file) during logon of a user. As every AppStack will be attached sequentially, it will take some time for this process to finish. With every AppStack that gets attached, the filter driver that comes with the App Volumes agent has to do some work to make sure you are able to run the applications inside the AppStack. For instance, if attaching a single AppStack takes 5 seconds, imagine what happens if you attach 8 of them. Please note that the process of attaching them is executed during logon. After the last one is attached, the logon process continues, and you are presented with a desktop, not sooner. Imagine what happens if your logon process will take over a minute because of a large number of AppStacks. So, from a user experience perspective, App Volumes might not always be the way to go. This is the main reason why I always advise customers to use App Volumes, but not for all of their applications (unless they agree to a logon process delay).

On the previous page, I explained the layering strategy. Why just not deploy a single app in an AppStack you may ask? It's simply because of the limited number of AppStacks you are able to attach on a virtual machine and still make it workable. In an ideal situation, AppStacks would be containing a single app only, and during logon (or the start of an application), the AppStack is attached and merged with the already attached one (so you are able to run apps that require one another to work). Sounds familiar? If not, use your search engine and check out "App Volumes 3.0". I'm still hoping that VMware is going to bring out the features of App Volumes 3.0 in a solution that is able to run in an on-premises VDI. App Volumes 3.0 contained a lot of features such as the merging-technology I just mentioned, a technology called *App Blocking* which can hide a specific application from an AppStack if a user doesn't have permissions, and many more. If these features aren't available in future releases, finding the right layering strategy will remain a challenge in every project.

It's not all negative. Not at all. App Volumes can be a great solution, if used in the right way, with the right expectations.

## Considerations

- Like with every form of delivery, it's important to know thy app.
- Because of the logon delay, you want to keep the number of AppStacks to a bare minimum. Try to use App Volumes only for the applications that are deployed to the majority of users.
- Combine apps that belong to a logical group in your organization in an AppStack.
- The maximum advised size of an AppStack is 20 GB. The size isn't set in stone, but the more apps the AppStack contains, the more the filter driver has to do when attaching it. Consider smaller sized AppStacks, instead.
- Applications mentioned in the section about installing in the base image are on average the ones that won't run in an AppStack, so installing them in a base image is the solution for this.
- Like every form of layering or virtualizing applications, use a clean provisioning machine to make sure the container or bubble doesn't contain any junk.
- AppStacks built in one operating system might work in another as well but could also not work. Be sure to test this! Simple apps like 7zip and Paint .NET will absolutely work on Windows 7, Windows 10 and Windows Server 2016. Microsoft Office is a completely different ballgame.
- If you are designing App Volumes in a multi-site VDI, make sure to follow the Horizon Enterprise Multi-Site Reference Architecture recommendations (check the *References* section for more information).

- Try to automate the creation of AppStack as much as possible. When a new version of an application is released, it is smarter to run the setup fresh instead of upgrading an application (as it might break). In some cases, it might also be quicker to rebuild an AppStack instead of restoring from a backup (in case of a failure).

## App Volumes Writable Volumes

A Writable Volumes basically is the same as a regular AppStack, but with two major differences: it's not read-only and it's attached to a single desktop only which make them usable for users that require some form of persistence.

A Writable Volume is also a VMDK file that resides on the shared storage. It's also attached during logon of the user. The filter driver will record what changes were made during a session and will save the files in the Writable Volume instead of the desktop.

The Writable Volume is a real powerful tool to create a persistent user experience on top of a non-persistent desktop. Users are able to install apps, can be offered elevated permissions and might even be able to use complex applications in a non-persistent desktop that wouldn't be possible without Writable Volumes. Perfect use cases are OneDrive and Outlook. Both of those apps aren't really suitable to run them inside a non-persistent desktop: OneDrive because it tries to download/sync files to the profile of the user, Outlook because of the cache that it would like to sync to the same location. By using Writable Volumes, both of those applications can be configured to save their data there and would be able to run in a non-persistent desktop.

As explained in the *Persistency and Non-persistency* section, using Writable Volumes has the same downsides in terms of performance as AppStacks. The only advantage is that it's just one instead of many. But, they can be combined with AppStacks, which causes the same logon/user experience issues when implemented wrong.

Another major downside of a Writable Volume is when used in a multi-site scenario. Consider the following:

1. Developer John Connor signs into his non-persistent desktop in Site A.
2. His Writable Volume is attached, containing all of his development tools and database (which are over 10 GB in size).
3. He upgrades all his tools and reindexes his database.
4. After 5 minutes of him being ready with this, Site A goes black.
5. He reconnects to the VDI and gets a virtual desktop in site B, but it doesn't contain his development tools and data.

10 GB of changed data is not easily synchronized to another datacenter in such a short time. In case your RPO is 15 minutes and RTO is as well (which are relatively normal values), you need to check whether all of that data can be synchronized to the secondary datacenter in time. For one user it might be possible, but what happens if you have 500 of them? The only way to momentarily solve this, is by running your Writable Volumes on a metro cluster with synchronous replication, which is a very expensive solution if you ask me and **possibly not even supported**.

Another way to approach this risk is to add a different value to the RPO/RTO requirements of the data in Writable Volumes and make sure the user is aware. This risk is similar with persistent Full Clones, but now you will be able to run those use cases on a non-persistent desktop.

## Considerations

- Only a single Writable Volume can be used with a desktop at a time.
- If you are going to use Writable Volumes, make sure the RPO and RTO requirements are still respected.

- In order for a user to install apps inside the Writable Volume, elevated permissions are required to make it happen.

# ThinApp

Once known as Thinstall, ThinApp was VMware's first successful approach to application virtualization. Application virtualization is a technology to fully decouple an application from the operating system and put it in an isolated container, called a bubble. Everything the apps needs to start (like the file set, shortcuts, registry information, etc.) is stored in a single exe file and can be started on any device. The runtime ThinApp requires to start the bubble is compiled inside the exe file, so no additional client is required to start a ThinApp.

ThinApps can be stored on a file share, on a thumb drive or any other location. The cool thing is that they can be run on virtual machines and physical machines, which makes them versatile.

Changes which are made to a virtualized application, are stored in a sandbox that can be saved in the user's profile or any other location. Throwing the sandbox away, will restore the application to its initial state.

The process of creating a ThinApp is quite similar to that of an AppStack, including many of the same considerations. There is only one main difference: ThinApps contain (in general) a single application only. This makes them a lot easier to deploy to end-users as you don't have to group them based on logical groups or such.

## Considerations

- Building a ThinApp is quite similar to building an AppStack, but because it only contains a single app, testing an app will be less time consuming.
- If an app requires a certain version of middleware or reporting engine, include them in the same ThinApp.
- Consider distributing large ThinApps through an AppStack to reduce network traffic and slow application start times.
- Create ThinApps on a same, clean VM as you would be creating AppStacks.
- ThinApps built on operating system A might work on operating system B, but it's always wise to test it first.
- Automate the creation of your ThinApps as much as possible. Similarly to AppStacks, it will be a better option to create a new ThinApp if an application has a new release instead of opening up the ThinApp, upgrading it and closing it again. In this way, you will have more junk in the ThinApp and chances are that setups will break.

## Regular Deployment

Although not a deployment methodology that is offered by VMware in the Horizon Enterprise Suite, deploying applications like you did before might be the best solution possible. Especially for persistent Full Clones, using a solution like SCCM to deploy applications might be suitable. I would still try to deliver applications to Full Clones through one of the named delivery methods in the previous sections, but certain apps might just not be suitable for any of them. A persistent Full Clone with regularly deployed apps could eventually be your best friend. I do think you should use this option as your worst-case scenario.

I've also seen customers using a regular deployment to non-persistent use cases where they deployed the apps at every refresh of a pool, which was once a week. It will work, but I think it's a bad plan.

## Considerations

- Like every other deployment methodology, automate as much as possible.

## User Environment Manager

People long enough in the server-based computing industry might remember the Flex Profile Kit, developed by Jeroen van de Kamp. In the early days, it was a free utility that let you synchronize only the bare minimum required files and registry settings an application or desktop required to a profile. So, instead of completely synchronizing a roaming profile, you could use a mandatory profile and sync the files and registry keys from the network into your fresh profile. Many years later, after becoming a successful company called Immidio, VMware acquired the solution and renamed it into User Environment Manager. Some of the former employees of Immidio are still working at VMware, such as Pim van de Vis and Raymond Wiesemann.

User Environment Manager (UEM) is essential to any of the deployment technology chosen. Independent of the methodology you choose, when you deploy those apps in a base image, AppStack or ThinApp, you need to make sure UEM is able to configure those apps and extract the settings again when you finished running your applications or session.

UEM is not only capable of making your applications persistent in a non-persistent desktop, it can also do this based on conditions. I had a customer once in Belgium that had an application which needed to support both the Dutch and French languages. With UEM, I was able to create a condition that injected a Dutch or French language pack depending on an Active Directory property.

Another great feature of UEM, is the ability to set up the user environment (hence the name). Things like shortcuts, file type association, printers and file shares can all be dynamically configured and refreshed if the context of the user's changes. If a user works from the third floor in an office building and has a printer connected, UEM can make sure a different printer is connected if he moves to the first floor.

UEM works based on file shares that reside on a file server. As Microsoft isn't really the best in building file shares that are synchronous replicated between datacenters, creating a UEM design that is able to run multi-site requires some more components. Following the guidelines in the Horizon Enterprise Multi-site Reference Architecture is recommended.

## Considerations

- Use the reference architecture to deploy UEM (either multi-site or single-site).
- Like the AppStacks and ThinApps, make sure to create UEM templates on a clean machine.
- UEM templates could be dependent on a certain version of the application or operating system, so be sure to test the profiles with every upgrade of an application.
- There is an online repository of UEM templates built by the community. Although it's hosted at the VMware community pages, searching for the right one will be easier through http://uemtemplates.com, created by Ivan de Mes.

## Creating Shortcuts

Some apps are just awesome for not having to be deployed. Apps that run from the network or SaaS and web-based apps could easily be "distributed" by creating a shortcut on the desktops, start menu or favorites. User Environment Manager could be used to do that for network apps or web-based apps.

There is a different methodology to deliver web-based apps to an end-user, though. If your web-based app supports Single Sign-On

(SSO) through SAML (Security Assertion Markup Language) integration, the application could also be delivered through a solution like VMware Identity Manager (vIDM). vIDM is a portal that acts like an Identity provider (IDP). An IDP is a single point of authentication that federates your identity to another application. Office 365 is a great example. If you start Office 365, you first need to authenticate to a portal. In most cases that is Azure Active Directory, but when designing Horizon Enterprise, vIDM is included in the license which could offer the same functionality. Independent of the solution you might choose, having a central portal to offer you all of your apps and federating identity is a must-have if you ask me. More about vIDM can be found in the security section.

## Delivery Methodology

One method of deployment isn't better than the other. App Volumes is great, but possibly not suitable for all use cases. The same is the case with Writable Volumes and ThinApp. Combining all of the methods described in the previous sections will create a basis for a methodology that should be able to handle most (if not, all) of your applications.

The methodology I use is based on the one that can be downloaded from my blog. Although that one covers all solutions in the Workspace ONE Enterprise Suite, the following methodology only covers the ones that can be applied to the Horizon Enterprise Suite.

You can download the full Workspace ONE version here: https://vhojan.nl/application-delivery-decision-diagram/

The delivery methodology will guide you through every step and will give you a predictive outcome which was about right in 95% of every project I finished with it.

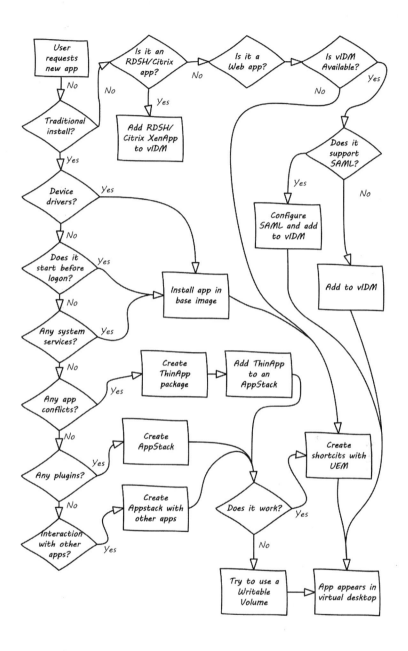

## Considerations

- As mentioned, 95% of the applications will work when you use this prediction model. Unfortunately, there will always be apps that work a bit differently. In that case, I would always try to add them to an AppStack. If that doesn't work, try a ThinApp or installing in the base image instead.
- You are not alone. If you have an application and you have no idea what to do with it, reach out to the VMware EUC community. Chances are that someone else has already built or documented something around your app.
- There are other solutions out there that are capable of delivering apps as well. Solutions like Liquidware FlexApp, FSLogix or Microsoft App-V might be suitable as well for your specific application landscape.
- If you have a constraint because you already own a delivery solution like the ones mentioned above, just remember that independent of the chosen technology, apps will behave the same in a container, layer or bubble. Creating those should be done by following the same guidelines.

# LIFECYCLE MANAGEMENT

Migrating hundreds of applications to VDI is one thing, maintaining them is another. Having 500 different applications on VDI is still a challenge, using the delivery methodology in the previous section or not. On average, a single admin or packager could manage around 100 apps. If your application vendor decides to increase the number of updates from let's say 4 per year to maybe 12 per year, the pressure on the packagers will only increase. So, it's very, very important to automate the packaging process as much as possible. I know I may sound annoying by constantly repeating this, but it is the only way to make it successful. PowerShell and PowerCLI are free tools which can help you automate. A lot of resources can be found on the internet and in the community.

# GENERAL APPLICATION DELIVERY

# CONSIDERATIONS

Applications can cause a lot of headaches if delivered incorrectly. Please take the following into account when designing a delivery strategy:

- Make sure to document your delivery methods to ensure your applications can be supported if a packager or admin decides to leave your organization or customer.
- With every 100 apps, on average, an additional packager might be required. Please take this into account before moving towards VDI.
- Rationalizing your landscape before migrating to a new delivery methodology is very important and will eventually save you time and money. Rationalizing could either mean you consolidate multiple versions of an app into a single one or possible phase out an app.
- Migrating from traditional apps towards SaaS and web-based apps might be the best idea because you won't have to package the app ever again.
- Apps are part of the user experience. This means that a user needs to be happy to use a certain app. If that's not the case, migrating towards another one could be a solution to get a better user experience.
- Make sure to monitor your applications for performance and things like user count to be on top of the user experience.
- Use the reference architecture from VMware (Horizon Enterprise and Horizon Enterprise Multi-site) for deployment best practices.
- If your VDI is multi-site and your applications have an availability requirement that forces you to run active/active, make sure the back-end is also capable of running in both sites.

- Keep the delivery as simple as possible. Don't overdo stuff. If you don't need a component, don't design and deploy it. Your VDI could easily work without App Volumes and instead run perfectly with ThinApp or applications installed in the base image.

# GRAPHICS AND REMOTE

# PROTOCOLS

During the design of VDI, there are a couple of components that require some extra attention. Especially the ones that have a direct impact on user experience when sized or designed incorrectly are the ones to give some extra love. Graphics and remote protocols are two of those components. A lot has happened in the remote graphics space over the past years and this section is dedicated to helping you get some insights into what many consider as an unknown territory. Since my first VDI design and deploy, the number of projects where GPUs were used increased drastically. But is a GPU really necessary for a good user experience? What about the choice between Blast Extreme and PCoIP? Is one better than the other? Is it really true that VMware stopped investing in PCoIP? These are all questions that I will try to answer in this section.

# GPUS

Let's talk about cool stuff first: GPUs. GPUs are awesome and can be found in many different devices (even the trusty Commodore 64 had a 16 color GPU☺). Basically, every device that attaches to or has a TFT/LED/IPS display also has a GPU, including smart watches, phones, car audio systems and computers of course. But not only graphical related workloads can be enhanced through the use of a GPU. Cryptocurrency mining rigs benefit heavily from the power of GPU cores and the speed of its memory. Nowadays, even Docker containers can run on a GPU to benefit from its power and utilize CUDA cores.

There are currently three companies that develop GPUs: Intel, AMD, and NVIDIA. The first two offer GPUs that are capable of delivering graphical acceleration in VDI, but NVIDIA became a market leader in this space by developing the first real GPU that could be shared amongst multiple users, concurrently in a single host.

First, let's go back in time a couple of years.

If you played first-person shooters in the 90's such as Quake and Doom, you must remember *the* moment when you first saw those games running on a Diamond Monster 3D card. To me, that was the same feeling as seeing my first vMotion. It was a total shift in how video was rendered and showed what a difference it could be when using a dedicated GPU for suitable tasks. In this case, a special API called Glide could benefit from a daisy-chained PCI card that had 4MB of RAM attached to it and was purposely built to render 3D graphics. 3DFX, the company responsible for these remarkable cards, got acquired in 2002 by NVIDIA which brought an end to a great era. Since then, a lot has happened in the GPU space.

As users became more demanding in terms of user experience, GPU vendors had to bring their A-game to continuously improve performance, resolution and detail that could be achieved when playing games. Especially when playing online in massive multiplayer games with like Half Life Counterstrike or Team

Fortress Classic, the slightest improvement of detail or a single millisecond of latency could make a difference in killing or be killed. Back then, it felt a little bit as if those of my generation were pioneers in the area of graphical user experience. Getting the most out of what was possible in the user experience space was what made a difference in gaming.

If you look at how graphical user experience was applied in the corporate world, things were pretty straightforward. 95% of all users were running their apps on a Windows NT/2000 based desktop and in the other 5%, they were either running on terminals or possibly remote with Windows Terminal Server or Citrix Winframe/Metaframe. No real demand for an enhanced graphical interface existed in most use cases.

A lot has happened since then. With every release of Linux or Windows operating systems, the demand for more resources increases and this includes graphical resources. In 1999 I had my first CRT monitor that was able to produce a resolution of 1280 x 1024, I'm currently using a 4K monitor where 1280 x 1024 feels like a little stamp on a big postcard. If you realize that, and also know that more (business) applications have the ability to offload specific tasks to a GPU, it is starting to make more sense to use GPUs in that space, as well. Another movement that might justify the use of GPUs in the corporate world is Bring Your Own Device (BYOD). Most of the students that graduate from university, have been using their own device to run their student applications during their time at the university – the same device they might use to watch Netflix and run their banking applications. The device itself is equipped with a GPU and in most cases either Windows 10 or macOS. All of those ingredients spoil the user in terms of user experience.

If you take this knowledge a step further, to the point at which you are designing VDI, it becomes complex. A GPU for home use is quite often relatively cheap. For around 100 – 150 euros (120 – 180 US dollars), you can buy a GPU that is able to play games, offload video decoding and can use multiple monitors at high resolutions (4K+). A GPU for shared use starts at around 2,000 euros (2,500 US dollars) (excluding licenses) and is able to be shared amongst up to eight users. The next question would be how your corporate IT environment would benefit from it? As always, it's all about use cases and requirements.

# VMWARE & GRAPHICAL

# ACCELERATION

To answer to the increasing demand for improved graphics, VMware developed multiple ways to utilize the physical GPU in a virtual desktop. The following section is taken from the VMware GPU guide and describes the different flavors of graphical acceleration.

## Virtual Shared Graphics Acceleration

Virtual Shared Graphics Acceleration (vSGA) allows you to share a GPU across multiple virtual desktops. It is an attractive solution for users who require the GPUs full potential during brief periods. However, vSGA can create bottlenecks depending on which applications are used and the resources the applications require. This type of graphics acceleration is generally used for knowledge workers and occasionally for power users. With vSGA, the host's physical GPUs are virtualized and shared across multiple guest virtual machines. You must install a vendor driver in the hypervisor. Each guest virtual machine uses a proprietary VMware vSGA 3D driver that communicates with the vendor driver in VMware vSphere. Drawbacks of vSGA are that applications might need to be recertified to be supported, API support is limited, and support is restricted to OpenGL (2.1) and DirectX (version 9.0c SM3).

# Virtual Dedicated Graphics Acceleration

Virtual Dedicated Graphics Acceleration (vDGA) technology, also known as *GPU pass-through,* provides each user with unrestricted, fully dedicated access to one of the host's GPUs. Although dedicated access has some consolidation and management trade-offs, vDGA offers the highest level of performance for users with the most intensive graphics computing needs. The hypervisor passes the GPUs directly to individual guest virtual machines. No special drivers are required in the hypervisor. However, to enable graphics acceleration, you must install the appropriate vendor driver on each guest virtual machine. The installation procedures are the same as for physical machines. Drawbacks of vDGA are the lack of vMotion support and a low consolidation ratio on a single GPU.

# Virtual Shared Pass-Through Graphics Acceleration

Virtual Shared Pass-Through Graphics Acceleration allows you to share a GPU across multiple virtual desktops instead of focusing on only one user. Unlike vSGA, it does not use the proprietary VMware 3D driver, and most graphics card features are supported.

You must install the appropriate vendor driver on the guest virtual machine. All graphics commands are passed directly to the GPU without having to be translated by the hypervisor. On the hypervisor, a vSphere Installation Bundle (VIB) is installed, which aids or performs the scheduling. Depending on the card and the use case, up to 64 virtual machines can share a single card (some cards have multiple GPUs). Calculating the number of desktops or users per GPU depends on the type of card, application requirements, screen resolution, number of displays, and frame rate, measured in frames per second (FPS).

The amount of framebuffer (VRAM) per virtual machine (VM) is fixed, and the GPU engines are shared between VMs. Virtual shared pass-through technology provides better performance than vSGA and higher consolidation ratios than Virtual Dedicated Graphics Acceleration (vDGA). It is a useful technology for low-, mid-, and advanced-level engineers and designers and power users with 3D application requirements. Its drawback is that the technology might require applications to be recertified to be supported.

From a supportability perspective, the following table (which is taken from the VMware GPU guide) displays the feature comparison for the different types of graphical acceleration that VMware can offer.

| Type | Virtual Shared Graphics Acceleration | Virtual Shared Pass-through Graphics Acceleration | Virtual Dedicated Graphics Acceleration |
|---|---|---|---|
| Abbreviation | vSGA | vGPU | vDGA |
| Consolidation | High (limited by video memory) | Up to 1:32 per GPU card | None (1:1) |
| Performance | Lightweight | Lightweight or workstation | Workstation |
| Compatibility | Limited | Full, but not all apps are certified | Full |
| Direct X level | 9.0c SM3 only | All supported versions | All supported versions |
| OpenGL version | 2.1 only | All supported versions | All supported versions |
| Video encoding and decoding | Software | Hardware | Hardware |

| Type | Virtual Shared Graphics Acceleration | Virtual Shared Pass-through Graphics Acceleration | Virtual Dedicated Graphics Acceleration |
|---|---|---|---|
| OpenCL or CUDA | No | Yes | Yes |
| vSphere vMotion support | Yes | Not yet | No |

In the above table, there are some details that stand out. Since it has limited support for Direct X, OpenGL, and CUDA, I do not really see any advantage in using vSGA over vGPU. The one advantage for a long time was vMotion, but since version 7.5 of Horizon, 6.7 of vSphere and 6.1 of NVIDIA vGPU, suspend and resume is supported as well (with vMotion probably coming very soon), so availability won't be a requirement to choose vSGA. vDGA has its advantages in terms of performance, but in that case vMotion isn't possible. As vDGA will allocate an entire GPU to a single desktop, it isn't suitable for a solution in which you would like to achieve a high density.

# NVIDIA VIRTUAL GPU

Late 2012, NVIDIA decided to jump into the VDI space and introduced two GPUs which could be shared amongst multiple users at the same time. The GRID K1 and K2 were based on the Kepler architecture. From a VMware perspective, vGPU wasn't born yet. Virtual Shared Graphics Acceleration (vSGA) was VMware's primary solution to enable shared GPU graphical acceleration. With vSGA it is possible to share the framebuffer of a GPU amongst all users running on a single host. For some time, vSGA was a fine solution, but it lacked support for use cases that required more resources and graphical acceleration like a Quadro card does. vDGA was born for that specific reason. By passing through a physical GPU to a single VM, the VM has full access to all of the resources that the GPU has to offer. When it comes to performance and running workloads that require a lot of resources, vDGA does the job. Today, vDGA is still the most powerful way to enable a desktop with graphical acceleration as no process is used to schedule cycles of graphical workloads which are requested by different desktops on a single GPU. The downside, of course, is that vDGA limits the density of graphical accelerated users on a single host and it lacks vMotion support. When Horizon 6.1 came out, it had support for vSphere 6. vSphere 6 was the first VMware Hypervisor that had support for NVIDIA Virtual GPU (vGPU), the new holy grail for shared GPU graphical acceleration.

If you are entirely new in the field of graphical acceleration, the first thing you might ask yourself is: *Why should I implement a technology that shares a GPU amongst users?*
The answer is relatively simple. A GPU is built out of many components of which the cores and the framebuffer (the RAM on the GPU) are the most important ones. If you add a GPU like an NVIDIA Tesla P40 to a single physical machine, the chance is quite significant that you won't utilize all of the resources that the card has to offer. By sharing the card with more than one user, it will probably be better utilized. Compare it to when virtualization was introduced. By adding a hypervisor to a single host, the resources on that host can be shared by multiple VMs. The result is that the resources of the physical host are better utilized.
So, that's exactly what NVIDIA vGPU does. It's a GPU resources scheduler running next to the hypervisor, scheduling physical GPU resources which are requested by virtual desktops.

The following figure shows the NVIDIA vGPU architecture:

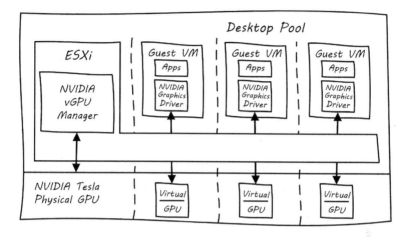

The virtual desktops are using the vGPU in the same way as when a physical GPU is passed through to the virtual desktop. A driver needs to be installed in the virtual desktop to utilize the virtual GPU.

When a new virtual desktop is created that includes a vGPU, an allocation of all or part of a framebuffer will be made for that desktop. The allocation is set through *profiles*. The framebuffer will be exclusively allocated (through a profile) for a specific virtual desktop until it is destroyed.

Other components on the physical card are time shared amongst other vGPU profiles such as the graphics engine and encode/decode engines by the GPU scheduler (which is covered in one of the next sections).

The following diagram shows some more details of the shared components of the NVIDIA vGPU architecture:

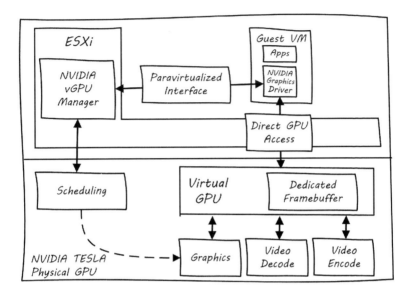

The framebuffer from a single GPU engine on an NVIDIA Tesla GPU card can only be equally divided into vGPUs that have the same profile. So, if you have 8 GB of framebuffer, you are able to divide it in 8 x 1 GB, 4 x 2 GB or 2 x 4 GB, etc. Mixing different types of profiles on a single physical GPU isn't currently possible.

The following diagram shows some more details on a valid profile allocation for a card with multiple GPUs:

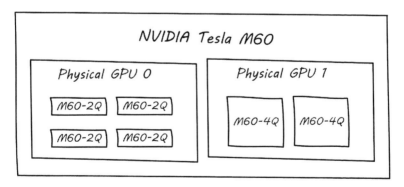

The following diagram shows an invalid profile allocation for a card with multiple GPUs:

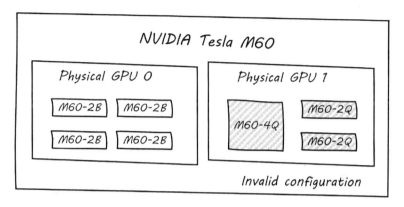

More about these profile names will be explained in a later section.

## GPU Hardware

Since 2012, a lot has happened in the GPU virtualization space in terms of hardware. In this section, I would like to explain some more about the different cards you might come across in either your own environment or that from a customer.

Although considered legacy, the first cards I would like to mention here are the Kepler-based cards. The Kepler cards (GRID K1 and GRID K2) contained multiple GPUs on one card and had a total of 16GB (K1) or 8GB (K2) framebuffer. The K1 was a more purposely built card for density because of the larger framebuffer and 4 (less powerful) GPUs. The K2 "only" contained 2 GPUs and 8 GB of framebuffer, but it was a card capable of great performance. The challenge with the card was the limited framebuffer size of 4 GB per profile. Especially for use cases requiring more memory, this was a big limitation.

Another challenge with the Kepler-based cards was that they weren't purposely built for encoding Blast Extreme traffic (which leverages H.264 encoding). They could do it, but the result wasn't the same as with the newer architectures. Still, for a long time, the

Kepler architecture with vGPU ruled the world. But as time went by and NVIDIA continued building bigger, better and faster GPU architectures, something needed to happen in the vGPU space. And it did.

One of the disadvantages of the K1 and K2 cards was the limited density on a single card when larger framebuffers per desktop began to be the standard. Therefore, when NVIDIA came out with the NVIDIA Maxwell architecture, one of the new GPU virtualization cards announced was the Tesla M10 – a single card that had 4 GPUs with 8 GB framebuffer per GPU. This card was purposely designed for density. When using Windows 7 with 512MB profiles, up to 64 users could share a single card. Most systems from vendors like HP and Dell could easily fit two M10s in a single host (with 3 cards becoming a new standard since 2018), so 128 users could be running on that same host, including graphical acceleration. Great stuff! Also based on the Maxwell architecture, was the more higher-end Tesla M60. The M60 had 2 GPUs with 8GB framebuffer per GPU and was primarily meant for use cases that required more power (such as engineering designers).

The Maxwell architecture also brought cards that could be used with blade servers. The M6 contained a single GPU (the same as the M60 has) and had 8GB of framebuffer. As just one M6 could fit in a regular blade server, it is not a card built to create a high density of graphical accelerated users on a single host. There are workstation blades that have options to include more than one card, but they aren't really mainstream for VDI workloads.

Another great feature of the Maxwell-based cards was that they were also built to encode H.264 streams. Besides lowering CPU usage on a desktop (because rendering could be offloaded to the GPU), encoding could also be offloaded.

Maxwell's successor was the NVIDIA Pascal architecture, a more powerful architecture which has brought the P-series cards. The Tesla P40 and the Tesla P4 are also built for the somewhat more demanding use cases. The P40 and P4 both have a single GPU, but the P40 has 24 GB of framebuffer and its smaller half-height and single slot cousin has 8GB of framebuffer. With the 24 GB of framebuffer linked to a single GPU, the P40 is the only card that could offer you a massive framebuffer of 24 GB for a single desktop if a use case requires this. Another innovation that the Pascal architecture brought, is *Hardware Preemption Support*. In the Maxwell and Kepler architectures, CUDA support was only available when using the maximum Q profile (MXX-8Q for a Maxwell card or KX80Q for a Kepler card). This dedicated an entire GPU to a single virtual desktop and let you benefit from the CUDA cores on the cards.

With hardware preemption support, Pascal cards will allow you to support CUDA on all profiles. This enables high-end applications to use smaller NVIDIA Virtual Datacenter Workstation (Quadro vDWS) profiles instead of having to have an entire GPU dedicated to that specific user.

Early in 2018, NVIDIA announced the NVIDIA Volta architecture. The Tesla V100 is the first GPU based on the Volta architecture that can be used for graphical acceleration in VDI. It is (of course) faster and more powerful than the cards with the Pascal architecture and could have a massive 32 GB of framebuffer on a single GPU.

To give you an idea of what the difference in specifications is, I created a table that shows specifications like the number of GPUs, framebuffer, encoding streams, etc. All cards are displayed starting with the Kepler architecture and newer.

| Card | GPU | CUDA Cores | Framebuffer size | Encoding\decoding | Max profiles | Form factor | Power | Cooling |
|---|---|---|---|---|---|---|---|---|
| GRID K1 | 4 x Kepler | 768 | 16 GB DDR3 (4 GB per GPU) | 360 FPS | 32 | Dual PCIe | 130 W | Passive |

| Card | GPU | CUDA Cores | Framebuffer size | Encoding\decoding | Max profiles | Form factor | Power | Cooling |
|---|---|---|---|---|---|---|---|---|
| GRID K2 | 2 x Kepler (high-end) | 3,072 | 8 GB DDR3 (4 GB per GPU) | 180 FPS | 16 | Dual PCIe | 225 W | Passive |
| Tesla M10 | 4 x Mid-level Maxwell | 2,560 | 32 GB DDR5 (8 per GPU) | 840 FPS | 32 | Dual PCIe | 240 W – 300 W | Passive |
| Tesla M6 | 1 x High-end Maxwell | 1,536 | 8 GB DDR5 | 540 FPS | 8 | MX M | 100 W | Relies on blade cooling |
| Tesla M60 | 2 x High-end Maxwell | 4,096 | 16 GB DDR5 (8 per GPU) | 1080 FPS | 16 | Dual PCIe | 240 W – 300 W | Active/ Passive |
| Tesla P6 | 1 x Pascal | 2,048 | 16 GB DDR5 | 720 FPS | 16 | MX M | 90W | Relies on blade cooling |
| Tesla P4 | 1 x Pascal | 2,560 | 8 GB DDR5 | 720 FPS | 8 | Single PCIe | 75W | Passive |
| Tesla P40 | 1 x Pascal | 3,840 | 24 GB DDR5 | 720 FPS | 24 | Dual PCIe | 250 W | Passive |
| Tesla P100 | 1 x Pascal | 3,584 | 16 GB CoWos HBM2 | 1080 FPS | 16 | Dual PCIe | 250 W | Passive |
| Tesla V100 | 1 x Volta | 5,120 | 16 GB CoWos HBM2 | 1080 FPS | 16 | Dual PCIe | 250 W | Passive |
| Tesla V100 | 1 x Volta | 5,120 | 32 GB CoWos HBM2 | 1080 FPS | 16 | Dual PCIe | 250 W | Passive |

The following table displays the profile specifications for every card:

| Card | vGPU Profile | Use case | Framebuffer size | Virtual display heads | Resolution per display | Max vGPUs per GPU | Max vGPUs per card | Required license |
|------|------|------|------|------|------|------|------|------|
| GRID K1 | K120Q | Power user | 512 MB | 2 | 2560 x 1600 | 8 | 32 | - |
| GRID K1 | K140Q | Power user | 1 GB | 2 | 2560 x 1600 | 4 | 16 | - |
| GRID K1 | K160Q | Power user | 2 GB | 4 | 2560 x 1600 | 2 | 8 | - |
| GRID K1 | K180Q | Light designer | 4 GB | 4 | 2560 x 1600 | 1 | 4 | - |
| GRID K2 | K220Q | Power user | 512 MB | 2 | 2560 x 1600 | 8 | 16 | - |
| GRID K2 | K240Q | Power user | 1 GB | 2 | 2560 x 1600 | 4 | 8 | - |
| GRID K2 | K260Q | Power user | 2 GB | 4 | 2560 x 1600 | 2 | 4 | - |
| GRID K2 | K280Q | Power user | 4 GB | 4 | 2560 x 1600 | 1 | 2 | - |
| Tesla M10 | M10-1A | RDS Apps | 1 GB | 1 | 1280 x 1024 | 8 | 32 | vApp |
| Tesla M10 | M10-2A | RDS Apps | 2 GB | 1 | 1280 x 1024 | 4 | 16 | vApp |
| Tesla M10 | M10-4A | RDS Apps | 4 GB | 1 | 1280 x 1024 | 2 | 8 | vApp |
| Tesla M10 | M10-8A | RDS Apps | 8 GB | 1 | 1280 x 1024 | 1 | 4 | vApp |
| Tesla M10[1] | M10-0B | Power user | 512 MB | 2 | 2560 x 1600 | 16 | 64 | vPC |

| Card | vGPU Profile | Use case | Framebuffer size | Virtual display heads | Resolution per display | Max vGPUs per GPU | Max vGPUs per card | Max vGPUs per GPU | Required license |
|---|---|---|---|---|---|---|---|---|---|
| Tesla M10 | M10-1B | Power user | 1 GB | 4 | 2560 x 1600 | | 8 | 32 | vPC |
| Tesla M10 | M10-2B | Power user | 2 GB | 4 | 4096 x 2160 | | 4 | 16 | vPC |
| Tesla M10 | M10-0Q | Power user / designer | 512 MB | 2 | 2560 x 1600 | | 16 | 64 | vDWS |
| Tesla M10 | M10-1Q | Power user / designer | 1 GB | 2 | 4096 x 2160 | | 8 | 32 | vDWS |
| Tesla M10 | M10-2Q | Designer | 2 GB | 4 | 4096 x 2160 | | 4 | 16 | vDWS |
| Tesla M10 | M10-4Q | Designer | 4 GB | 4 | 4096 x 2160 | | 2 | 8 | vDWS |
| Tesla M10 | M10-8Q | Designer | 8 GB | 4 | 4096 x 2160 | | 1 | 4 | vDWS |
| Tesla M6 | M6-1A | RDS Apps | 1 GB | 1 | 1280 x 1024 | | 8 | 8 | vApp |
| Tesla M6 | M6-2A | RDS Apps | 2 GB | 1 | 1280 x 1024 | | 4 | 4 | vApp |
| Tesla M6 | M6-4A | RDS Apps | 4 GB | 1 | 1280 x 1024 | | 2 | 2 | vApp |
| Tesla M6 | M6-8A | RDS Apps | 8 GB | 1 | 1280 x 1024 | | 1 | 1 | vApp |
| Tesla M6 [1] | M6-0B | Power user | 512 MB | 2 | 2560 x 1600 | | 16 | 16 | vPC |
| Tesla M6 | M6-1B | Power user | 1 GB | 4 | 2560 x 1600 | | 8 | 8 | vPC |
| Tesla M6 | M6-2B | Power user | 2 GB | 2 | 4096 x 2160 | | 4 | 4 | vPC |

| Card | vGPU Profile | Use case | Framebuffer size | Virtual display heads | Resolution per display | Max vGPUs per GPU | Max vGPUs per card | Required license |
|---|---|---|---|---|---|---|---|---|
| Tesla M10 | M6-0Q | Power user / designer | 512 MB | 2 | 2560 x 1600 | 16 | 16 | vDWS |
| Tesla M6 | M6-1Q | Power user / designer | 1 GB | 2 | 4096 x 2160 | 8 | 8 | vDWS |
| Tesla M6 | M6-2Q | Designer | 2 GB | 4 | 4096 x 2160 | 4 | 4 | vDWS |
| Tesla M6 | M6-4Q | Designer | 4 GB | 4 | 4096 x 2160 | 2 | 2 | vDWS |
| Tesla M6 | M6-8Q | Designer | 8 GB | 4 | 4096 x 2160 | 1 | 1 | vDWS |
| Tesla M60 | M60-1A | RDS Apps | 1 GB | 1 | 1280 x 1024 | 8 | 16 | vApp |
| Tesla M60 | M60-2A | RDS Apps | 2 GB | 1 | 1280 x 1024 | 4 | 8 | vApp |
| Tesla M60 | M60-4A | RDS Apps | 4 GB | 1 | 1280 x 1024 | 2 | 4 | vApp |
| Tesla M60 | M60-8A | RDS Apps | 8 GB | 1 | 1280 x 1024 | 1 | 2 | vApp |
| Tesla M60 [1] | M60-0B | Power user | 512 MB | 2 | 2560 x 1600 | 16 | 32 | vPC |
| Tesla M60 | M60-1B | Power user | 1 GB | 4 | 2560 x 1600 | 8 | 16 | vPC |
| Tesla M60 | M60-2B | Power user | 2 GB | 2 | 4096 x 2160 | 4 | 8 | vPC |
| Tesla M10 | M60-0Q | Power user / designer | 512 MB | 2 | 2560 x 1600 | 16 | 32 | vDWS |
| Tesla M60 | M60-1Q | Power user / designer | 1 GB | 2 | 4096 x 2160 | 8 | 16 | vDWS |

| Card | vGPU Profile | Use case | Framebuffer size | Virtual display heads | Resolution per display | Max vGPUs per GPU | Max vGPUs per card | Required license |
|---|---|---|---|---|---|---|---|---|
| Tesla M60 | M60-2Q | Designer | 2 GB | 4 | 4096 x 2160 | 4 | 8 | vDWS |
| Tesla M60 | M60-4Q | Designer | 4 GB | 4 | 4096 x 2160 | 2 | 4 | vDWS |
| Tesla M60 | M60-8Q | Designer | 8 GB | 4 | 4096 x 2160 | 1 | 2 | vDWS |
| Tesla P6 | P6-1A | RDS Apps | 1 GB | 1 | 1280 x 1024 | 16 | 16 | vApp |
| Tesla P6 | P6-2A | RDS Apps | 2 GB | 1 | 1280 x 1024 | 8 | 8 | vApp |
| Tesla P6 | P6-4A | RDS Apps | 4 GB | 1 | 1280 x 1024 | 4 | 4 | vApp |
| Tesla P6 | P6-8A | RDS Apps | 8 GB | 1 | 1280 x 1024 | 2 | 2 | vApp |
| Tesla P6 | P6-16A | RDS Apps | 16 GB | 1 | 1280 x 1024 | 1 | 1 | vApp |
| Tesla P6 | P6-1B | Power user | 1 GB | 4 | 2560 x 1600 | 16 | 16 | vPC |
| Tesla P6 | P6-2B | Power user | 2 GB | 2 | 4096 x 2160 | 8 | 8 | vPC |
| Tesla P6 | P6-1Q | Power user / designer | 1 GB | 2 | 4096 x 2160 | 16 | 16 | vDWS |
| Tesla P6 | P6-2Q | Designer | 2 GB | 4 | 4096 x 2160 | 8 | 8 | vDWS |
| Tesla P6 | P6-4Q | Designer | 4 GB | 4 | 4096 x 2160 | 4 | 4 | vDWS |
| Tesla P6 | P6-8Q | Designer | 8 GB | 4 | 4096 x 2160 | 2 | 2 | vDWS |

| Card | vGPU Profile | Use case | Framebuffer size | Virtual display heads | Resolution per display | Max vGPUs per GPU | Max vGPUs per card | Required license |
|---|---|---|---|---|---|---|---|---|
| Tesla P6 | P6-16Q | Designer | 16 GB | 4 | 4096 x 2160 | 1 | 1 | vDWS |
| Tesla P4 | P4-1A | RDS Apps | 1 GB | 1 | 1280 x 1024 | 8 | 8 | vApp |
| Tesla P4 | P4-2A | RDS Apps | 2 GB | 1 | 1280 x 1024 | 4 | 4 | vApp |
| Tesla P4 | P4-4A | RDS Apps | 4 GB | 1 | 1280 x 1024 | 2 | 2 | vApp |
| Tesla P4 | P4-8A | RDS Apps | 8 GB | 1 | 1280 x 1024 | 1 | 1 | vApp |
| Tesla P4 | P4-1B | Power user | 1 GB | 4 | 2560 x 1600 | 8 | 8 | vPC |
| Tesla P4 | P4-2B | Power user | 2 GB | 2 | 4096 x 2160 | 4 | 4 | vPC |
| Tesla P4 | P4-1Q | Power user / designer | 1 GB | 2 | 4096 x 2160 | 8 | 8 | vDWS |
| Tesla P4 | P4-2Q | Designer | 2 GB | 4 | 4096 x 2160 | 4 | 4 | vDWS |
| Tesla P4 | P4-4Q | Designer | 4 GB | 4 | 4096 x 2160 | 2 | 2 | vDWS |
| Tesla P4 | P4-8Q | Designer | 8 GB | 4 | 4096 x 2160 | 1 | 1 | vDWS |
| Tesla P40 | P40-1A | RDS Apps | 1 GB | 1 | 1280 x 1024 | 24 | 24 | vApp |
| Tesla P40 | P40-2A | RDS Apps | 2 GB | 1 | 1280 x 1024 | 12 | 12 | vApp |
| Tesla P40 | P40-4A | RDS Apps | 4 GB | 1 | 1280 x 1024 | 6 | 6 | vApp |

| Card | vGPU Profile | Use case | Framebuffer size | Virtual display heads | Resolution per display | Max vGPUs per GPU | Max vGPUs per card | Required license |
|------|-------------|----------|-----------------|----------------------|----------------------|-------------------|--------------------|------------------|
| Tesla P40 | P40-8A | RDS Apps | 8 GB | 1 | 1280 x 1024 | 3 | 3 | vApp |
| Tesla P40 | P40-12A | RDS Apps | 12 GB | 1 | 1280 x 1024 | 2 | 2 | vApp |
| Tesla P40 | P40-24A | RDS Apps | 24 GB | 1 | 1280 x 1024 | 1 | 1 | vApp |
| Tesla P40 | P40-1B | Power user | 1 GB | 4 | 2560 x 1600 | 24 | 24 | vPC |
| Tesla P40 | P40-2B | Power user | 2 GB | 2 | 4096 x 2160 | 12 | 12 | vPC |
| Tesla P40 | P40-1Q | Power user / designer | 1 GB | 2 | 4096 x 2160 | 24 | 24 | vDWS |
| Tesla P40 | P40-2Q | Designer | 2 GB | 4 | 4096 x 2160 | 12 | 12 | vDWS |
| Tesla P40 | P40-4Q | Designer | 4 GB | 4 | 4096 x 2160 | 6 | 6 | vDWS |
| Tesla P40 | P40-8Q | Designer | 8 GB | 4 | 4096 x 2160 | 3 | 3 | vDWS |
| Tesla P40 | P40-12Q | Designer | 12 GB | 4 | 4096 x 2160 | 2 | 2 | vDWS |
| Tesla P40 | P40-24Q | Designer | 24 GB | 4 | 4096 x 2160 | 1 | 1 | vDWS |
| Tesla P100 | P100-1A | RDS Apps | 1 GB | 1 | 1280 x 1024 | 16 | 16 | vApp |
| Tesla P100 | P100-2A | RDS Apps | 2 GB | 1 | 1280 x 1024 | 8 | 8 | vApp |
| Tesla P100 | P100-4A | RDS Apps | 4 GB | 1 | 1280 x 1024 | 4 | 4 | vApp |

| Card | vGPU Profile | Use case | Framebuffer size | Virtual display heads | Resolution per display | Max vGPUs per GPU | Max vGPUs per card | Required license |
|---|---|---|---|---|---|---|---|---|
| Tesla P100 | P100-8A | RDS Apps | 8 GB | 1 | 1280 x 1024 | 2 | 2 | vApp |
| Tesla P100 | P100-16A | RDS Apps | 16 GB | 1 | 1280 x 1024 | 1 | 1 | vApp |
| Tesla P100 | P100-1B | Power user | 1 GB | 4 | 2560 x 1600 | 16 | 16 | vPC |
| Tesla P100 | P100-2B | Power user | 2 GB | 2 | 4096 x 2160 | 8 | 8 | vPC |
| Tesla P100 | P100-1Q | Power user / designer | 1 GB | 2 | 4096 x 2160 | 16 | 16 | vDWS |
| Tesla P100 | P100-2Q | Designer | 2 GB | 4 | 4096 x 2160 | 8 | 8 | vDWS |
| Tesla P100 | P100-4Q | Designer | 4 GB | 4 | 4096 x 2160 | 4 | 4 | vDWS |
| Tesla P100 | P100-8Q | Designer | 8 GB | 4 | 4096 x 2160 | 2 | 2 | vDWS |
| Tesla P100 | P100-16Q | Designer | 16 GB | 4 | 4096 x 2160 | 1 | 1 | vDWS |
| Tesla V100 | V100-1A | RDS Apps | 1 GB | 1 | 1280 x 1024 | 16 | 16 | vApp |
| Tesla V100 | V100-2A | RDS Apps | 2 GB | 1 | 1280 x 1024 | 8 | 8 | vApp |
| Tesla V100 | V100-4A | RDS Apps | 4 GB | 1 | 1280 x 1024 | 4 | 4 | vApp |
| Tesla V100 | V100-8A | RDS Apps | 8 GB | 1 | 1280 x 1024 | 2 | 2 | vApp |
| Tesla V100 | V100-16A | RDS Apps | 16 GB | 1 | 1280 x 1024 | 1 | 1 | vApp |

| Card | vGPU Profile | Use case | Framebuffer size | Virtual display heads | Resolution per display | Max vGPUs per GPU | Max vGPUs per card | Max vGPUs per card | Required license |
|------|-------------|----------|-------------|-------|-------------|------|------|------|------|
| Tesla V100 | V100-32A | RDS Apps | 32 GB | 1 | 1280 x 1024 | 1 | 1 | | vApp |
| Tesla V100 | V100-1B | Power user | 1 GB | 4 | 2560 x 1600 | 16 | 16 | | vPC |
| Tesla V100 | V100-2B | Power user | 2 GB | 2 | 4096 x 2160 | 8 | 8 | | vPC |
| Tesla V100 | V100-1Q | Power user / designer | 1 GB | 2 | 4096 x 2160 | 16 | 16 | | vDWS |
| Tesla V100 | V100-2Q | Designer | 2 GB | 4 | 4096 x 2160 | 8 | 8 | | vDWS |
| Tesla V100 | V100-4Q | Designer | 4 GB | 4 | 4096 x 2160 | 4 | 4 | | vDWS |
| Tesla V100 | V100-8Q | Designer | 8 GB | 4 | 4096 x 2160 | 2 | 2 | | vDWS |
| Tesla V100 | V100-16Q | Designer | 16 GB | 4 | 4096 x 2160 | 1 | 1 | | vDWS |
| Tesla V100 | V100-32Q | Designer | 32 GB | 4 | 4096 x 2160 | 1 | 1 | | vDWS |

[1] Only supported by the Maxwell architecture, but as Windows 7 with multiple displays or Windows 10 with a single display easily takes more than 512 MB of framebuffer, use cases are limited.

As more architectures are released and updates of the virtual GPU software could contain additional features or updated ones, it's always wise to check the NVIDIA online documentation at: https://docs.nvidia.com/grid/latest/grid-vgpu-user-guide/

The name of the profiles that can be assigned to a virtual desktop is based on the type of the card (first couple of letters) followed by a dash and the framebuffer size (first number) and the type of virtual GPU license last letter). More about licensing can be found in the licensing section.

# GPU Scheduler

Let's dive a little bit deeper into the architecture. Like I explained, scheduling the resources on a GPU works a little bit like how vSphere handles its hardware resources (like CPU and RAM). Like a hypervisor, the type of scheduler to use will depend on your use case. There are three different scheduling modes that can be used and they all have their specific use cases.

## Best Effort

This was the first scheduling mode that NVIDIA developed to share GPU resources amongst multiple virtual desktops. The *Best Effort* scheduler is based on a time sliced round robin mechanism which means that it divides the GPU resources to virtual desktops based on the demand. If in a single cycle, 3 virtual desktops request resources, the scheduler will allocate those resources on a first come, first serve basis. VM 1 requests 62.5% of the resources, VM 2 requests 25% of the resources and VM 3 requests 12.5% of the resources. If, in this case, a fourth virtual desktop will request resources, it has to wait until the next cycle.

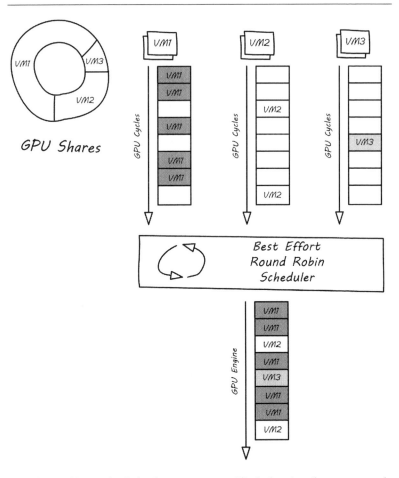

GPU Shares

Best Effort
Round Robin
Scheduler

The best effort scheduler has some specific behavior that you need to take into account before you might consider this scheduling mode. First of all, the advantage is that all virtual desktops will be able to utilize the full GPU engine during a cycle. Also, the GPU engine will be constantly busy as no idle cycles are allocated to virtual desktops.

This has also some disadvantages, though. If (hypothetically speaking) a virtual desktop is requesting resources, but the GPU engine is busy handling the resources from other virtual desktops, this will impact your graphical performance. Compare it to *ready times* in a virtual machine. If a physical CPU is too busy, it won't be able to schedule the virtual CPU cycles in time and the virtual desktop has to wait (which causes performance issues). When the GPU is rendering graphics to be displayed on the remote display, this scheduler method generally works well because the GPU can typically complete all the work in the allotted time slice. CUDA jobs, however, pose a challenge because jobs can take hours to complete. Without the ability to preempt the running jobs, the CUDA jobs could fail when the time slice expired.

Another disadvantage is that no resources can be pre-allocated. If you would like to reserve resources for some of your high demanding virtual desktops, you will have a challenge. The Best Effort scheduler isn't able to protect you from *noisy neighbors*. If a virtual desktop is demanding a lot of resources, it might impact the performance of other virtual desktops, as no resources can be allocated to every virtual desktop that utilizes a single GPU. Noisy neighbor issues are quite uncommon, but hypothetically can happen, so keep this in mind. To minimize the risk, Maxwell boards have a Frame Rate Limiter (FRL).

Overall, the Best Effort scheduler performs great. It allows the maximum output of the GPU with still a high QoS. For some use cases, the scheduler might be less suitable. This scheduler is the only one supported for Kepler and Maxwell-based cards. If you are requiring CUDA, please note that the Kepler and Maxwell-based cards together with the Best Effort scheduler aren't your best pick.

## Equal Share

The *Equal Share* scheduler mode offers a different mechanism to schedule tasks on the GPU. As the name suggests, it aims at making sure each virtual desktop gets an equal share of the GPU cycles.

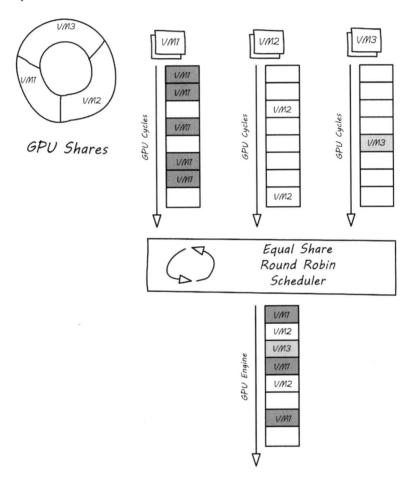

As the diagram shows, the scheduler still uses a round robin mechanism to schedule tasks from VMs but differs from the Best Effort scheduler because it assigns a time slice to every virtual desktop whose round robin turn comes up. If the virtual desktop has no task, then the GPU sits idle for that duration. This leads to a different execution sequence on the GPU engine. As you can see, the GPU Engine toggles between the 3 VMs for the exact duration of its time slice, leading to a fair division of the GPU cycles per virtual desktop.

When a virtual desktop is added or removed on a host with graphical acceleration enabled, the GPU cycles will now get shared amongst the remaining virtual desktops still active on the host. In the example above when VM 3 is removed, the remaining two VMs share the GPU cycles equally.

The advantage of the Equal Share scheduler mode is that it supports both graphical rendering tasks as well as CUDA-related tasks. It will also support a kind of Quality of Service, as it will allocate GPU resources based on the virtual desktops that demand resources. So, if eight virtual desktops can utilize the GPU, the scheduler will divide the resources among those eight if they are all running workloads that demand graphical acceleration. If one is not, the GPU will be shared amongst the seven that are running.

Another advantage is that the Equal Share scheduler has a form of noisy neighbor protection because it will make sure that every virtual machine will get an equal chunk of resources during a single cycle.

*Please note that the Equal Share scheduler is only available for the Pascal and later architectures.*

## Fixed Share

The *Fixed Share* scheduler mode is the latest addition to the scheduler architecture and offers a different mechanism to schedule tasks on the GPU. Like the other scheduler, the fixed share scheduler is also based on round robin. As the name suggests, it aims at making sure each virtual desktop gets a fixed share of the GPU cycles.

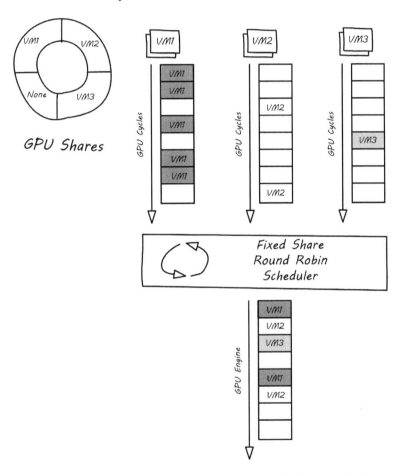

In this diagram, the scheduler still uses a round robin mechanism to schedule tasks from virtual desktops. Where it differs from the equal share scheduler is that it schedules a virtual desktop's GPU workloads based on its allocated share (irrespective of any other virtual desktops on the GPU). If the virtual desktop has no task, then the GPU sits idle for that duration.

This way of scheduling (like the others) has both advantages and disadvantages and should be used in specific use cases. The first major disadvantage is that the allocated GPU shares can't be used by other virtual desktops when a virtual desktop is idle. The GPU engine is completely pre-allocated. Of course, this is expected behavior. but this makes it also usable for use cases where you need to guarantee that a virtual desktop receives the resources it needs. The most important use case that comes to mind is a Desktop as a Service-based virtual desktop. If a customer pays for a guaranteed GPU performance and receives a Quality of Service in return, this will be the scheduler mode to pick. Another use case that might benefit would be for traders. If a trader (especially a micro trader) has a tiny latency, it could already cost money to a trading company. This is a perfect example of a use case that requires a guaranteed GPU performance.

*Like the Equal Share scheduler, the Fixed Share scheduler is only available for Pascal and later architectures.*

# LICENSING

The NVIDIA vGPU solution doesn't only rely on hardware, the scheduler, and drivers. It also has a licensing component that enables feature sets and is also required to use the GPU in general. The licensing component was introduced in NVIDIA vGPU release version 2 and based on the type of use cases, different licenses might be used. As of release version 6, the licensing model looks like this:

| Feature | GRID Virtual Apps (GRID vApp) | GRID Virtual PC (GRID vPC) | Quadro Virtual Datacenter Workstation (Quadro vDWS) |
|---|---|---|---|
| Concurrent user (CCU) | Yes | Yes | Yes |
| Desktop virtualization | - | Yes | Yes |
| RDSH App hosting | Yes | Yes | Yes [1] |
| Windows guest operating system | Yes | Yes | Yes |
| Linux guest operating system | - | Yes | Yes |
| Max displays | 1 | 2 at 4096 x 2160 4 at 2560 x 1600 | 4 |
| Max resolution | - | 4096 x 2160 | 4096 x 2160 |
| Quadro performance features and optimization | - | No | Yes |
| CUDA | Yes [2] | No | Yes [3] |
| OpenCL | Yes [2] | No | Yes [3] |
| GPU pass-through | Yes | No | Yes |
| Baremetal support | Yes | No | Yes |
| 1 GB profile support | Yes | Yes | Yes |
| 2 GB profile support | Yes | Yes | Yes |
| 4 GB profile support | Yes | - | Yes |
| 6 GB profile support | Yes | - | Yes |
| 8 GB profile support | Yes | - | Yes |

| Feature | GRID Virtual Apps (GRID vApp) | GRID Virtual PC (GRID vPC) | Quadro Virtual Datacenter Workstation (Quadro vDWS) |
|---|---|---|---|
| 12 GB profile support [4] | Yes | - | Yes |
| 16 GB profile support [5] | Yes | - | Yes |
| 24 GB profile support [4] | Yes | - | Yes |
| 32 GB profile support [6] | Yes | - | Yes |

[1] Packaged GRID vApps license required
[2] Only supported for Maxwell 8A profile on GRID 4.x and earlier releases
[3] Supported on 8GB 1:1 profile on Maxwell and all profiles on Pascal
[4] Only supported by the Tesla P40 cards
[5] Only supported by the Tesla P6, P100 and V100 cards
[5] Only supported by the V100 cards with 32 GB

There are three different license types available that all have their own price tag and specific use case. GRID Virtual Apps is the one specifically designed for RDSH (so, just Remote Apps). GRID Virtual PC is suitable for use cases that don't require powerful GPU support and Quadro features. Quadro Virtual Datacenter Workstation is specifically for use cases that normally also use a Quadro-based GPU in their physical desktop and require a framebuffer that isn't limited to 2 GB (since GRID Virtual PC is limited to 2 GB only).

More about licensing (including the different models, such as educational licenses), can be found in the NVIDIA vGPU licensing guide:

https://images.nvidia.com/content/grid/pdf/161207-GRID-Packaging-and-Licensing-Guide.pdf

More about licensing from a technical perspective can be found here:

https://docs.nvidia.com/grid/latest/grid-licensing-user-guide/index.html

## Licensing Server

One of the components in the NVIDIA vGPU deployment is the license server. The license server can either run on a Windows or Linux server and due to availability demands, it is very wise to run it inside a VM. If your requirements will demand a higher availability, a secondary license server can be deployed as a backup in an active/passive setup.

If you are designing the license server in HA mode, please take the following into account:

- Both servers must run the same version of the NVIDIA vGPU Software License Server software.
- The clocks on both servers must be accurate and synchronized. NTP is recommended.
- The same license configuration file must be installed on both servers. This file is configured to include the Ethernet MAC addresses of both servers.

Please check the following link for more information on how to implement a secondary license server including failover capabilities:

https://docs.nvidia.com/grid/latest/grid-license-server-user-guide/index.html#enabling-failover-support-primary-secondary-servers

# USE CASES

In the process of figuring out what use cases might benefit from a GPU, it will (again) help to run a desktop and application assessment first. Based on the outcome of the assessment, you should be able to add them to one of the following three categories.

## Use Cases that Require a GPU

These are the easiest if you ask me. If you take away the VDI part and focus on how a particular use case (such as a graphical designer) is doing the job right now, would it make sense to do this without a GPU? If the answer is no, then this user belongs to this use case.

The following list describes the applications of which history has told us that running them without a GPU is an evil plan.

| Application name |
|---|
| 3DEXCITE |
| Adobe Creative Suite |
| ArcGIS |
| AUTODESK AUTOCAD |
| AUTODESK MAYA |
| AUTODESK REVIT |
| CATIA |
| Petrel |
| Siemens NX |
| SOLIDWORKS |

Each of these applications can benefit from a GPU since they can leverage the power of a supporting API (such as CUDA, OpenGL, Direct3D).

A full list of these applications can be found on the following location:

http://www.nvidia.com/content/gpu-applications/PDF/gpu-applications-catalog.pdf

Please note that to perform reasonably, some applications, such as SOLIDWORKS, requires Quadro support and hence will dictate the type of profile and license needed!

## Use Cases that can definitely work without a GPU

Users that belong to this use case are the next in line if you talk *easy*. A GPU isn't required to achieve an expected user experience. For these use cases, a GPU would mean that you are overdoing stuff. A kiosk pc is a good example. I've seen customers add a Virtual PC type license and accompanied GRID profile to a virtual desktop pool of kiosk desktops. If the kiosk pc doesn't run any applications that are listed in the previous section or the assessment output wouldn't demand any graphical acceleration, it wouldn't make any sense. The one thing you need to remember is that you need to take specific limitations in user experience into account. Don't expect a 4K resolution and 60 FPS. If you are aware of these constraints and accept them, you are all good. A GPU wouldn't make any sense and will only improve in terms of a somewhat smoother experience (which the average kiosk pc user isn't expecting, anyway).

## Use Cases that might work without a GPU

There are certain use cases that might work without a GPU, but the question is what the impact will be? Are users still able to work like they were used to on a physical desktop? Are they experiencing the same user experience? And what about sizing and density? What impact will the possible increase of CPU load mean to the overall performance and density of the VDI solution? These are a lot of questions that might be difficult to answer. In this section, I am going to give you some more guidance that will help you get a better understanding of the impact of a GPU (or the decision to design without them).

The biggest cause for an unclear answer to these questions is Windows 10 and applications purposely built for this latest Microsoft operating system. When companies were still running on Windows 7, everything was pretty straightforward. Windows 7 itself didn't require a GPU to run pretty smoothly, even with 2 monitors on 1080p. Everything became different when Microsoft decided that Windows 10 and applications that are made for Windows 10 should be using DirectX and OpenGL to basically render EVERYTHING. Windows 10 was built with hardware acceleration in mind. Without a physical GPU, the CPU and RAM of a virtual desktop will have to endure more because a GPU will be emulated. Unfortunately, this goes for modern browsers and apps like Microsoft Office 2016 as well. It doesn't mean that it won't work, but you do have to set expectations with your end-users. This makes it the hardest use case to decide if they require a GPU.

In terms of requirements, the decision on whether to use a GPU or not can be made easier. The following requirements will most likely force you into using GPUs:

- Video content needs to be streamed with resolutions over 720p with at least a smooth 30 FPS.
- 2+ monitors need to be supported.
- 4K needs to be supported.
- Applications require the use of an API (like OpenGL and CUDA).
- Skype for Business (or a similar application) needs to be included with A/V integration (and offloading to a Windows endpoint isn't possible).
- The images should be displayed uncompressed (or lossless).

The above requirements are all undebatable, as they are factual. If you decide to run without a GPU, you will have a challenge. If you exceed 2 monitors, you will see the user experience drop. If you have to run WebGL without a GPU, you will see the user experience drop. Streaming 1080p video at 60 FPS is almost undoable without a GPU. It's simple. It might work for a single session, but what happens if you run fifty of them on the same host without a GPU? It will end up in a very unpleasant situation.

There are some debatable requirements as well.

- The user experience must be equal or better after migrating from a physical to a virtual desktop.
- Users must not experience any delays in their daily work.
- Windows 10 must be used as the virtual desktop operating system.

If you have to fill in these requirements, it's not set in stone that a GPU is required. If a customer demands that the user experience is at least as good as it is on their physical machine, does that require a GPU? The obvious answer is again *it depends*. With that requirement alone, you aren't able to fill this in. You need additional information to be able to create a solid advice, especially information as to what the user is expecting. That is where you should take up this discussion. Get as many details as possible to get a perfect understanding of what the user is going to expect. As soon as something is open to interpretation, it might end up in a displeased customer. Questions that absolutely need to be answered are:

- What is the user doing?
- What kind of applications?
- Are there features in the application that can benefit from acceleration by a GPU?
- Are they browser-based? Which browser?
- How often are they using this?
- Where is he doing this from?
    - All possible (network) locations should be taken into account.
- What kind of devices is the user using?
- What kind of physical hardware and resources?
- What kind of operating system?

- How is the user viewing this?
- What kind of monitors?
- Resolution per monitor?
- Required frame rate?
- Is it compressed?
- Is the user satisfied with this current situation? (It won't be the first situation in which the customer is requesting a similar or better user experience without knowing that the end-users are actually complaining about the current user experience)

These questions are an example of what to find out. There might be other questions that pertain to your specific situation.

Some of these questions could be answered from the assessment output, but a couple of crucial questions to user experience can't. That's why you should interact with users. Talk to them. Meet with a representative of a use case so you are 100% absolutely sure what they are expecting.

Knowing what to ask for is one thing, but what to do with the answers? If you look at the answers, I think you need to ask yourself the following questions:

- If you weren't designing VDI but were replacing the user's physical desktop with a new one, would the user also be satisfied if I wouldn't add a GPU to a physical machine?
- Are you able to tweak the user experience of a desktop so it will run as like expected by the end-user, without a GPU?

There are also some recorded differences when you look at the density of a host with and without a GPU. NVIDIA and Lakeside have used the information of over three million desktops to see what the impact of GPUs is. On an average, CPU usage can be decreased with 17% if a GPU is used. That may sound like a low number, but it all depends on the type of applications used. NVIDIA released a whitepaper which showed the difference in user experience for a couple of tasks that an average use case might perform. The user experience was measured by asking the user how they experienced the task (on a per-task basis). They could answer by selecting one of the following answers:

- 5: Outstanding. As good (or almost) as physical
- 4: Pretty good (for a virtual desktop)
- 3: Tolerable, I guess I can make do
- 2: Barely usable, borderline, I'll get tired of this soon
- 1: Unacceptable, unusable (fire someone in IT)

The tasks they performed:

- Find an email in your inbox that includes a long thread. Scroll all the way through the thread. Try a couple of times with 2 - 3 different emails. Use outlook search to find emails with specific subjects and scroll to the bottom of the list and read the email.
- Open up Internet Explorer and visit msn.com. Scroll to the bottom of the page. Use keyboard shortcuts to zoom in the page. Visit YouTube, find a movie trailer on the main page and watch it for 15 - 30 seconds. Visit the Yahoo! stocks page and open up the NVIDIA stocks.
- Use Windows Search to locate a program such as PowerPoint.
- Open PowerPoint, create a new presentation and fill it with an image. Resize the image. Copy some email data and paste it into the presentation.
- Open up Internet Explorer and visit a WebGL application such as the Hello Racer. Interact with the WebGL application.
- Open up Internet Explorer and visit Google Maps. Locate a specific address. Click on street view and interact in the street view mode (look around, pan, zoom, etc.).

The actions were performed on virtual desktops running on top of pretty straightforward VDI hardware and software.

Server specifications:

- HP DL380 Gen9
- 2 x E5-2697 v4 with 18 cores @ 2.3GHz
- 768 GM RAM
- XtremeIO All-Flash SAN
- 10 Gbit ethernet
- 2 x NVIDIA Tesla M10 GPU

Virtualization specifications:

- VMware vSphere 6.0.0 version 3620759
- Horizon 7.0.2 with Blast Extreme
- VM hardware version 11
- Windows 10 64 bit
- 2 x vCPU
- 4 GB RAM
- M10-1B vGPU profile

GRID specifications:

- GRID version 4.0
- NVIDIA vGPU driver version 369.43
- NVIDIA VM driver version 369.17

Endpoint specifications:

- Chromebooks and laptops
- 1 Full HD monitor

The results were interesting. Testing two identical VDI environments, one with GPU acceleration and one without, showed that the environment with GPU acceleration with NVENC provided an average positive increase to user experience of 34%.

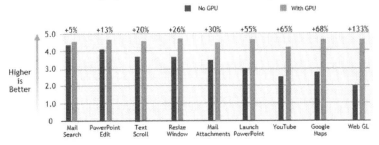

The thing that I find interesting in the previous chart is that most of the applications are usable without a GPU. But the thing is that you need to set the right expectations. Everyone was using a single display at 1080p. Based on those specs, you'd even consider not to use a GPU. But what happens if a second display or higher resolution is required? The user experience for the non-GPU sessions will most likely decrease and the benefit of a GPU will be bigger.

I know there isn't a hard number that I could give you when deciding to use a GPU or not. In case you aren't sure, try to run a proof of concept. Setting up a PoC is fairly simple. Defining a goal for the PoC is quite important. When will the PoC be successful? Define your own tests and set a minimal user experience limit. If the outcome of the tests without a GPU is below the user experience limit, you should consider using GPUs. If the outcome without GPUs exceeds your expectations, you might not consider using GPUs. It's that simple. But don't forget to test at scale! Running a single session on a host will not give you the results you need to make a good decision.

# SIZING

If you decided to go for GPUs, it's important to properly size your infrastructure. When sizing, there are a couple of different metrics and parameters you need to take into account:

- Framebuffer – the physical video memory required per desktop
- Encoding streams – the number of encoding streams per host
- Quadro – features, and functionality that requires a Quadro-based GPU and corresponding licensing

The first metric is the easiest of all. Like I explained in the general sizing section, framebuffer won't be overprovisioned. It actually *can't* be overprovisioned. Every new desktop that will be created receives a fixed part of the framebuffer that belongs to a GPU. If the framebuffer is fully allocated to existing desktops, no new desktops can be created. Thus, the limiting factor here is the number of cards that you are able to run in a particular system. Take the total size of framebuffer memory that exists on a single host and divide it by the profile size per desktop. The outcome is the maximum density of accelerated desktops on a single host. For a Tesla M10, that will be 64 if you run 1 GB profiles for GRID vPC use cases with only two cards in the host. The bigger the profile, the lower the density you will achieve. Please note that both accelerated desktops and non-accelerated desktops can run on a single host. So, the total density might be higher (accelerated + non-accelerated desktops).

The next metric is somewhat more challenging. An encoding stream is a single session that can be encoded at host level and decoded at endpoint level. The reason why this is somewhat more challenging is that the number of encoding streams on a single card isn't fixed. The number of *frames per second* that a card can encode actually is. In most GPU specification sheets, you can see that a Tesla M10, for instance, can run an average of 28 streams on 1080P with 30 frames per second. The average is based on the fact that the M10 has a maximum number of 840 frames per second that it's able to encode. If you limit your session to 15 frames per second, you would hypothetically be able to encode 56 of these streams on a single card. If (for some reason) the limit is reached, the NVENC engine will become oversaturated. As a result, roundtrip latency will increase, plus you might experience frame drops. So, please take this metric into account when sizing for GPUs. Before choosing a certain GPU, make sure that you know what the maximum number of streams is and compare it with the required frame rate. To give you an idea, if a user is only working in Microsoft Office applications and isn't watching a video, an FPS limit of 15 might be quite suitable. If the user is watching a lot of videos, you should be looking at 25 – 30 FPS.

The last item of the three, is Quadro. If you have users that require Quadro features, you need to choose the proper card(s) to run your desktops on and size the profiles according to the specifications of the application vendor. As we know from the past, the advice that vendors give might be a little exaggerated. We saw (and still see) that when vendors define CPU/RAM specifications and it might be no different with GPUs.

When sizing your GPUs, the trick is to follow your assessment data. Unfortunately, the only metric that can be assessed by the majority of solutions, is framebuffer. So, start with that. The peak average framebuffer is a good indication of what the profile size should be. Do check within the recorded metrics if users exist that have a peak that exceeds the average peak a lot. In that case, a different profile with a bigger framebuffer might be required for that use case.

To validate if the proper profile has been chosen, it's a great idea to run a pilot. After deploying the pools and GPU settings to your desktops, you can validate if the profiles were properly sized by running a community build tool called *GPUSizer* (get it at https://gpusizer.com). The GPUSizer will collect metrics like framebuffer and GPU load and will give you an advice based on the result of the collection. The advice is presented as follows:

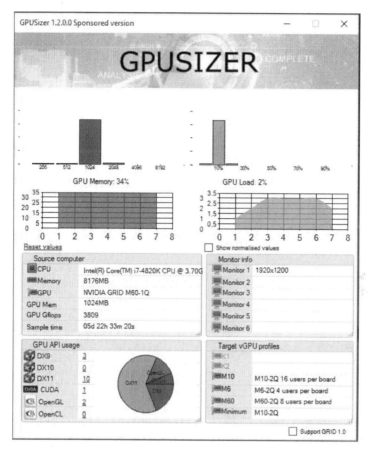

In the right bottom box, the target vGPU profiles are displayed that you could use to satisfy your GPU resource requirements. Another interesting feature is that based on your required API features, it will also advise you if Quadro features are necessary. Thus, the GPUSizer is a great tool to validate your proposed Quadro profiles, as well.

*Please note that as of this writing, the Pascal and Volta architectures weren't added yet, but the tool will still give you an advice in terms of API requirements and framebuffer size.*

From a sizing perspective, sizing for encoding streams works a bit differently. On average (and even peak average), users aren't utilizing the full power of the encoding engine. From a practical perspective, a user will only utilize the full power of the engine when watching videos or running high-end applications at a high frame rate. The frame rate, in general, might say something about the user experience. But, the question here is if a user will notice is if the video is rendered in 26 FPS instead of 30. My advice here is to also validate this by running another great community-built tool called the Remote Display Analyzer (get it at https://www.rdanalyzer.com).

The Remote Display Analyzer lets you adjust your Blast Extreme or PCoIP settings on-the-fly. The result is that you are actually able to adjust FPS settings and validate the user experience with the end-user. Other settings that can be manipulated are the minimum and maximum image quality and the encoder (switch between the software encoder and NVENC).

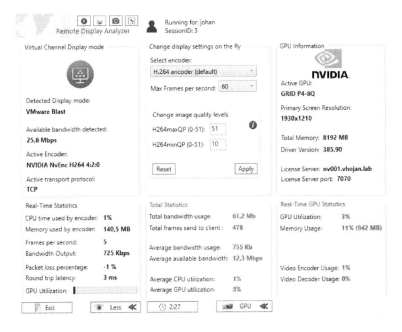

*If you are tuning the image quality, one misconception about the H264maxQP and H264minQP parameters is that 51 is the highest value and therefore, has the highest image quality. Please note that the lower the value, the higher the quality becomes. There is no guidance in terms of specific values being best practices for specific use cases, but I always*

*start with a H264maxQP of 28 and a H264minQP of 10. Adjusting the H264maxQP with higher values will result in lower image quality and less bandwidth usage.*

After tuning the FPS for a certain user or group of users (through a GPO), it is important to check the video encoder usage to make sure the encoder engine isn't being oversaturated.

Since NVIDIA has created the NVIDIA Windows Management Instrumentation (NWMI) engine to extract real-time information from the GPU and its related resources, there are multiple solutions that will help you display those metrics and possibly alert when something gets oversaturated or hits a threshold. Three examples of solutions with these capabilities are vRealize Operations (with the Management Pack for vGPU), Goliath Technologies Performance Monitor for NVIDIA vGPU and Liquidware Stratusphere UX.

All of these solutions have the ability to build a dashboard that displays the required metrics like encoder/decoder utilization, GPU utilization, and framebuffer utilization. These solutions also let you monitor individual vGPU profiles and linked desktop sessions.

Be sure to always monitor your GPUs and vGPU profiles to avoid failure and degraded performance!

The next question would be what kind of impact this might have on protocol choices.

# BLAST EXTREME AND PCOIP

Since Blast Extreme came out, one of the most asked questions around protocol choices is *Which one is better?* I don't believe one is better than the other; I believe both satisfy different use cases. A misconception quite often heard is that VMware isn't developing in PCoIP anymore. There is both a fact here as well as a bit of ignorance. First of all, I think it's true that most of the development is being done in Blast Extreme. But, have you ever thought why that is? The answer is fairly simple: PCoIP has a full, rich feature set including lots of channels that support a wide variety of use cases. Another reason might be that VMware doesn't own the PCoIP protocol, but rather, Teradici does. I'm not aware of what the license to use the protocol costs, but it's always more expensive than building, maintaining and improving your own protocol (Blast Extreme). So, would it make any sense for VMware to continue investing heavily in PCoIP? I don't think so.

I think it's all about use cases, requirements and constraints. Both protocols are really good and bring different constraints to the table. PCoIP, for instance, runs on TCP/UDP port 4172. It's impossible to tunnel it over HTTPS (443) without the use of a VPN, so in case a customer has a security requirement that all external traffic must be tunneled over HTTPS, you are unable to use PCoIP. Another perfect example is the use of zero clients as an endpoint. If a zero client model is used that requires PCoIP, you are unable to switch to Blast Extreme as most zero clients have proprietary hardware that runs PCoIP connection without an additional operating system (like a Linux or Windows operating system adjusted to run on a thin client).

Let's look at the two protocols to understand some more as to when to choose which one. PCoIP and Blast Extreme have a comparable feature set, but also some differences. The following features are equal for both protocols (and taken from the VMware Horizon documentation):

- Users outside the corporate firewall can use this protocol with your company's virtual private network (VPN), or users can make secure, encrypted connections to a security server or Unified Access Gateway appliance in the corporate DMZ.
- Advanced Encryption Standard (AES) 128-bit encryption is supported and is turned on by default. You can, however, change the encryption key cipher to AES-256.
- Connections from most types of client devices.
- Optimization controls for reducing bandwidth usage on the LAN and WAN.
- 32-bit color is supported for virtual displays.
- ClearType fonts are supported.

- Audio redirection with dynamic audio quality adjustment for LAN and WAN.
- Real-Time Audio-Video for using webcams and microphones on some client types.
- Copy and paste of text and, on some clients, images between the client operating system and a remote application or desktop. For other client types, only copy and paste of plain text is supported. You cannot copy and paste system objects such as folders and files between systems.
- Multiple monitors are supported for some client types. On some clients, you can use up to 4 monitors with a resolution of up to 2560 x 1600 per display or up to 3 monitors with a resolution of 4K (3840 x 2160) for Windows 7 remote desktops with Aero disabled. Pivot display and autofit are also supported.
- When the 3D feature is enabled, up to 2 monitors are supported with a resolution of up to 1920 x 1200 or one monitor with a resolution of 4K (3840 x 2160).
- USB redirection is supported for some client types.
- MMR redirection is supported for some Windows client operating systems and some remote desktop operating systems (with Horizon Agent installed).

As already mentioned, there are also some key differences. The differences from a PCoIP perspective are:

- PCoIP is a lossless connection protocol with the possibility to transfer pixel data uncompressed.
- Encoding and decoding of PCoIP streams can be offloaded, but specific hardware is required. For hosts, Teradici PCoIP APEX cards can be used to offload encoding. On endpoints, Teradici PCoIP decoding chips are required (which can be found in multiple types of zero & thin clients.
- Because the protocol can be transferred lossless, bandwidth consumption can be high (I have seen sessions easily running over 120 Mbps, if not tuned correctly).
- PCoIP uses TCP/UDP port 4172 for client connectivity.

The differences from a Blast Extreme perspective are:

- Blast Extreme is a lossy and compressed connection protocol that can't transfer lossless images.
- Encoding and decoding can be done in two different ways; either by JPG/PNG or H.264. When choosing JPG/PNG, encoding and decoding will always be done by the CPU as no offloading to hardware is possible. When choosing H.264, you have the ability to offload encoding and decoding to hardware (as explained in the previous section). Offloading the decoding of a stream on an endpoint is also possible as most "relatively" new endpoints support H.264 decoding natively through a GPU (like a Raspberry Pi for instance). It is also possible to decode through CPU without an enormous increase of CPU usage (but this depends on the number of displays, display resolutions and frames per second).
- In terms of bandwidth consumption, Blast Extreme is much more efficient. Especially when looking at large video streams, Blast Extreme could easily save you over 300% in bandwidth. Of course, this is partly due to the fact that the protocol doesn't have the possibility of being lossless.
- Blast Extreme uses port TCP port 8443 by default and 443 to tunnel, but HTTPS/443 can be used for both.
- Blast Extreme supports a technology called *Blast Extreme Adaptive Transport* (BEAT). BEAT will automatically switch from TCP to UDP in case the network connection between an endpoint and virtual desktop has a high latency and packet loss. TCP is intolerant to packet loss which in case of connectivity between applications and database servers is great (because you want to make sure that data is guaranteed to be transferred securely and successfully). In case of video playback, it doesn't really matter if a frame drops because the user probably doesn't notice the difference between 25 and 22 frames.
- Since Horizon 7.5, Blast Extreme has an additional feature called Blast Extreme Network Intelligent Transport (BENIT). BENIT enables you to use multiple transports dynamically based on the network conditions. It will always choose the best of the transports in terms of latency

and available bandwidth. As a result, you don't have to setup your connection type at client-level (poor, typical or excellent).

- As of this writing, H.265 and H.266 support isn't available in any of the connection protocols of Horizon. My estimate is that since H.264 encoding is supported in Horizon from a Blast Extreme perspective, H.265 and H.266 encoding might be supported, as well, in Blast Extreme.

More technical details about the Blast Extreme protocol can be found at VMware's TechZone:

https://techzone.vmware.com/resource/blast-extreme-display-protocol-vmware-horizon-7

To help you in getting an idea of what the difference is between the two protocols in terms of bandwidth, CPU usage, encoder usage, etcetera, I did a lot of research. During the research, I took a Windows 10 virtual desktop with 4 CPUs, 8 Gb of RAM and a P4-1B profile. I played a YouTube video called *Peru 8K 60FPS* (https://youtu.be/1La4QzGeaaQ) with Google Chrome and limited the frame rate to 30 FPS with RD Analyzer. The display quality in all tests was set to the highest possible. I tested Blast Extreme (including Chroma Subsampling on 4:4:4), PCoIP with and without Build to Lossless enabled. The network connection was based on LAN and the bandwidth between the endpoint and the virtual desktop was 1 GB. The following table shows some of the results.

| Metric | Blast Extreme | PCoIP with Build to Lossless disabled | PCoIP with Build to Lossless enabled |
|---|---|---|---|
| Average bandwidth usage | 10.1 Mbs | 31.6 Mbps | 59.7 Mbps |
| Average FPS | 30 | 29 | 28 |
| RTT latency | 4 ms | 12 ms | 42 ms |
| Average CPU utilization | 4% | 6% | 7% |

| Metric | Blast Extreme | PCoIP with Build to Lossless disabled | PCoIP with Build to Lossless enabled |
|---|---|---|---|
| Average GPU utilization | 11% | 22% | 25% |
| Average framebuffer usage | 994 MB | 927 MB | 930 MB |
| CPU usage time by encoder | 3% | 15% | 17% |

The video playback had the same user experience in all three different test cases. But, as you can see in the table, Blast Extreme outperforms on all different metrics (except for one little difference in framebuffer). Because of the lower outcome of the Blast Extreme metrics, Blast Extreme may let you achieve a higher density on a single host comparing to PCoIP.

As mentioned, the choice of protocol depends on your use cases, requirements and constraints. The following list shows examples of requirements that force you into choosing PCoIP over Blast Extreme:

- The solution must be able to work with Zero clients (that aren't able to run Blast Extreme).
- The solution must be able to display remote graphics uncompressed due to (medical) regulations.

If those requirements don't exist, I would always start with Blast Extreme as your primary display protocol. There are some examples of requirements and constraints, that force you into choosing Blast Extreme over PCoIP:

- The solution must be able to run all incoming traffic securely over port TCP 443 (HTTPS).
- The solution must be able to run in locations that may have high network latency and low available bandwidth.

There might be additional reasons in your specific situation. If you aren't sure which protocol to choose, it's always wise to run a proof of concept and find out.

# INTERVIEW WITH RUBEN SPRUIJT

Years back, when I was in the search of a solution that was able to run different versions of a same (dramatically) written legacy application, a young guy named Ruben Spruijt came over to show me Softricity Softgrid. I think it was around 2006 and after he demonstrated three different versions of Microsoft Office running on the same desktop, I was sold. It felt a bit like watching your first vMotion.

I kept following Ruben on the web as he started to get really involved in all kinds of communities. Being that involved would bring him a lot of recognition as he became the first European person who was acknowledged as a VMware vExpert, a Microsoft MVP and a Citrix CTP.

Ruben also (co)founded Project Virtual Reality Check (VRC) and Team RGE, which are two community groups that focus on VDI, remote graphics and applications. He was also one of the inaugural members of the NVIDIA vGPU Community Advisors (NGCA) program (like yours truly).

To me, Ruben is one of the world's best experts in the area of remote graphics and that why I asked him a couple of questions about this topic.

Me: Why did you become so involved in the remote graphics space?

Ruben: I believe it's smart to start conversations more often with *why*, so a great start ☺. That being said, there isn't a single reason why I got so involved in remote graphics space, it's a mixture of gifts, people, passion and *Just DO IT* mentality. Let me share some stories and lessons learned. I started many years ago sharing the knowledge I gained in customer and vendor engagements, product evaluation and performance benchmarking. As a result, various different *Smackdown white papers* have been created, I presented 300+ sessions at various community and leading worldwide industry events and started different community groups. Groups such as AppVirtGURU, ProjectVRC, VDILikeAPro, WhatMatrix, TeamRGE. All these activities are centered around end-user computing solutions with vendors such as AMD, Citrix, Microsoft, NVIDIA, VMware and its ecosystem. It's awesome to work closely with other experts and geeks in our industry. Starting and leading these community groups also developing and presenting new content is often done with others in our EUC industry. It truly is a team effort, so credits to my friends and team members, as well. Without them I couldn't do it. Why is this teamwork important? Iron sharpens iron – you learn a lot from others. If you don't want to learn you need to step out of IT and do something else. It's also great and a responsibility to mentor others – men and women in IT.

All these activities and community groups are about *Virtual Client Computing* – remote applications and virtual desktops running on-premises, co-located or running in public clouds. Why do I like these technologies? Because it is impacting you and me – business consumers directly on a daily basis. End-user computing is as close to the business consumers as can be. This is where the action is, where the rubber meets the road.

Close to 15 years ago I met Benny Tritsch, Shawn Bass, Ron Oglesby, Brian Madden, Jeroen van de Kamp, Rick Dehlinger along with others at BriForum. During the years we talked and shared 'crazy ideas' at various events. One of them was about benchmarking EUC platform solutions. This is how projectVRC started - a conversation with Jeroen, a crazy idea and "Just DO IT" resulted in awesome results which had a positive impact in the community, business and personal life. Shawn and Benny started benchmarking VDI/SBC with focus on user experience and developed their own software to record and analyze the user experience. Over time our two worlds connected and the community body *Team Remote Graphics Experts* was started, why? because it's fun to work together, learn from each other and it was a great excuse to drink a beer and have a BBQ together on the other side of the world. Also, in these days, NVIDIA introduced their first vGPU technology for EUC, I think this was 2012. We saw the potential and asked ourselves, "How does it work, what is the user experience impact of adding GPUs in? Why not buy 'some' hardware for our home-labs and execute 'some' tests, record the outcome and share with others across the globe". This idea sounds simple but then the reality is different; serious time and $$ investment, we created 1000s of videos, learned and shared a ton of insights, received awesome feedback from customers and peers and sometimes got a message from a vendor who wasn't happy. Above all, great friendships formed. My simple summary: I received a few gifts and developed these over time, took the opportunity, met awesome people who helped me in my journey, focused on a few areas, gave back and 'Just did it' without asking what the impact is. I enjoyed and still very much enjoy IT, which is the most important reason.

Me: Smooth Remote Graphics are key to a great user experience. Do you think it is possible to achieve such a great user experience without the use of GPUs?

Ruben: The modern PC and mobile devices we use at home are often the experience baseline for you and me, our business consumers. These modern devices all have a GPU and flash storage. Why deliver applications and desktops on-premises and public clouds while not using GPUs and flash? "*Do you think it is possible to achieve such a great user experience without the use of GPUs?*" No, modern applications, operating systems, and remoting protocols do use and benefit of GPUs. Windows 10, Office 2016, Windows Server 2016, modern remoting protocols from Citrix, Frame, Microsoft, and VMware do benefit from encoding in GPUs. For sure and no discussion, in my opinion, there are some scenarios where GPUs don't make sense, true legacy applications or applications without any real graphics interaction. So, start with 'why' applies here as well.

Me: What do you think are the main challenges when deciding to go for GPUs or not?

Ruben: Unfortunately, there isn't a single main challenge, it often is a combination of challenges such as a perception that applications don't benefit from GPUs or not knowing what the application exactly requires. Also, the perception that the user experience is good enough by just using CPUs, cost of adding GPUs is too high and GPUs are only needed when running high-end applications. These are the main challenges I see, the question is: how to solve these challenges? My advice: understand the use case and applications. Also involve users and execute a 'Pepsi vs Coca-Cola test'. Record, analyze and share user experience results with management. These ingredients will support you in creating a sound business case.

Me: We are seeing that GPUs are becoming more useful for other tasks than just graphical acceleration. Where do you see this development going?

Ruben: Virtual Reality (VR) is awesome, it requires a high-end GPU or multiple GPUs for the best experience. That won't change anywhere soon especially with higher resolutions and refresh-rates. The biggest challenge with mainstream VR usage is the use case, it is and will stay a niche. Applications which benefit from parallel computing such as AI, Machine- and Deep Learning also have a huge potential and many developments are happening here. I also see smaller/cheaper and more mobile GPUs and AI-optimized solutions moving to the edge. The new 'Intel inside' for many autonomous vehicles is the GPU, real-time computing with a bulk of sensors and associated data generation requires edge-computing.

Me: Do you think the Cloud has an impact on this development?

Ruben: Yes, no doubt about it and also public cloud and edge do walk hand in hand in many scenarios, hybrid solutions are real now and in the future. Public cloud has a huge impact on today's development because many want to execute their cloud-first approach and want to switch from OpEx to CapEx. The cloud with its (almost) unlimited scale, its global availability, enable pay-per-use and is relatively easy to use. These are main reasons why public cloud adoption and solution development is skyrocketing. For many organizations as mentioned earlier, the reality is a hybrid approach, especially in the Virtual Client Computing space. The main reasons for this are integration with on-premises solutions because of a classic application stack, cost and limited cloud options to run e.g. GPUs in the cloud. More competition and product developments in this space will help to address these challenges.

Me: What would be you key takeaway in terms of designing VDI that includes GPUs?

Ruben: The biggest competitor of Virtual Client Computing is the physical PC, the biggest competitor of PC and Virtual Client Computer is mobile/SaaS/web. The modern workspace is a combination of these solutions now and in the future. Understand the exceptions using a CPU only approach instead of using GPU when designing or re-designing your VDI solution both on-premises or using cloud services, GPU is the new normal. Understand the advantages, downsides and the fast pace of developments in public cloud services such as Amazon, Citrix, Frame, Google, Microsoft, VMware. It will help you make the right choice for your consumers.

# CLIENTS AND

# ENDPOINTS

Throughout the years, endpoints have evolved. Obviously, this is due to the fact that we, as users have evolved, as well. Would you ever have thought ten years ago that you would require integration with a fingerprint reader or retina scanner inside your VDI? What about the number and size of your displays? Ever thought that 4K would become a standard? And what about mobility? Would you have thought ten years ago that you would be able to perform your job from basically every single place on earth where there is an internet connection? All of these workplace innovations are enabled because of technological innovations and the supporting infrastructure. Sure, not every use case would be able to work from every location (like nurses or people in retail), but it is good to know that from a technological standpoint a lot is possible. Finding the right endpoint to fit the job is the trick here.

So, what is an endpoint? An endpoint could be anything that has the ability to connect to a remote desktop. The most common ones are fat clients (normal PCs), laptops, MacBooks, tablets, smartphones, Raspberry Pis, wearables and even Teslas could be an endpoint. With so much to choose from, I can imagine it could be a challenge to find the right one that fits the job. Every type of endpoint has its pros and cons, which I will explain in the next sections.

# FULL CLIENT VS HTML CLIENT

There are two ways of connecting to a desktop. The first (and most feature-rich) is the Horizon Client. The Horizon Client is an installable client that provides the end-user with the UI to connect to desktops and applications. It can interact with the operating system on the endpoint, so you are able to add file type associations, provide client drive redirection and connect to locally installed printers. These features are all developed to create the best user experience possible.

The other option is to use a web browser with HTML5 capability to access desktops and applications. In theory, every device that has a browser that supports HTML5 is able to do this without installing software on the endpoint. By simply just entering the external URL of Horizon, the user is presented with a portal in which he or she can enter credentials and sign in. Sounds pretty awesome, right?

Well, for some use cases it is indeed awesome. But it has its downsides as well. Because it runs inside a browser, it has limited interaction possibilities compared to the full Horizon Client. Things like Skype for Business integration aren't going to work with the HTML5 client. Multi-monitor support is another feature that is better supported with the full Horizon Client on a Windows machine or Apple macOS.

Before you make any decisions on which client to use for which use case, it would be very wise to check out the feature set of the different clients. If a feature isn't supported on a specific client, it's better to know this before you start deploying (to avoid disappointment with the end-user).

The following endpoints have an official Horizon Client.

- Windows-based devices (laptops and desktops)
- macOS-based devices
- Windows IoT-based devices (thin clients)
- Linux-based devices (laptops, desktops and thin clients)
- Zero clients
- iOS-based devices (iPhones and iPads)
- Android-based devices (phones and tablets)
- ChromeOS-based devices (Chrome book)

These clients have specific features that let you integrate the client of the endpoint with specific features of the device. Of course, not every device is suitable to run a session with a virtual desktop on it, including certain of applications. Just because you can run a remote desktop with AutoCAD on an Apple iPhone, doesn't mean you should.

# ENDPOINTS

Deciding on which client to use is important, but a client is nothing without an endpoint. Choosing an endpoint that fits a client can be a challenge because in a lot of cases, devices are being managed by different teams or might even require you to create a new device strategy if this is going to be your first VDI project. This is why it's important to involve your entire organization with the choice of endpoints. As you read in the previous section, there are a lot of different types of endpoint and each has its own specific use case. Some might even be used for different use cases. The following section will guide you through the different types of endpoints, including some examples of requirements and possible constraints or risks.

# Windows-based Devices

I think these are the easiest of all devices in terms of extensibility. Windows devices (in general) are versatile. If you take a laptop of each of the big OEMs such as HPE, Dell or Lenovo, you will have a device that contains enough RAM and a CPU capable of running business apps locally. Quite often those devices contain a GPU (based on NVIDIA, Intel or AMD) so it will be able to run (web)apps that are capable of offloading to the GPU.

## Use Cases

Windows-based endpoints are quite often used in environments where a mixture of VDI workloads and locally installed applications are required. If you are planning a solution on which 100% of the applications are going to run in the virtual desktop, a Windows-based endpoint might not be the best choice. Because the device runs a full Windows operating system and is capable of running those business applications locally, it might have an overkill of resources to just run VDI.

On the other hand, Windows endpoints are able to use the VMware Horizon Client for Windows, which has the most complete feature set. The Horizon Client is able to redirect most of the USB-connected devices like webcams, printers, HID devices, scanners, etc. And, I'm shitting you not, for a couple of VMUGs and other events like *ITQ Transform!*, we (myself together with a couple of ITQ colleagues) build an F1 Playseat complete with 4K monitor, steering wheel, and pedals. The steering wheel and pedals were adapted through USB redirection and with latencies up to 5ms we were able to run F1 racing games without noticing we were running the game in VDI. I think this shows the power, extensibility, and versatility of Windows-based endpoints.

It's not all awesomeness, though. Extensibility is great, but it also introduces risks. Imagine users being able to redirect flash drives with malicious software. Who would do that you might ask? Your company doesn't have any interesting data, right? Well, research has been done about IT security risks by several investigators such as *Experience Dynamics*. On an average, it's not the hacker who is directly involved in installing the malicious software. It's your end-user who (unintendedly) used a flash drive that they didn't know contained the malicious software. That's why I think that unintended security risks must be avoided at all costs. Security, in general, is a challenge for most companies and I think it's all about avoiding instead of remediating. More about security can be found in the NSX and Security sections.

Another challenge when using Windows-based endpoints is the management of the endpoints. Thin clients and zero clients have big advantages in terms of management as these endpoints include management solutions that are able to completely manipulate every setting on those devices (More about that in the thin clients/zero clients sections). Another challenge in terms of management is the operating system that I see with customers. On average, customers haven't completely migrated to Windows 10 yet for their endpoints. Windows 7 can't be properly managed through *Modern Management* solutions like VMware AirWatch or Microsoft Intune. This means that traditional solutions like Microsoft SCCM are still required to manage those devices. The adoption of modern management solutions will probably be better as soon as Window 7 is at end-of-life.

If you already migrated towards a modern management solution, your organization might also be ready to introduce a *Bring Your Own Device (BYOD) policy*. By an increasing demand from end-users (especially from Generation X and younger), I see customers in Europe introducing a BYOD policy on quite an impressive scale. With a BYOD policy, end-users are able to simply buy a device from the PC store on the corner of the street and bring it to the office to work. Or even better, they can use it from home (or any other location) to work from there. Windows-based endpoints are the most popular because of their price, ease of use and general availability, so expect these to be used by the majority of users.

## Considerations

The following requirements could drive your decision towards Windows-based endpoint:

- The device must be able to run both VDI applications as well as local applications.
- The device must be able to run applications during offline use (like in a plane or other location without connectivity).
- The VDI must be able to handle certain local devices (such as scanners, special HID devices, serial devices, etc).

If existing devices must be used (for most customers, this is the case), this will be a major constraint. Make sure that a proper solution exists to manage those devices or at least assume it to avoid an increase in operational expenses. In some cases, a certain version of an operating system (such as Windows 10 LTSB) must be used, but these will force you to similar decisions (in terms of management). Another thing to look out for in this case is to assure supportability with all used hardware and software (such as the Horizon Client for Windows).

Deciding to go for Windows-based endpoints could create the following risks:

- Redirecting devices such as flash drives can pose a security risk. Mitigate this by implementing a GPO or UEM Smart Policy to just enable certain types of devices.
- Storing data on the local device can pose a GDPR/privacy/data loss related risk. Mitigate this by reducing permissions on the endpoint. If local use is necessary for a specific use case, make sure to encrypt the local storage and implement a modern management solution to be in control of what happens on the local endpoint. Also, make sure the user recognizes that he or she is working on a virtual desktop instead of the local desktop. I have seen it too often that a user is mistaken and tries to work on the local device with (SaaS) applications that have a different user experience or just don't work.

## macOS-based Devices

These are my personal favorite endpoints, but I might be a little biased. I've used Apple products for over 10 years and have seen great support from VMware since I've used the VMware Horizon View client since 2014. As the time went by, the VMware Horizon Client for macOS evolved in what it is now with almost the same feature set as the one for Windows. I'm seeing an increase in the number of Apple devices as many customers are introducing a Bring Your Own Device strategy (although Apple devices are generally spoken somewhat more expensive). Modern Management solutions like VMware AirWatch (called VMware Unified Endpoint Management nowadays), reduce the number of endpoint solutions to manage different types of devices. And so, managing Apple devices or Windows 10 devices is quite similar with such tools.

## Use Cases

I think the use cases for macOS-based devices are similar to Windows-based devices, especially when a modern management solution is in place. Because of their small form factor and long battery life, they are generally suitable for users who need to be mobile (like salespersons, consultants, and management).

Besides those use cases, I personally don't think an Apple device is suitable for general use. The biggest reason is the price. On an average, a Windows 10 laptop might be 40% cheaper with comparable specs and form factor. Imagine the financial impact when 4,000 users require such an endpoint?

## Considerations

Although they have a comparable feature set to Windows 10 devices, there are some considerations when going for Apple macOS devices.

A modern management solution must be in place to ensure the devices are kept secure and access to your corporate resources is completely managed. Also, a modern management solution will enable users to enroll their device by themselves, which is essential if you are going to introduce a Bring Your Own Device strategy.

The majority of users are capable enough to work with Windows operating systems. One of the challenges I see customers are facing, is the knowledge gap with their users. Sure, you can offer a shiny device with an Apple logo on it, but if your supporting IT team gets impacted by an increase of requests, you might end up with a lot of angry people.

If you have a budget constraint, you might want to consider going for other endpoints because of the higher price per unit. On the other hand, a budget constraint could be an enabler for a BYOD strategy, so take this into account.

## Thin Clients

They are probably the most common endpoint for VDI deployment: thin clients. Years back, in the era of mainframes, thin devices like terminal PCs were also a common thing. Just basically take a pc, strip off everything you don't need (in terms of compute resources) and make sure it is able to run the applications from your mainframe. The downside of these thin devices was that they were unable to display somewhat more complex graphics (other than ASCII art). So, when vendors were developing systems that required those complex graphics, the thin client was born. Believe it or not, the term *Thin Client* was originally created in 1993 by Tim Negris, VP of Server Marketing when Oracle was launching its Oracle 7 system.

Thin clients exist in all sorts and shapes. From all-in-one machines to devices being just a little bit bigger than a matchbox. What kind of thin client to use totally depends on your use cases. The same goes for the operating system you run on the thin client. Windows-based thin clients can be useful, but I see some of the bigger thin client vendors developing their products mainly with Linux-based operating systems. All have their advantages and downsides.

## Use cases

There are tons of use cases for thin clients. Especially use cases that work primarily from an office location are really suitable. Connect a thin client to an external monitor, attach a mouse and keyboard, and presto: you are done. A thin client can be configured to only connect to your VDI, without any additional options. Just push the power button and the next screen you will see asks you for your VDI credentials. It's that simple. But, like I mentioned, thin clients come in different shapes and sizes. Laptop-shaped thin clients are becoming more popular as they offer a mobile user a similar user experience as the conventional thin client, but with the advantage of mobility. When equipping them with a mobile internet connection, you are basically able to work on a virtual desktop from every location that has mobile reception. But why go that way instead of just buying normal laptops? The answer can be found in a couple of things. First of all, a thin client is completely locked down. So, from a security perspective, the device is one of the most secure possible. The device also doesn't contain any corporate data, so again a great advantage from a security perspective.

## Considerations

- Thin clients are quite often used to reduce the number of endpoints. If you have use cases that work in shifts and are able to work from an office location (such as call center use cases), a single endpoint can be shared by multiple employees.

- There are some downsides to thin clients as well. If the VDI is unavailable, a thin client is nothing more than a brick. In some cases, customers are able to run their business-critical application on an endpoint in case of a DR scenario. If you choose this option, thin clients will probably not fit.
- If your endpoint of choice is a thin client, you would normally do that for a certain number of endpoints. Thin clients need to be managed. As modern management solutions aren't yet mature enough (in 2018) to manage thin clients as well as conventional devices, you need to introduce a point solution to manage them. Believe me, you don't want to manage them individually by hand. If you just have a really small percentage of use cases that would benefit from a thin client, consider using normal Windows endpoint that could be managed by your existing endpoint management solution.
- Choose thin clients that are able to run the proposed workloads. Going for Raspberry Pis sound like a great idea but running 4K workloads on them isn't going to work.
- I would recommend getting demo units to test out if all of your requirements can be met. Test them thoroughly including the accompanied management solution.

## Windows-based Thin Clients

Windows-based thin clients are the most versatile in terms of supported features. Windows 10-based thin clients use the full version of the Horizon Client for Windows, which is the most complete one in terms of features but have the form factor of a thin client. You could either consider this as "The best of both worlds" or consider this being quite useless – useless as in you could possibly buy a Windows 10-based fat client for a similar price. Both could be true, but (again) all depends on your requirements.

I'm very sorry if you are starting to get annoyed by this answer, but requirements are just really important.

## Considerations

Next to the general considerations for thin clients, take the following considerations into account when choosing Windows-based thin clients.

- The Horizon Client for Windows is the most versatile one. If you need the form factor and advantages of a thin client (such as power consumption), but the versatility of the Horizon Client for Windows, this could be your pick.
- Because of required licenses, Windows-based thin clients could be more expensive than the same models based on Linux.
- If your endpoint of choice needs to run additional software such as CMDB tools or remote viewers like TeamViewer, the Windows-based thin client might be suitable as well. Do check if the thin client of choice has enough resources to do so.

## Linux-based Thin Clients

When using a search engine in your browser to find thin clients, the first few results just show the traditional OEMs that build thin clients such as HPE and Dell EMC. For a long time, those might have delivered your primary thin client of choice, but times have changed. Emerging thin client vendors such as IGEL and 10ZIG are gaining market share and offer great thin clients, which are by default preloaded with a Linux operating system. The Linux operating system is configured to be used as a thin client and best of all is that it can be fully managed by an accompanied management solution. Almost every setting of a client can centrally be manipulated, which will save you tons of time. The thin client uses the Horizon Client for Linux, which offers a great feature set (although less complete compared with the Windows-based thin client).

Like the other types of thin clients, Linux-based ones come in all sorts of shapes and sizes. What client to choose from, depends on the use cases. IGEL even has a USB thumb drive-sized client, which can be used to transform most of the modern endpoints in a thin client that can be managed by their management solution.

## Considerations

Linux-based thin clients are becoming the most popular and as their feature set is quite rich, they might be suitable for the job.

- Not every Linux-based thin client vendor offers a management solution that is able to completely configure the thin client remotely. Be sure to check this.
- Check if the features that your use cases require are supported on the Linux-based thin client of choice.
- Running additional software on a Linux-based thin client can be a challenge because they are quite often hardened or preloaded with a specific distribution of Linux.
- From a security perspective, these devices might be a better fit as the average user isn't able to run or install software on the endpoint. The only thing that shows when the device is booted, is the Horizon Client which is asking for credentials. This is possible for Windows-based thin clients as well, but somewhat more work to achieve.
- Linux is less known for possible malware, virus or other exploits. Because of this, using Linux-based thin clients can be considered as a more secure option.

# Zero Clients

Whoever ran VDI in the early days with PCoIP as the main connection protocol, might also have used zero clients as endpoints. Zero clients were pretty awesome for a really long time because of a variety of reasons. First of all, they are purposely built for one task only: connect over PCoIP to a virtual desktop. The only thing that runs on the zero client, is a tiny operating system. No ability to run software on it, other than the proprietary Horizon Client. Like a thin client, zero clients are managed through a management solution. From a security perspective, zero clients are awesome. As there is no option to install software or configure the device, there isn't an option, either, to compromise the device.

Unfortunately, zero clients have some downsides as well. As "real" zero clients are only able to run PCoIP, their use cases are becoming limited. If you see zero clients being offered on the internet that are capable of running Blast Extreme, they are just thin lients with a tiny operating system on them. The operating system is completely stripped down. Zero clients are less versatile as a lot of features in both thin clients and fat clients are simply not possible (like redirection of resources).

In order to use a zero client, PCoIP is mandatory. Offloading encoding and decoding of the PCoIP stream, Teradici hardware is required in both a host as well as the zero client. Most zero clients are equipped with so-called Teradici offloading chips.

## Considerations

I do think there might be specific use cases that would require zero clients, but like mentioned the use cases are becoming limited.

- As we are seeing great development of the Blast Extreme protocol, you might want to consider using this as your main protocol and only use PCoIP when absolutely necessary. To simplify your endpoint strategy, you might want to choose endpoints that are capable of running both protocols.

- Security requirements might force you into choosing a completely stripped down and hardened endpoint. In this case, a zero client might still be an option. VMware won't end the support any time soon for the PCoIP protocol, but make sure the endpoint vendor of choice won't end support either.

- Zero clients have less support for extensibility features as redirection of certain types of devices. Take a webcam for instance. If you are using a webcam from an endpoint that supports the AV channel in PCoIP, the USB stream will be converted into an AV stream which is by default compressed and takes less bandwidth. Zero clients aren't capable of those features and thus will use the webcam in the redirected USB channel. Imagine 80 MBps instead of maybe 800 KBps being transferred for every endpoint using a webcam. Get the point?

- Some zero clients are useless without a management solution. Be sure to choose zero clients that are capable of saving a Horizon configuration to the local devices so, in case of failing management solution, your users are still able to work.

## Linux-based Devices

Although it is somewhat expected, Linux as an operating system for fat clients isn't gaining any popularity with projects I have run in the past. I'm also not really seeing it gaining popularity in the future, to be honest. Linux as a desktop operating system is somewhat more complex to deploy and manage remotely. The modern management solutions like VMware AirWatch and Microsoft Intune aren't capable of managing Linux, so the question is if you should choose Linux as an endpoint for fat clients. Even accepting them in a Bring Your Own Device policy might be a risk because enrolling such a device isn't possible without the use of specific point solutions.

There is a Horizon Client available for Linux though. It's the same as the Horizon Client for Linux-based thin clients. It does offer a great feature set, so it is capable of offering a great user experience. The challenge is still security though. Would you like to accept endpoints in your corporate environment that are hard to manage or require additional effort to do so?

## Considerations

To be honest, I would only consider Linux-based fat clients if you are running into specific constraints.

- The endpoints you are forced into using, require specific applications or solutions that run on the local endpoints and can't run on any other type of device.
- Linux-based fat clients might require a higher skill set from the end-user as they have a different user experience than a Windows-based fat client or any thin client.
- Linux doesn't require a license (except for certain distributions). If a really, really tight budget forces you into fat clients without Windows, it might be a possibility to run Linux. Be sure to include a management solution, as well, to manage the endpoints.

# Mobile Devices

The world of mobile devices has exploded in the last ten years. Before that time, there were a couple of pioneers in that space that made some legendary devices:

- In 1997, Palm released the PalmPilot (one of the first mobile computing devices with a portrait-shaped display and stylus).
- The Psion Series 5mx was my most favorite gadget in the late 90s and my first laptop-shaped pocket computer that I used for most of my daily agenda and contacts stuff.
- The Compaq iPAQ was one of the first PDAs (Pocket Digital Assistant) running a Windows Mobile operating system and was announced in 2000.

Mobile devices have had different forms, shapes and operating systems. My first smartphone was a Windows Phone-based O2 XDA II that I got in 2003 and nearly required an MCSE certification in order to completely know how to run it. It came with a stylus, which was basically the only way to navigate through the device. Although this may sound a bit negative, back then it was an awesome device. I could run my navigation software on it to guide me from customer to customer and the browser was capable of running most websites. It was the first, great but unsuccessful attempt to create a mainstream smartphone. Something in which Apple did succeed in 2007 with the launch of the first iPhone. The iPhone was the first device I have used that used a different type of touch screen (which wasn't relying on a stylus to be operated). I think this made the biggest difference. Funny enough, this is another great example of what user experience can do for a solution or product in this case. Apple's coolness factor together with the fact they were the first with a smartphone that was powerful, had a great ecosystem of apps and accessories around it, had hardware and software from the same factory and a smooth UI, made it a great success and I think laid the foundation of how we use our devices nowadays.

In 2008, Google tried to compete in the smartphone market by releasing the first public version of the Android OS. Other than

Apple, Android could run on devices from other vendors, as well. This made it probably an even greater success in terms of market share. The total number of devices running Android compared to Apple's iOS is far greater. If you have powerful vendors such as Samsung, HTC, LG and Huawei running your operating system, you can imagine the success this might have.

Nowadays, my estimate is that there are just a handful of people not using a smartphone. The ease of use has changed in the past couple of years, which increased the adoption.

Next to smartphones, tablets have become popular devices, as well. Although Apple wasn't the first one to release a device with a similar look and feel as a smartphone, just a lot bigger, they were the first to release one that was built for the masses. The iPad ran the same kind of hardware as the iPhone, but with a bigger screen and also without a stylus being required for navigation. Both the iPhone and the iPad started a revolution in how we use devices.

The question really is: are these devices with their powerful hardware suitable to be used as an endpoint for your VDI? Of course, the answer is it depends.

Working on VDI requires a mouse and a keyboard if your virtual desktop is based on a Windows operating system. This causes the first challenge. The touchscreen on these devices isn't purposely built to navigate through a virtual desktop and because it uses your fingertips, it's just not suitable to use all day. These mobile devices can be used as an endpoint for VDI though, you just need the proper tools. Android devices are able to use a mouse and keyboard when running a VDI session. Take the Samsung DEX, for instance. It's basically a docking station that turns a Samsung smartphone into a powerful endpoint for VDI. With Apple devices, you are able to do the same by simply connecting a Bluetooth keyboard and the Swiftpoint GT mouse (which is the only mouse that can be used with the Horizon Client for iOS). Although small and hard to use in the beginning, I'm used to the device now and I love it, to be honest. The downside is that it is relatively expensive if you compare it with a normal mouse.

## Considerations

I think we will see a shift in the future in terms of endpoints for VDI or in general. Laptops are getting smaller, smartphones are getting bigger and tablets are somewhat stuck in the middle. Having a single device that can be used for all of your daily work, will eventually be a reality. As a Samsung smartphone combined with a DEX is already capable now, I don't think a device like that is built for the masses. If you do want to see what possibilities exist, you might consider the following:

- Navigation inside VDI requires a mouse and keyboard in order to have an acceptable user experience.
- Most applications running inside a virtual desktop aren't optimized for mobile devices. Navigating through them with just your fingers in a small screen is a challenge.
- Just because you can run every application from a smartphone, doesn't mean you have to (or should!).
- If you would consider mobile devices, the screen size and resolution of a tablet might be more useful than the one of a smartphone.
- Horizon Clients exist for both iOS and Android. Please note that some of the features in the Windows, macOS, and Linux clients aren't available.
- Managing mobile devices requires modern management solutions like AirWatch/Workspace ONE. Although they can manage most of the mobile device, the Horizon Client can't be easily prepopulated with connection settings. This will require an App SDK to do so. It would probably be better set up via a connection from the Horizon web client, instead.

## Chrome OS-based Devices

In 2011, the first devices containing Google's Chrome OS, were released. Chrome OS (which isn't related to Android in any way) is basically a complete stripped-down operating system which is based on a browser. In order to use applications on the device (which is called a Google Chromebook), an internet connection is required. No applications are "really" installed locally. They are more or less plugins for the Chrome browser running on the device and require an internet connection because they are almost all based on SaaS applications. Things like your office-type of applications are fully based on the cloud-version like Microsoft Office Online. Of course, you need to be online in order to connect to VDI anyway, so this might not be a deal breaker.

Google Chromebooks are quite often cheaper than normal laptops and are widely spread available. Almost every electronics store in the Netherlands offers Chromebooks.

## Considerations

I think Chromebooks have a great use case, I'm just not sure if VDI is the right one.

- The number one requirement when going for Chromebooks would be mobility. The advantages of the devices are the almost-never-ending battery life. I have heard customers telling me their device easily lasted over 15 hours without charging, which might be something to consider.
- Managing Chrome OS-based devices will require a modern management solution, but like the Horizon Client for mobile devices, this one is quite hard or even impossible to prepopulate with connection settings. Using a Chromebook would mean that you might want to use the Horizon web client as your primary client, instead.
- Chromebooks are quite often cheaper. The reason being that cheaper hardware can be used as well as a lack of required operating system licenses.
- If mobility is a requirement, but you want to avoid using Windows-based laptops, a Chromebook could be your choice. Please note that I do think that alternatives exist (like turning a cheap laptop into a Linux-based thin client).

317

In this way, you can still manage the device like the other thin clients.

## Wearables

This is where the future of the endpoint will be if you ask me. Don't panic, I'm not implicating you should run a VDI session from a smartwatch. The first wearable device I have seen that was able to run a Horizon Client, is Microsoft's HoloLens. If you don't know what a HoloLens is, stop now, go to YouTube and view some demo videos first.

Done? Cool. This is the future of wearable tech as I see it. By using augmented reality, you would, for instance, be able to create a Digital Workspace where the user will be able to work from any location but with a complete virtual workspace that is always the same. Imagine having your colleagues virtually next to you but physically separated by thousands of kilometers. That would be very cool, right?

There is only one big challenge with tech like that. It doesn't work with traditional applications, just like a traditional app doesn't work on a smartphone. That's where the use case for VDI is an excellent one. Being able to run your traditional apps from a virtual workspace and control them through gestures, eye tracking, and other cool integrations is going to happen, I'm positive!

## CONCLUSION

I hope this section gave you the information required to help you decide what endpoint to choose in what situation. At the end, it's all about the user. So again, talk to your users to see what they require and see how that could be converted to design choices.

# SECURITY

Securing IT systems is one of the top priorities in enterprise IT departments today. Many systems contain sensitive or proprietary data, including customer financial data. These systems may be targeted by malicious actors looking to access and sell this data for personal gain.

Security is at the center of virtual desktop deployments. Virtual desktops can provide remote access to enterprise applications and datacenters, so data sensitive corporate data does not have to leave the datacenter. Virtual desktop solutions also need to be secure. Unauthorized access to virtual desktops or applications would allow malicious users to access sensitive data.

VMware Horizon designs need to include security as a core design component. Security needs to be considered at multiple layers in the design to ensure that the Horizon infrastructure, remote access, and virtual desktops are all protected.

# AUTHORIZATION

Authorization is the rule set specifying who can do what in a system. It is specifying specific access rights or system privileges to resources. In other words, it is providing access control within Horizon. Authorization within Horizon occurs on multiple levels. Administrators are granted roles within Horizon that provide them with access to the Horizon Administrator Console and the ability to perform specific tasks based on their assigned role. End-users are entitled, or granted access, to virtual desktops, published applications, and the ability to access the environment remotely. Microsoft Active Directory is the primary authentication and authorization source for VMware Horizon environments. Entitlements and administrative access are tied closely to Active Directory user accounts or groups.

Active Directory Groups are the primary authorization method for desktop pools and published applications. Horizon resources are entitled to specific groups, and members of the entitled group receive access to the resources. Active Directory Groups are preferred over directly entitling users for two reasons. First, it simplifies management. Users can be granted access to desktops or applications by simply adding them to a group. Administrators do not need to open the Horizon administrator console to perform these tasks. The second reason is auditability. Administrators and auditors can easily see who has access to specific desktop pools or applications by viewing the membership of the group.

Users who are authenticated through the Horizon Client or the Horizon web client can only view resources that they have been given access to. If a user attempts to access a resource that they are not entitled to, which is possible by launching the Horizon Client through the command line, they receive an error.

Active Directory is also used for managing authorization to the backend Horizon administrative consoles. This includes Horizon Administrator, Horizon Help Desk, and the new Horizon HTML5 administrative interface. Active Directory users or groups can be assigned administrative roles within Horizon that allows them access to specific administrative features or the ability to complete administrative tasks.

# AUTHENTICATION

Imagine that you're flying somewhere on a vacation. You print your airplane ticket, grab your passport, and down to the airport you go. When you get to the airport, you hand your ticket and your identification to the security guy. He reviews everything, hands your documents back to you, and waves your through. Your ticket was your authorization. It showed that you were a valid passenger with a specific seat on a specific flight on that day. Your identification was your authentication – it validated that you were the person on the ticket.

Authentication is the process of validating the identity of the user. This process occurs when the user attempts to access a system, and they must provide their name and something that only that user would have or know to validate their identity.

VMware Horizon utilizes Active Directory for handling user authentication. Horizon Connection servers are members of an Active Directory domain, and each user who accesses Horizon is authenticated against this domain. Horizon can also enumerate and authenticate users against any domain where a one-way or two-way domain or forest trust is in place. When a one-way trust is used, the domain that the Connection server belongs to must trust the domain where the user account credentials are located.

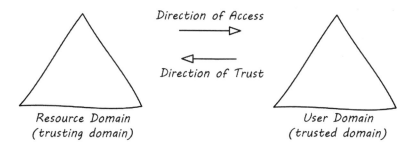

# Multi-Factor Authentication

Active Directory Authentication only requires a username and password when accessing Horizon. Multi-factor Authentication (or MFA) is supported when additional security is required. MFA relies on having at least two authentication factors when accessing the system – something the user knows, their password, and something the user has – an authentication token. The authentication token can take the form of proprietary devices, smartphone apps, one-time passwords sent via email or text message, or phone calls.

*Please note that SMS and phone call-based MFA is very much frowned upon in the security industry, especially in the USA. Bad actors can very easily get a phone number transferred to a spare SIM card in their possession by calling the phone company and using social engineering techniques.*

Horizon supports two forms of multi-factor authentication – RSA SecurID and RADIUS. Both options require an external server that acts as an authentication manager. When the user signs in, they are prompted for their username, password, and the code from their two-factor authentication token. All three are required to successfully authenticate.

There are two methods for setting up multi-factor authentication in Horizon. It's important to understand the differences between the two ways that MFA is configured as it impacts the architecture and configuration of Horizon.

The first method for enabling MFA is to enable it on a per-Connection server basis. In this configuration, MFA is enabled and configured on specific Connection servers in the Horizon Pod. Any user that connects to that Connection server is prompted for MFA as part of the login process. This method is primarily used when the Horizon Security server is deployed, and MFA is only enabled on the Connection servers that are paired with a Security server. This approach requires twice as many Connection servers to be deployed as highly available MFA and non-MFA enabled Connection servers are needed.

The second method requires the Unified Access Gateway (UAG) appliance to be used in place of the Security server. When the UAG is deployed, it can be configured to handle MFA, offloading it from the Connection servers. When users sign in, the UAG processes the MFA request prior to asking for the user's Active Directory credentials. The UAG approach allows for fewer Connection servers when using MFA since it does not need to be enabled on a per-Connection server basis.

## Workspace ONE Integration with SAML

Workspace ONE is VMware's overarching EUC product solution set. It contains the modern management solution built around AirWatch and identity management and a workspace portal through VMware Identity Manager (vIDM).

Horizon can integrate with Workspace ONE to provide a single portal experience where users access their Horizon desktops and published applications alongside cloud-based SaaS applications. When Horizon is integrated into vIDM and Workspace ONE, user authentication is handled by the vIDM solution. VMware Identity Manager interacts with Active Directory, and potentially the multi-factor authentication configuration to authenticate users and provide them with the resources they are authorized to use. So how is Horizon authenticating users if Workspace ONE is handling any primary and/or secondary authentication? How do users know which pools or published applications they are entitled to access?

VMware Identity Manager integrates with Horizon through the Security Assertion Markup Language, or SAML for short. SAML is an open standard that defines a method for exchanging authentication and authorization data between two systems. In SAML, the authentication and authorization data is called an *assertion*. An assertion is a package of data that contains information about the user attempting to access the system. Assertions are issued by an identity provider (IdP), or a system that creates, maintains, and manages identity information and provides authentication services. The assertion is consumed by a service provider (SP), and based on the contents of the assertion, makes an authorization decision.

I you are going to use SAML integration with vIDM, the user is not prompted for their username, password, and multifactor authentication if they are already signed into the Workspace ONE application. When accessing Horizon, a SAML assertion is sent from vIDM to Horizon, and Horizon authenticates the user based on what vIDM was sent.

Although user authentication into Horizon is being handled differently in this model, users are still authenticated against an Active Directory service that is trusted by Horizon.

# VIRTUAL DESKTOP SECURITY

Security doesn't stop at authentication and authorization. Once users are authenticated, they are granted access to virtual desktops or servers that usually run Microsoft Windows.

The virtual desktop or RDSH server operating system needs to be hardened and secured to protect against potential malware attacks. The best defense against malware infection is defense-in-depth with multiple layers of protection. This starts at the network edge with network appliances that have anti-malware capabilities and intrusion detection and prevention and has multiple layers of security on the virtual machine. This can include anti-virus software, data loss prevention software, enhanced system event monitoring, and restricting administrative rights.

## Anti-virus Software

Anti-virus or anti-malware software is one of the most common endpoint and virtual desktop security solutions. This software attempts to identify and block malicious software from running on the endpoints or virtual machines where it is active. Anti-virus software for virtual desktops comes in three forms. The first form is the traditional signature-based anti-virus. This software has its roots in the antimalware software that runs on desktop computers. Detection of malicious software is typically signature-based. Traditional anti-virus applications tend to run full scans of all files on the system, and this can cause storage performance issues in virtual environments.

In terms of a traditional anti-virus application, it's important to review the vendor guide for optimizing the application for best performance. Vendors provide recommendations around optimizing the anti-virus application, and these steps can include policies that stagger full disk scanning, file and folder exclusions, and tools that mark scanned files as safe or remove unique identifiers for Linked Clone or Instant Clone desktops.

Examples of traditional anti-virus applications include the typical anti-virus vendors such as Symantec, Kaspersky, Trend Micro, and McAfee. Microsoft also includes traditional anti-virus in Windows 10 in the form of Windows Defender.

The second form of virtual desktop anti-virus is anti-virus offload with NSX. This technology utilizes NSX and the Guest Introspection Driver in VMware Tools to offload anti-virus and anti-malware processing to vendor specific virtual appliances. The virtual appliances are always online, and they continuously receive the latest vendor signatures, and new VMs that utilize the NSX anti-virus offload are protected as soon as they come online. It can also improve the performance of the virtual desktop environment by removing anti-virus components from each virtual machine.

Not all vendors support NSX Guest Introspection and anti-virus offload, and vendors that do support it may not support all features that are available in their traditional anti-virus software. Trend Micro Deep Security and McAfee MOVE are examples of anti-virus or anti-malware software that support NSX agentless anti-virus.

The third anti-virus software is modern endpoint protection. Like traditional anti-virus software, it requires an agent or application to be installed on each virtual machine. Unlike traditional anti-virus software, however, detection of malicious software or activity is not signature-based. Malware detection is behavior-based, and it looks at application behavior when determining if an application is malicious. Because these applications look at application behavior, they may also provide a forensic chain to show how an infection or breech occurred.

While modern endpoint protection requires fewer resources to run than traditional anti-virus and can protect against a wider range of threats, it can be more expensive than traditional anti-virus. It may not also be widespread, as corporate security organizations may not have evaluated it.

Carbon Black Defense, Cylance, and Palo Alto Traps are examples of modern endpoint protection software.

## Considerations

Which option to include in your design, depends on your requirements. If your design includes NSX, my preference would be to go for a solution that integrates with it. I think the most important goal here, is to make sure that your users will still have a normal user experience. So, be aware of the possible impact on performance if you run any of the solutions mentioned. As no customer is the same, I would recommend to run a proof of concept with a couple of solution (if you have the time).

## Forensics

Sometimes, something just gets through multiple layers of defenses and infects a machine. It can even happen in the most security-conscious organizations. To understand what happened and how to prevent it in the future, the security team will often collect forensic data using their toolkit of choice. The toolkits can vary widely by environment, and some examples of forensic tools include:

- FLARE VM – A Windows malware analysis tool
- Kali Linux
- Carbon Black Response
- Microsoft Sysmon and Windows Event Log Forwarding

The purpose of these tools is to provide an understanding of what suspected malware did.

Non-persistent desktops can pose a challenge to collecting forensic data. These desktops are often destroyed when the user logs out, and if the machine was infected, any forensic data would be lost. Some of these tools also require the machine to be rebooted in order to perform forensic data gathering and malware analysis. Tools like Carbon Black Response and Microsoft Sysmon can record this data and store it in a central server, so administrators or security professional can review the data and provide security recommendations.

## Application Whitelisting

Application whitelisting is the process of configuring the desktop or server to run only specified or selected applications. Applications that are not on the list will be blocked from running. This could potentially block a significant amount of malware from running on the system.

Application whitelisting can be configured through Microsoft Group Policy or preferably by tools like VMware User Environment Manager. Effectively building application whitelists requires a good understanding of what applications users run.

Implementing a proper whitelisting strategy could be a lot of work at first but may save you a lot of time in the long run. Recovering from malware or viruses isn't fun and could be a lot of work. Prevention is the keyword here. Whitelisting is a great way of prevention!

*Please note that application whitelisting should only be configured after performing a proper assessment of the application landscape, so know thy application.*

## Event Management

Security doesn't just exist at a single point in time on a single system. Any security incident could take place over hours, days, or months, and it could involve multiple systems. This includes Horizon and the virtual desktops or servers accessed through Horizon.

A comprehensive security solution includes centralizing all logs into a single system so that events can be correlated across systems. This kind of system is known as a SIEM, or a Security Information and Event Management system. Horizon tracks and records all activity that occurs in the system. This includes user logins, desktop or application requests, and changes in the administrative consoles. This data can be stored in an events database. It can also be forwarded to a syslog collector for aggregation in a SIEM. When events are stored in the Horizon Events database, they can be displayed or reviewed in the Horizon Administrator console.

Windows does not have a way to natively send logs to a SIEM, if capturing Windows logs is important, a third-party agent is required. One example would be the VMware Log Insight Agent. There are other third-party options available, as well.

# VSPHERE FEATURES

Environment security doesn't stop with the Horizon infrastructure or the virtual machines. Horizon is built upon VMware vSphere, and some environments may require additional security to be implemented in the hypervisor layer.

While vSphere itself is fairly secure, VMware provides a Security Configuration Guide that outlines the various security settings that can be enabled in the environment to improve security. The Hardening Guide for vSphere 6.5 is available at https://blogs.vmware.com/vsphere/2017/04/vsphere-6-5-security-configuration-guide-hardening-guide-release-candidate.html.

It's important to note that the Security Configuration Guide is not a policy that can be implemented as it stands. Organizations should review the contents of the Security Configuration Guide and only implement the items that do not conflict with the management of the environment or the required Horizon features.

VMware is also adding encryption into vSphere. Encryption comes in multiple places in the environment including encrypting the network traffic for vMotion, encrypting VSAN datastores, and encrypting individual virtual machines. This can improve the overall security of the environment by preventing data theft from network snooping or hardware theft. Encryption comes with a price, though. Encryption can have a performance penalty, so be sure to run a proof of concept with encryption on the required level before using it in production.

VMware places some limits around virtual machine encryption and Horizon. Virtual machine encryption can only be used on full Clone desktops when the View Storage Accelerator, or Content-Based Read Cache (CRBC) is not used. It cannot be used on Linked Clone or Instant Clone desktops.

# NETWORK

# VIRTUALIZATION

Everyone working in IT understands the difficulties when it comes to networking, e.g. a requested new network can take weeks to be implemented. Even with compute and storage virtualization, our applications are still shackled to the physical network infrastructure. As a result, an automated VM deployment can still rely on manual steps on the physical layer, which make deployments slow and expensive. What if we could solve this by breaking the shackles between the physical network and applications?

This is where network virtualization comes into play. Network virtualization is the process of combining physical hardware and software network resources and network services into a software-based administrative entity also known as a virtual network. But please be aware, it does not replace the physical network! It only abstracts networking services from the physical layer.

But it doesn't stop there; companies are facing three key major challenges around security that are driving the adoption of network virtualization even harder. The first one of these challenges is the risk of data breaches. The second is the push to deliver applications and services faster. And the third is the constant pressure to do more with fewer human resources.

Within the VMware Software-Defined Datacenter (SDDC) stack, VMware NSX was introduced in 2014 as the secret sauce to solve the network abstraction and security issues described above. The services that come with VMware NSX include a complete set of layer 2 to layer 7 networking services e.g., switching, routing, firewalling, extensibility and load balancing, all driven by software.

There are currently two varieties of VMware NSX Data Center available: VMware NSX-v and VMware NSX-T. NSX-v is currently the mainstream version of network virtualization for a VMware-based SDDC infrastructure. As the demand to manage other objects and use cases such as cloud-native applications, containers, multi-datacenter infrastructures and public cloud services increased, VMware released NSX-T. NSX-T is the network virtualization product for multi-hypervisor and multi-cloud platforms. NSX-T is designed to handle those use cases which are already part of some VMware offerings like VMware Cloud on AWS (VMC) and is key for platforms running Pivotal Container Service (PKS) and Pivotal Application Service (PAS). NSX-T is likely to replace NSX-v in the future, but as not all of the security features required for VDI are included yet, the focus for now will still be on NSX-v.

In the next couple of sections, we will go in-depth, how VMware NSX can be leveraged to create a secure and stable foundation for VMware Horizon and add security to the Horizon desktop workloads in a simple and agile way.

# VMWARE NSX COMPONENTS

The NSX architecture itself has separation of the data, control, and management layers. This separation allows the NSX architecture to be resilient and scale without impacting workload. Each layer and its specific details are described in the following diagram.

Cloud
Consumption

Management
Plane — NSX Manager

Control
Plane — NSX Controller

Data
Plane — NSX Edge

VDS — VDS VDS VDS

Logical Switch · Distributed Logical Router · Firewall

Hosts — CPU RAM · Net · vSAN

Logical Network

Physical Network — Switch, Switch, Switch, Switch, Switch, Switch, Switch, Switch

## Data Plane

The NSX data plane consists of the vSphere Distributed Switch (VDS) with additional components to enable services. NSX kernel modules, User World agents, configuration files, and install scripts are packaged in VIBs and run within the hypervisor kernel to provide services such as distributed routing and logical firewall and to enable VXLAN bridging capabilities. The NSX Edge Services Gateway (ESG) provides not only North-South routing to upstream routers outside the virtual boundary, but also services such as firewall, NAT, DHCP, VPN, load balancing, and high availability. The NSX Distributed Logical Router (DLR) provides East-West distributed routing. Workloads that reside on the same host on different subnets can communicate with one another without having to traverse a traditional routing interface.

## Control Plane

The NSX control plane runs in the NSX Controller cluster. NSX Controller is an advanced distributed state management system that provides control plane functions for NSX logical switching and routing functions. It is the central control point for all logical switches within a network and maintains information about all hosts, logical switches (VXLANs) and distributed logical routers.

## Management Plane

The NSX management plane is built by the NSX Manager, the centralized network management component of NSX. It provides the single point of configuration and REST API entry-points.

# Consumption Platform

The consumption of NSX can be driven directly through the NSX Manager user interface, which is available in the vSphere Web Client. Typically, end-users tie network virtualization to their cloud management platform for deploying applications. NSX provides rich integration into virtually any CMP through REST APIs. Out-of-the-box integration is also available through VMware vRealize Automation, vCloud Director, OpenStack with the Neutron plug-in for NSX and many other Cloud Management Platforms.

## Network Abstraction

As previously described, VMware NSX provides core-networking services in software like switching and routing that can be automatically provisioned to create various topologies as required. This allows for a quick and agile way to spin up or down new desktop pools or expand existing desktop pools on an existing infrastructure.

## Network Services

VMware NSX provides software-based networking services like load balancers, VPN termination, SSL offloads and NAT capabilities. In addition to that, NSX integrates with physical services like load balancers and DHCP servers to allow customers to use their existing infrastructure or use NSX built-in services to deploy virtual desktops.

## Network Security

Nowadays most companies have done a good job creating a solid perimeter around their infrastructure for traffic going in and out of the datacenter; these traffic movements are also known as North-South traffic. But if that perimeter is breached and a malicious person or software is on the inside, he, she or it is then able to move freely over networks from server to server as there is less security available on the inside. This lateral movement of traffic is also known as East-West traffic. To secure this East-West traffic, one could introduce numerous firewalls to secure traffic between all components, but then it would quickly become operationally infeasible to manage all of these firewalls and firewall rules.

This is where Micro-segmentation and zero-trust come into the picture. Micro-segmentation and zero-trust are much often mixed up but are quite different.

- Micro-segmentation is the ability to apply fine-grained security policies on different layers down to application or workload level.
- Zero-trust simply means nothing is trusted, and thus denied unless else is specified and leverages Micro-segmentation to achieve this.

# CREATING A SECURITY FRAMEWORK

When developing a Security Framework there are four typical methods that are used to construct firewall rules.

- Network-based rules
    o Policies are network-centric
    o Based mainly on IP Addresses and MAC addresses
- Infrastructure-based rules
    o Policies are SDDC infrastructure centric
    o Based mainly on SDDC objects like VMs, port groups and logical Switches
- Application-based rules
    o Policies are application-centric
    o Based mainly on dynamic sources rules
- Identity-Based rules

o Policies are user-centric or group-centric
o Based mainly on group membership

## Network-based Rules

Network based firewall rules are the type of rules that are used in a typical networking environment. These rules rely on a static source and destination IPs or MAC addresses to create static firewall rules. The firewall rules are applied to specific addresses regardless of the user who is currently using them.

## Infrastructure-based Rules

In a Software-Defined Datacenter it is possible to use the logical constructs to setup static firewall rules based around infrastructure services. NSX can apply firewall rules to logical constructs within vCenter to control access based on the attributes of a given VM or other vCenter object.

## Application-based Rules

Application based firewall rules are focused on providing access to specific applications. Rule sets are created based on a range of criteria that can be applied without prior knowledge of the source IP address. This allows firewall rules to follow for example a user's identity instead of being constrained to a specific address.

## Identity-based Rules

The Identity Based Firewall was introduced in NSX 6.0. It monitors which desktop an Active Directory user is logged onto and maps the Active Directory user to an IP address. This then can be used to create DFW rules based on Active Directory security groups or users. There are two methods of obtaining the user identity, through the Guest Introspection and Active Directory Log Scraping. The Guest Introspection method depends on a Thin Agent that can be installed along with the VMware Tools, the Active Directory Event Log Scraper is pointed at an instance of your Active Directory Domain Controller. The NSX Manager will then pull the events from the Active Directory security event log. Both options can be used in an environment, but both are exclusive, and they cannot work as each other's backup. Since NSX 6.4 there is also support for user sessions on remote desktop servers (RDSH) sharing a single IP address.

# SECURITY POLICY AND SECURITY

# GROUPS

The NSX Service Composer can help you provision and assign network and security services to applications in a virtual infrastructure. You then map these services to a security group, and then these services are applied to the objects in the security group. The Service Composer relies on Security Policies and Security Groups to accomplish this.

Security Policy - How you want to protect it
Security Group - What you want to protect

## Security Policy

A Security Policy is based on a set of Guest Introspection, firewall, and network introspection services that can be applied to a Security Group. The order in which the Security Policies are applied is determined by the weight associated with the policy. The profile part of a security policy can be used to publish policies back from the security vendors to NSX. This can then be used as service profiles for particular services to assign for example tags if a vulnerability is found on a VM.

## Security Group

A Security Group within NSX can be any combination of objects; it is based on all the inclusion (static & dynamic) criteria and static exclusion criteria defined by a user.

# SERVICE INSERTION

By leveraging *Service Insertion* and *Chaining* it is possible to steer predefined traffic via the Distributed Firewall (DFW) through one or more Service Virtual Machines (SVMs). These Service Virtual Machines can be for example a Layer 7 firewall or Intrusion Detection System (IDS) and Intrusion Prevention System (IPS). It all depends on the requirement how thoroughly the traffic needs to be filtered.

Sometimes it is difficult to understand how it all comes together; as an example, imagine the following scenario:

- Traffic exits a desktop VM and reaches the DFW for processing.
- A policy is configured to process all the desktop VM traffic, the DFW will forward traffic to the filtering module.

- If the filtering module allows the traffic to be redirected, then the traffic redirection steers traffic to the SVMs.
- Then the traffic is processed by the SVMs before it is sent to the destination.
- The SVM, in this case, a host-based anti-virus scanner, has detected malicious traffic from the desktop VM.
- The affected desktop VM is now assigned with a security tag "Virus_Found" by the anti-virus software policy.
- The DFW then directly blocks all traffic from and to the desktop VM due to the configured DFW rule linked to the security tag.
- The host-based anti-virus software then can take action to clean the VM.
- After the virus, that was the cause for the malicious traffic, has been cleaned from the VM, the security tag is removed and the Desktop VM can be accessed again.

This way, the desktop VM was quarantined until it has been remediated, mitigating the risk of the virus spreading quickly in the environment.

# DEPLOYMENT TOPOLOGY WITH NSX & HORIZON

The Horizon infrastructure and Horizon desktop pools can be deployed on VMware NSX created overlays. The Horizon infrastructure components will then be deployed in a *Management Domain* where the Horizon desktop pools will be deployed in a *Workload Domain*.

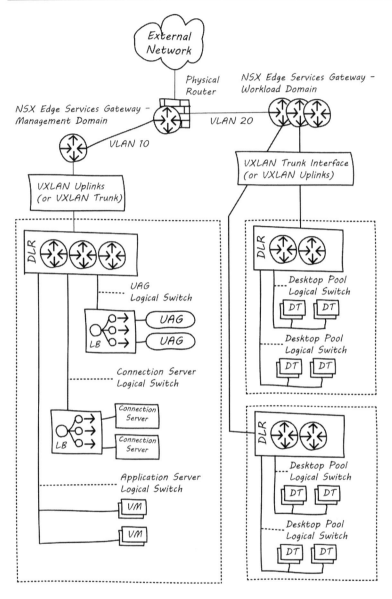

The biggest differences between the two domains will be that the management domain will be connected to a DLR for East-West optimization. For the desktop pools, you have a choice what you can do, as you do not require East-West optimization between the different desktop workloads. There are three available options on how to connect the Logical Switches to a DLR or to an ESG and route the traffic or to an ESG and NAT the traffic.

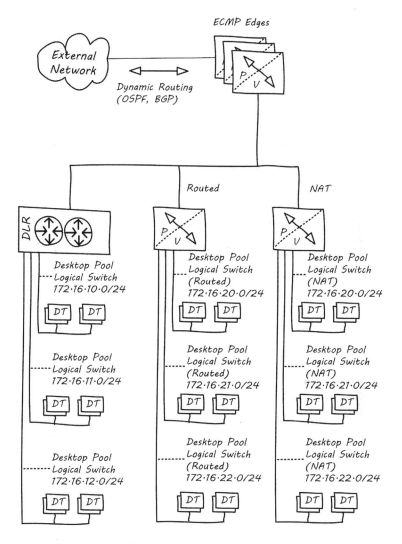

A way to create a scalable and flexible topology is to utilize a set of Equal Cost Multipath (ECMP) ESGs as "Tier-0" which will aggregate all the traffic to the external network. The desktop pools or tenant's logical switches can then be uplinked to a "Tier-1" ESG with NAT enabled if overlapping IPs are required or a set of "Tier-

1" ECMP ESGs if more bandwidth or a faster failover is required. The benefit of this topology is you can mix and match the different types of models with different characteristics in a single topology.

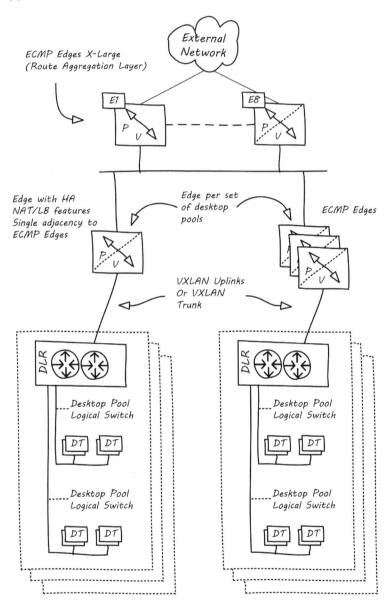

# Load Balancing

NSX can provide load balancing capabilities for Horizon components such as the Unified Access Gateway and the Connection servers. With NSX there are two different types of load balancing deployment topologies: *one-arm mode* (aka proxy mode) and *inline mode* (aka transparent mode). Both have different characteristics:

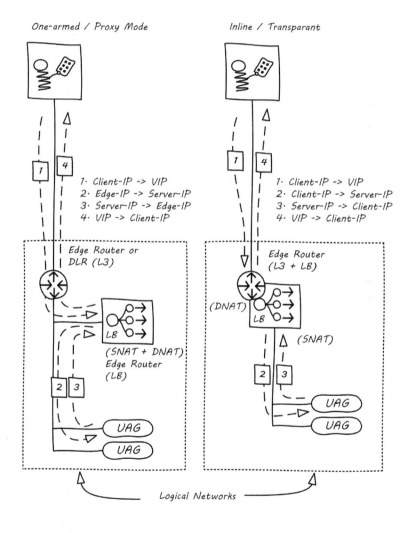

One-armed / Proxy Mode

1. Client-IP -> VIP
2. Edge-IP -> Server-IP
3. Server-IP -> Edge-IP
4. VIP -> Client-IP

Edge Router or DLR (L3)

LB

(SNAT + DNAT)
Edge Router (LB)

UAG
UAG

Inline / Transparant

1. Client-IP -> VIP
2. Client-IP -> Server-IP
3. Server-IP -> Client-IP
4. VIP -> Client-IP

Edge Router (L3 + LB)

(DNAT)

LB

(SNAT)

UAG
UAG

Logical Networks

One-arm mode is the easiest topology to use as it does not require any changes to the server gateways, the drawback is that the source IP address of the original client is lost. Please note that the IP address of the client can be inserted into the HTTP header before performing a SNAT (Secure Network Address Translation). This provides the servers visibility into the client IP address, but it is limited to HTTP traffic, only.

Inline mode requires the ESG to be the gateway for the server. It allows for the retention of the client IP address but requires the network topology to support it. Please note that if the ESG is deployed in a transparent topology the load balancing pool needs to be configured, as well, for transparent mode.

# CONSIDERATIONS

- Use a "keep it simple" principle when architecting the security policies and groups.
- For a scalable and flexible topology, use ECMP in your design.
- When using ECMP in your design, keep in mind that ECMP is stateless and therefore services like NAT and load balancing are not supported.
- ECMP relies on dynamic routing: OSPF or BGP is a must.
- Always make sure to spread the NSX Controllers across separate hosts with DRS Anti-Affinity rules.
- Always make sure to spread the NSX Edges in HA and ECMP mode across separate hosts with DRS Anti-Affinity rules.
- Sizing is key: make sure that the load balancer sizes match the number of concurrent sessions.
- When using Micro Segmentation, logging is key. Leverage tools like vRealize Log Insight or vRealize Network Insight to keep visibility in traffic flows.

# MONITORING

Designing and building VDI are the first steps in the process, keeping it healthy and your end-users happy are the next. But what is healthy? And how do you measure happiness? One is easier than the other, but there are some rules of thumb I will share in this section.

The first question related to monitoring customers ask me, is *What should be monitored?* Although it sounds like there are many answers to that question, I think you should go back to your requirements first, because the answer lies there. Customers expect you to design an architecture that fulfills their requirements. If your customer has an availability requirement, be sure to monitor the services that are included in the SLA which are linked to the requirement. If the customer demands that the logon process shouldn't take longer than 30 seconds, you have again a great example of what to monitor.

# SERVICE MONITORING

Everything starts with *Service Monitoring*. In the end, you are delivering a service called VDI that needs to be compliant to an SLA. I think service monitoring might be the easiest of all in terms of what to monitor. This is because the value of the service to monitor is binary. It's either on or off. The service is available or not. That's it. What items to include in you monitoring solution depend on the definition of your service, your SLA and availability requirements. The following metrics could be a great starting point:

- The external URL of your VDI service
- The internal URL of your VDI service
- The external URL of your vIDM service
- The internal URL of your vIDM service
- All VMware services running on your Connection servers
- All VMware services running on your View Composer servers
- The URL of your App Volumes service
- Microsoft SQL Database services
- All services running on your vCenter Appliances & PSCs
- All infrastructure services such as DHCP, DNS, AD and NTP
- The capacity of datastores becoming less than XX% in a cluster
- Memory resources becoming less than XX% on a host
- CPU resources becoming less than XX% on a host
- All services running on ESXi hosts
- All hardware components involved with the service such as switches, firewalls, load balancers and possibly storage appliances

There might be a lot more, but those depend on the infrastructure you are running on.

If one of these services isn't running, you could possibly have an outage. Since some of these components aren't really designed for failure, therefore it's very important to respond quickly and either resolve the issue or make sure the service is running.

The number of nines explained in the *Availability and Disaster Recovery* section determines the maximum time a service might be unavailable before you violate the SLA. The more nines, the shorter the time you have to act and the more important it becomes to automate alerting and possibly failover scenarios. One of the customers I have worked for had an on-call service outside of regular business hours to respond to possible outages during the night and weekend. At some point, in the middle of the night, the VDI decided to stop working because of snapshots that weren't removed after an upgrade they performed two weeks earlier. The result: in the active datacenter the datastores that contained Connection servers ran out of capacity and the virtual machines stopped working. The on-call engineer was supposed to get an alert on this phone so that he could to perform a failover. As Murphy's Law kicked in, his cell phone didn't have any reception and so, the VDI wasn't available until the next morning. Engineers arriving at the office noticed people were gathered around coffee machines instead of doing their job and found out the outage.

The VDI of this specific customer consisted out of a multi-site solution. But since a failover had to be performed manually, this became useless. During the project I did for the customer, I completely redesigned their solution and more important, their failover procedure. The most important part we changed was that next to an alert, the failover to the other datacenter was automatically executed after three failed attempts to check if the service was available again.

## Tools

Displaying service metrics in a monitoring dashboard is a good thing but doesn't resolve any availability issues. A good alerting system that isn't dependent on the same infrastructure as the VDI should be a must-have in any environment that heavily relies on those services.

Independent of the solution you choose to keep track of the services, you should be able to check if a service is available and if possible, even what the response time of a service is.

vRealize Operations for Horizon (V4H) comes with a standard number of dashboards and collectors which will keep track of all of the services which are essential. It's a great solution but doesn't offer out of the box support to send alerts over a completely different infrastructure in case the primary infrastructure fails. You won't be the first that has a sophisticated service monitoring solution which is running on the same infrastructure as the one that is being monitored. Building a solution next to V4H to collect SNMP traps and send out SMS messages would be the way to go. At the healthcare service provider I worked at, we had a completely separated cellular internet fabric running next to the MPLS networks that were used for incoming remote sessions. A Nagios appliance running on a different infrastructure collected all traps and sent out SMS messages in case of a failure right after sending out emails and push notifications. If the first on-call engineer didn't respond to an alert, his backup was alerted and afterwards his boss. If that doesn't work, what will, right?

So, my conclusion is that there isn't really a single solution that is able to handle all of the steps in service monitoring. Next to V4H, other common solutions are Splunk and Nagios.

# USER EXPERIENCE

How do you measure if a user is happy? It's quite hard to take pictures of a smile on their face. Although with Deep Learning technology, GPUs and webcams it could be possible to analyze what the expression of a user's face is and relate that to performance or usability issues. Until that will be the reality, we need to look at an alternative.

User experience itself is hard to measure, besides just asking the user on a regular basis what their experience is (which is a great idea by the way). Measuring things that could predict a good user experience is something that actually is possible. It's a good thing to start with metrics which have a direct impact on the user experience. The following metrics could be used as a starting point:

- CPU usage in a virtual desktop
- CPU wait times on the host for a specific desktop
- Memory usage in a virtual desktop
- IOPS of the virtual desktop
- Disk latency of the virtual desktop
- Round trip latency between the virtual desktop and the endpoint
- Packet drops between the virtual desktop and the endpoint
- Logon time of the session
- GPO loading time of the user
- Application start time
- GPU utilization
- Framebuffer utilization

Depending on your situation, other metrics might be useful, as well.

Other user experience components are quite hard to measure. If a user is annoyed by the fact that he or she has to sign in with every application that is started, you need to think of a process that makes you aware of this. Sending out (simple) surveys on a regular basis would be my advice here. Users in a VDI project are your number one stakeholder. If the users are unhappy, but the CFO is very happy because you saved your customer a ton of money on maintenance, the project will eventually fail. A survey could be very simple. Look at how Zoom is doing this. After every session, you will get a simple question: How was your session? You could respond with a "thumbs up" or a "thumbs down". If you respond with a "thumbs down", they might ask you additional questions to find out what it was that caused the bad user experience. I'm not saying you have to ask every user such questions at the end of every session, but I think it does help to stay in contact with your users.

Some customers find user experience to be mission critical. In some cases that might actually be true. The stockbrokers I mentioned in one of the previous sections are actually depending on a fast and consistent platform to execute buying and selling of stocks at the right moment. If they are too late to sell something because of latency, they might lose money. Other than such specific situations, I would always try to exclude the user experience from the SLA. The reason being that user experience can easily be impacted by external factors. Users connected over a crappy Wi-Fi connection can have a bad experience because of a microwave causing interference. If a user wants to watch 4K video from a virtual desktop, connected from a crappy laptop, you are sure to have them complain. I'm not saying it's not important, on the contrary, it's really important to ensure a great user experience. But just not mission critical. Explaining this during your requirement sessions will hopefully help.

## Tools

Displaying user experience metrics in a dashboard might make sense, but on average, monitoring solutions quite often have a delay of a couple of minutes before they display that something is wrong. If, that delay is five minutes and the user is experiencing a bad user experience for three minutes within the refresh interval, you might not notice it. That's why you need a tool that is able to help you troubleshoot user experience issues in (near) real-time. Being able to see what the user is experiencing on the spot, is essential in troubleshooting user experience. V4H isn't capable of doing this in real-time, but VMware has another solution called the Help Desk Tool which was introduced in Horizon 7.2. The Help Desk Tool collects user experience metrics with a retention of 15 minutes. The solution provides near real-time metrics with a delay of around 5 seconds and that's exactly what you need if a user calls you with a bad user experience.

Another solution, which is a bit more comprehensive, is the Goliath Performance Monitor by Goliath Technologies. This solution will show the same metrics as the Horizon Help Desk Tool but is able in addition to show a lot more. Things like GPU metrics, host metrics, storage metrics and network metrics are all collected and can be displayed in real-time.

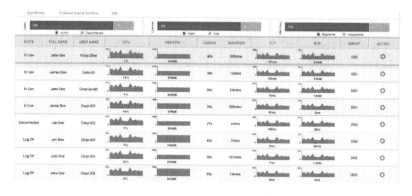

Another solution they offer to monitor user experience-related metrics is the Goliath Application Availability Monitor for Horizon. It runs a process every couple of seconds to simulate a session being brokered. The result should not be changing unless it is expected behavior. If, for some reason, an anomaly occurs (such as a changed logon duration or brokering of a desktop) the solution will report this to the VDI admin. With every iteration of the process, a screenshot is created from the result. In this case, you are also in control of user experience-related issues during things like changes in a change window.

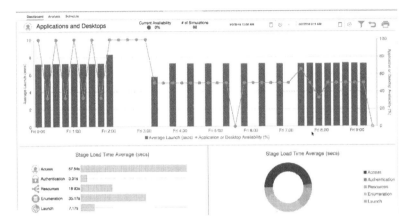

A solution like this can also publish some of the capacity management metrics, but I would rather use a different tool for that matter.

# CAPACITY MANAGEMENT

Managing your capacity is crucial to ensure a good user experience and running services. One of the most common issues I see at customers is resources related. For a long, long time, the business has treated a virtualization platform (like VDI) as a bottomless pit, a well of never-ending resources. That is, until their applications or virtual desktops became slow and sometimes unresponsive. As a service owner, it's very important to be in control of the resources that ensure a healthy service. If you are a farmer, you need to feed your cows continuously to ensure plenty of milk, right? The same is entirely true for virtualization resources. This is the exact goal of capacity management. Track the individual resources and make sure to anticipate in time if one of them is running out.

A VDI platform consists of a lot of resources. Not every one of them is measured in the same way, so know what to look for. The following metrics can be used as a good starting point to manage your capacity:

- RAM capacity in the cluster
- Average CPU usage per host
- Average CPU ready times per host (keep them under the 10% level at all times)
- Remaining datastore capacity per datastore
- Throughput on network components such as switches, load balancers, firewalls, etc.
- Available GPU resources per cluster (GPU profiles and encoder resources)
- The capacity of your file shares (for profiles, applications, etc)
- Reclaimable resources from existing virtual machines

Like the other metrics in the previous sections, the capacity management metrics are also depending on your situation. So include everything in your capacity management solution that might run out of capacity.

## Tools

If you don't decide to provision 500 extra desktops within the next 24 hours on an existing platform, you will most likely not run out of any resources on a very short notice. Because of this, a capacity management solution doesn't have to report anything in real-time. It's better to use a solution that is capable of running analytics on recorded metrics to help you create a capacity overview, including predictions. To a CIO or CFO, it isn't very useful to call out percentages or capacity measured in GBs or Mbps. In terms of reporting about capacity, it is much more useful to evaluate the time it takes before a platform becomes saturated. This is exactly what vRealize Operations for Horizon does. By running analytics on all of the collected metrics, it creates a prediction based on a growth trend. It will report these capacity trends on a per-metric basis, which (if you have done your sizing correctly) should be somewhat equal. But, don't break a sweat. In most of the projects I have finished, there was always a resource oversized (quite often it was CPU resources or storage). This is why I am convinced that Hyper-Converged Infrastructures are the most ideal platform for VDI. You are able to configure a host that is completely balanced in terms of required resources and makes scaling out easy.

Let's go back to V4H. V4H has a dashboard that is capable of producing those capacity metrics, which is really useful. It can either tell you how long it will take before the resources become saturated or how many virtual desktops you can grow before the same happens.

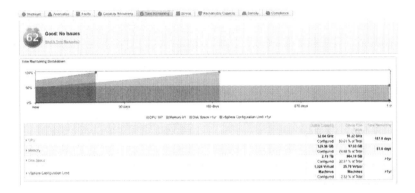

The dashboard shows you the time remaining, but also shows you if your resources aren't in balance, which could mean that adding memory and CPUs to a cluster could also solve your capacity issues. V4H is able to send these values to a customized report, so the IT management is always aware of what is happening in terms of capacity. This, to me, is essential to keep your VDI healthy.

# CONSIDERATIONS

- Service monitoring, user experience monitoring, and capacity management are three different things. You might be able to combine those three in a single tool but might lack important functionality. Using different tools that just do what they are good at might be a better idea.

- Be sure to include all three in your design or at least assume their existence. Don't forget to add risks, too, if the solutions aren't including in the project.
- If your business depends on the VDI platform, the inclusion of all of all three of the monitoring types is essential.
- The more nines are included in your availability requirement, the harder it will be to stay compliant if human interaction is essential in a DR. Include a risk in the design if this is still the case.
- Make sure the DR procedure doesn't depend on the same infrastructure to run as the platform you're monitoring, especially the alerting part of the procedure.
- Automate as much as possible to reduce your RTO and avoid human error.
- Use different forms of alerting to make sure that people are notified.
- Make sure the right people and enough people are tracking the general output of the monitoring process and understand its pieces well. Just because an alarm has not gone off, doesn't mean something does not need attention. This could be because trigger points were not set up with good values or something may have changed that requires new limits to be determined and set. They should also monitor the monitoring process to make sure a service has not stopped, or an important issue might go completely undetected!

# CONCLUSION

I hope this book gave you a good understanding of all of different things you could consider when designing VDI. As no process of designing an architecture is set in stone, I'm sure there might be more considerations you could think of. As I am always interested in *The Art of the Possible*, I would love to hear what kind of other challenges you have faced when designing your VDI.

What I also hope for is that the book has taken away all that was holding you back in going for the VCDX certification. If your personal goal for reading this book is to become a VMware Certified Design Expert on Desktop & Mobility, you should now be able to go for it and get that number!

# REFERENCES

State of the EUC union survey 2017
https://VDIlikeapro.com

State of the EUC union survey 2018
https://VDIlikeapro.com

Performance Best Practices for VMware vSphere 6.5
https://vmware.com

Horizon Enterprise Reference Architecture
https://www.vmware.com/content/dam/digitalmarketing/vmwar
e/en/pdf/techpaper/vmware-horizon-7-enterprise-validated-
integration-design-reference-architecture.pdf

Horizon Enterprise Multi-Site Reference Architecture,
https://techzone.vmware.com/sites/default/files/vmware-
horizon-7-enterprise-edition-reference-architecture-multi-
site_0.pdf

vSAN VDI Best Practices
https://cormachogan.com

Wikipedia.com

Assessment framework
https://vlenzker.com

vSAN Sizing Calculator
https://vmBaggum.nl

Lakeside Software, Inc. "Elevating user Experience Through GPU Acceleration: A Windows 10 versus Windows 7 Analysis." Lakeside Software White Paper. 2017 http://www.nvidia.com/object/lakeside-software-whitepaper-win10-vs-win7.html

NVIDIA. "See the Difference for Yourself: How to set up your own Windows 10 VDI test environment with NVIDIA Virtual GPU Solutions." NVIDIA Whitepaper. 2017 http://www.nvidia.com/object/setup-windows10-vdi-test-enviroment-nvidia-virtual-gpu-solutions.html

# INDEX

# BIO

I was born in 1982 (the year in which the Compact Disk and the Commodore 64 were released) and ever since I saw a computer for the first time (it was an original Pong game, which I still own), I had a fascination for the digital world.

From a professional perspective, my fascination for remote desktops and applications started off when I first touched Citrix WinFrame, somewhere in the late 90s. Citrix WinFrame was a Microsoft Windows NT 3.51-based Terminal Server solution and the very first successful attempt to create a Windows-based terminal emulator that could publish remote Window-based desktops and applications. Very much like Microsoft Remote App and Remote Desktops from the present. Connecting to a remote application with the Citrix WinFrame Client took over a minute or so because of a 56K modem ☺.

The ICA protocol that Citrix used (and still uses) was so impressive that the user experience of the remote desktop and applications blew my mind. How could it be that a desktop protocol was able to present a user with remote applications and desktops without the user even noticing it? And that was 20 years ago.

Over those 20 years, a lot has happened. I worked at various employers, but still with a focus on what became Server-Based Computing (SBC).

Somewhere in 2006, I worked at a company (as a system engineer) who wanted to build a Software as a Service platform that could offer hospitals, pharmacies and general practitioners a complete set of healthcare applications, hosted from a datacenter in Amsterdam. Those applications include a variety of office applications and in-house built ones. A great ambition, but like most of you might know, managing those applications and keeping them from conflicting with each other's middleware versions and DLLs is a real challenge. That's when I first got introduced to Softricity Softgrid. It was one of the first Application Virtualization tools which got acquired by Microsoft in 2008 and is now known as App-V. Like seeing your first remote desktop, this was also a game-changer. Without any hassle, we could run different versions of the same application on a single machine, without any conflicts. Again, very awesome. To create those Softgrid packages, which were called *Sequences*, I used a solution called VMware Workstation. With VMware Workstation, I could run a virtual desktop on top of my desktop and quickly restore my virtual desktop (after creating a Softgrid Sequence) to an initial state.

In that same time, my employer was heavily investing in a new datacenter architecture on which the SaaS applications and their servers were going to run. The architecture was based on a revolutionary new platform called VMware ESX. Four VMware ESX 2.5 hosts were connected through 4GB fiber channel interfaces to an EMC CX3 Shared Storage and the beauty of it all was that this new platform could reduce the number of physical hosts in the datacenter while providing a zero-downtime feature during maintenance on the hosts -- something with a new technology called *vMotion*.

Every person has those moments when he or she knew where they were when they heard that Michael Jackson passed away or of the tsunami disaster in Southeast Asia. I'm sure that every IT guy or girl that was born before 1985 also remembers where he or she was when they saw their first vMotion; vMotion was one of the biggest game changers in IT.

The cool thing was, that the more I got involved in the SaaS project, the more I got to spend time with the VMware ESX architecture. That's when I knew which way I wanted to take my career. Until 2013, I worked on the SaaS platform, which was running on VMware ESX 4, managed by vCenter Server, connected to an EMC Clarion CX4 shared storage. The Windows RDS machines were running on the platform in a big farm, load balanced with 2X and provisioned with applications by Microsoft App-V 4.5.

Late in 2013, it was time to make a career change. But what? It was kind of easy. When you mix server virtualization with SBC and application virtualization, what do you get? The answer is simple: end-user computing.

I applied for a job at ITQ Consultancy as a Virtualization Consultant, got hired and took my career to the next level. The four years after that were a rollercoaster. By blogging (on my own blog and the company blog), presenting and evangelizing VMware's products, I was rewarded as a vExpert since 2015 and as a VMware End-User Computing Champion since 2016. On top of that, I was recognized as an NVIDIA vGPU Community Advisor as well, which was a great honor!

By further specializing in VMware's End-User Computing products and doing exams, I achieved my VMware Certified Advanced Professional certification for both Datacenter Virtualization (DCV) as well as Desktop and Mobility (DTM). Those were the ideal basis to work towards my ultimate goal: become a VMware Certified Design Expert (VCDX) on Desktop and Mobility. The VCDX certification basically validates your skills as an architect. It's not a course with a lab- or quiz-based exam, but a path in gaining skills as an architect, using those skills in a real-life project and finally validating them in front of a panel. Kind-of how Luke became a Jedi. But instead of a panel, he had to show his skills to Yoda.

After achieving the VCDX certification, I wanted to pursue another dream: writing a book. But finding the right energy and making the final decision to start can be challenging too. With the help of Karlijn Bruns (a personal leadership coach), I got rid of all that was holding me back and started the journey in becoming an author.

As a VCDX I wanted to give something back to the EUC community. The community that helped *me* in achieving *my* goals. That's my primary goal for this book.

Made in the USA
San Bernardino, CA
29 July 2019